IMAGES
of Modern America

St. Joseph and Benton Harbor

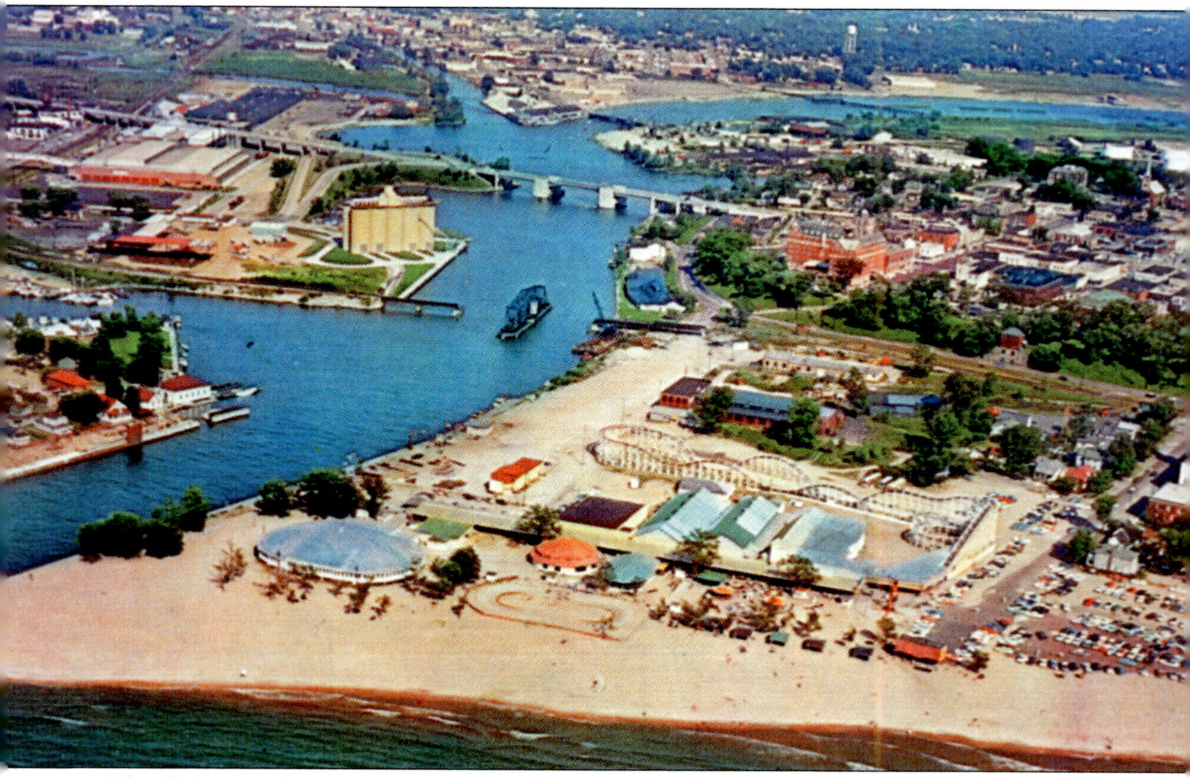

This 1960s east-facing aerial view shows twin cities with very different personalities. The red roofs of the Coast Guard station are visible across the channel. The tall cylinders of the Huron Cement silos and the long, low facilities of the Whirlpool Corporation at upper left characterize Benton Harbor's industrial and manufacturing economy. (Photograph by John Penrod, courtesy of Brian Ziebart.)

On the Front Cover: Clockwise from top left:
St. Joseph and Benton Harbor in the late 1980s (courtesy of the Maude Preston Palenske Memorial Library; see page 81), Miss Benton Harbor 2005 with her court (courtesy of Ashley Hampton; see page 89), Great Lakes towing tug *Wilfred M. Cohen* (courtesy of Jack Kinney; see page 72), beautifying Benton Harbor City Hall (author's collection; see page 94), Heathkit technician (courtesy of the Maude Preston Palenske Memorial Library; see page 33)

On the Back Cover: From left to right:
Farmers and Merchants Bank First drive-through branch, Benton Harbor (courtesy of Jim Willard; see page 39), Mabel and Edwin Damaske in front of their family grocery store (courtesy of the Heritage Museum and Cultural Center; see page 63), Boys and Girls Club drum line at the Harbor Market (author's collection; see page 90)

IMAGES
of Modern America

St. Joseph and Benton Harbor

Shannon McRae

ARCADIA PUBLISHING

ISBN 978-1-4671-1375-1

Published by Arcadia Publishing
Charleston, South Carolina

Printed in the United States of America

Library of Congress Control Number: 2014960002

For all general information, please contact Arcadia Publishing:
Telephone 843-853-2070
Fax 843-853-0044
E-mail sales@arcadiapublishing.com
For customer service and orders:
Toll-Free 1-888-313-2665

Visit us on the Internet at www.arcadiapublishing.com

To librarians, archivists, local historians, old-school journalists, and everyone who works against all odds to keep knowledge alive. You make all the difference.

Contents

ACKNOWLEDGMENTS

A community made this book, with generous gifts of stories, images, knowledge, and time. It would not have been possible without Jill Rauh at the Benton Harbor Public Library, Claire Gillespie at the Maud Preston Palenske Memorial Library in St. Joseph, or Mollie Kruck of the Heritage Museum and Cultural Center. Local historians Daryl Schlender and Kathryn Zerler both generously shared their extensive image collections and invaluable knowledge. Their excellent books on local history are required reading. Joseph Lodyga was a wealth of knowledge about life in St. Joseph and Silver Beach and Jack Kinney about the Central Dock and the Great Lakes shipping industry. Judge Ronald Taylor offered legal perspective on recent issues. Suz Schalon enthusiastically shared carousel lore. Ed and Jim Tiscornia's meticulous Auto Specialties scrapbooks are worthy of a serious separate study.

So many thanks to Angela Schrader Caldwell, Dixie Inocencio, Ken Ankli, Kathy Catania, Richard Hensel, and the other community builders and visionaries of the New Territory Arts Association for everything you have made possible. Additional thanks to Joshua Nowicki of the New Territory Arts Association for contributing his stunning photographs. Gratitude is due as well to John Penrod and Don Ames, whose professional photography over the decades has documented and preserved the charm and beauty of the region. I have credited their work when sources documented it.

Sessions at the Livery Microbrewery made research more fun, especially with Brian Ziebart's encyclopedic knowledge, extensive archival collection, and causing the world's problems over puddles of beer.

Thanks also to Larry and Sonja Podjan for beautiful images and fantastic blueberries; Jim Willard, Theresa Angelo-Immoos, the Eppelheimers, and the Mamminas for sharing family accomplishments; Joyce Hampton and her daughters, Ashley and Tanya, for their optimism and positive spirit; Candice Garman of Whirlpool Corporation; the inspiring community workers at the Mosaic Café and the Boys and Girls Club of Benton Harbor; Dave Smith and Martin Bishop of the Fairplain Plaza Cruisers; Grant Spitzke; and everybody who shared memories in the Benton Harbor and St. Joseph Stories Facebook group.

Finally, thank you to my patient editor Maggie Bullwinkel at Arcadia Publishing, colleagues at SUNY Fredonia for their encouragement, my mother, Maureen McRae, and my husband, Stephen Brandon, for feeding me and putting up with my whining when I got stuck.

Introduction

America was a different country after World War II. In the 1950s, the newly prosperous global superpower was driven by expansion, modernization, industrial production, technological development, and consumerism. The Great Lakes region offered good jobs in automobile and parts manufacture, steelwork, and shipping. These opportunities, and a hope of less culturally oppressive conditions, brought thousands of African Americans up north from the South in the Great Migration. Unions ensured good wages and safe working conditions, federal benefits such as the GI Bill assisted veterans with low-rate mortgages and college educations, and an abundance of newly built affordable housing made the American Dream seem attainable for many.

The reality was more complex. The cumulative effects of the Great Depression and a restricted wartime economy created infrastructure decay. The steady influx of workers into Northern cities and thousands of newly returned veterans meant overcrowding, poverty, and insufficient housing. The Housing Act of 1949, designed to address these issues, had mixed results. Federally funded urban renewal programs calling for lower-income neighborhoods to be leveled were often enacted with neither clear plans nor sufficient funds to relocate the residents. The fact that these residents were typically poor and black led poet Langston Hughes to famously refer to the program as "Negro Removal."

Black people attempting to find housing in white neighborhoods were typically not welcome. With urban centers demolished, new interstate construction that cut some towns through the middle and bypassed others, and city planning increasingly focused on cars moving quickly and efficiently between destinations, business owners relocated to newly built shopping centers and moved their families into the suburbs, taking the tax base with them. This phenomenon, called white flight, left many Northern urban centers impoverished, decayed, and crime-ridden by the 1970s.

To make matters worse, the heavy industries that brought prosperity also polluted the environment. Federal regulations designed to address the demonstrable dangers proved extremely costly for companies to implement. With growing consumer demand for automobiles increasing the demand for oil and gas, instability in the world's oil-producing regions, an unstable manufacturing economy, and a global energy crisis, the Northern industrial economy collapsed in the early 1980s.

Some regions, such as the financial centers New York and Chicago, recovered quickly. The oil and aerospace-rich Southwest and the research and technology sector in the south San Francisco Bay area known as Silicon Valley emerged as the new centers of the energy and information economy. The steel and automotive production centers located around the Great Lakes and the East Coast became the Rust Belt, settling into cultural and economic decay from which some regions have not yet recovered.

Others came back. Realizing that their city centers were the heart and soul of their communities, their citizens began to revive them. With the realization that the old manufacturing economy was gone for good, they reinvented themselves, became research and technology hubs, arts and cultural destinations, or tourist towns.

This American story is the story of St. Joseph and Benton Harbor, small adjacent cities in southwest Michigan on the Lake Michigan coast, some 90 miles from Chicago. This book chronicles how the citizens of the Twin Cities, through vision, effort, hard work, and cooperation, reinvented two struggling Rust Belt towns as thriving, unique, 21st-century destinations—St. Joseph through planned development that emphasized its hometown charm and attracted tourists, and Benton Harbor as a new urban center for the arts.

This book was a community effort. Residents, local historians, business owners, libraries, and historical societies in both cities contributed nearly all of the images. The stories are theirs, related in person or written in local history books and in newspaper accounts from the *News Palladium/Herald Press*, which later became the *Herald Palladium*. The enthusiasm, generosity, and wealth of knowledge of these contributors is extraordinary.

Some questioned whether the relatively recent events of the late 20th century counted as history. Particularly for older citizens who lived through what seemed a golden age of 1950s small-town American prosperity, history ended sometime in the late 1970s, brought down by economic forces and social changes largely beyond their control.

Others were concerned with how I intended to represent Benton Harbor. The town's recent history of racial tension, economic loss, slow recovery, and continued struggles remains difficult to discuss—a fact that has not been helped by periodic waves of negative and often sensational media attention. In 2003, a fatal altercation between a resident and a police officer resulted in rioting all too reminiscent of earlier upheavals in the 1960s and 1970s. When in 2010 it became one of the first cities in America to be run by a state-appointed emergency manager rather than its own elected officials, Benton Harbor was featured in the national spotlight once again, as were certain aspects of the recent Harbor Shores Golf Course development. Media representations that typically reduce complex issues to simplistic, one-sided assessments frustrate many locals because they do not capture a full, honest image of the city we know and love, where we work and play, attend church, and raise families like any other American city. More crucially, they do not show the remarkable and positive accomplishments achieved by community members successfully solving local problems together.

The tough times happened and are part of the story, but they are not the whole story. I grew up in Benton Harbor. I remember wonderful times. Childhood meant long summer days and cool evenings at the beach, sailing on Lake Michigan in summer, ice skating and sledding in winter, delicious ice cream and gentle old folks running the little train rides at the beautiful House of David Park, rides at Silver Beach Amusement Park and the romantic, haunted feeling of both after they closed. Teenage years meant Saturday nights with friends cruising in cars around Fairplain Plaza, shopping in the little boutiques there for something pretty to wear to a school dance or a party, haunting well-stocked bookstores, and entire afternoons reading in the St. Joseph Library or on a bench in the Bluff Park. Friday nights meant family evenings out in little taverns and restaurants, greeting friends over burgers, pizza, or perch dinners. It was the best place to grow up, and it is still the best place to come home to.

The recent story of Benton Harbor and St. Joseph is of two communities that weathered great change and came back again, because local individuals, community groups, and business philanthropists combined efforts, came together, faced challenges, and rebuilt for the 21st century. I am honored and delighted to tell that side of the story with this book.

One

Hometown Tourist Towns

Positioned on the sandy shores of Lake Michigan across from Chicago and on the major highway route between Chicago and Detroit, the twin cities of Benton Harbor and St. Joseph, although economically based in manufacturing, farming, and shipping, are also tourist towns. In the 19th century, both boasted large, graceful hotels with mineral baths and elegant accommodations. St. Joseph's Silver Beach and Benton Harbor's Israelite House of David Eden Springs Amusement Park competed for tourists for the entire first half of the 20th century.

Chicago tourists expecting first-rate entertainment and high style found it in any number of restaurants, nightclubs, and movie theaters. Miles of beautiful white sandy beaches offered summer weekends swimming and sunbathing. Freighters and barges brought asphalt and coal through the St. Joseph River Channel to the Central Dock, and steamships brought tourists, and the lively port offered ideal conditions for sailing and small-craft cruises.

For local families in the 1950s and 1960s, these same delights were part of everyday life. Benton Harbor and St. Joseph were both tourist towns, but they were also hometowns, with classic American main streets featuring shops and restaurants and small businesses owned and run by the same families for decades. Everyday life was pleasant, ordinary, and always a little bit magical.

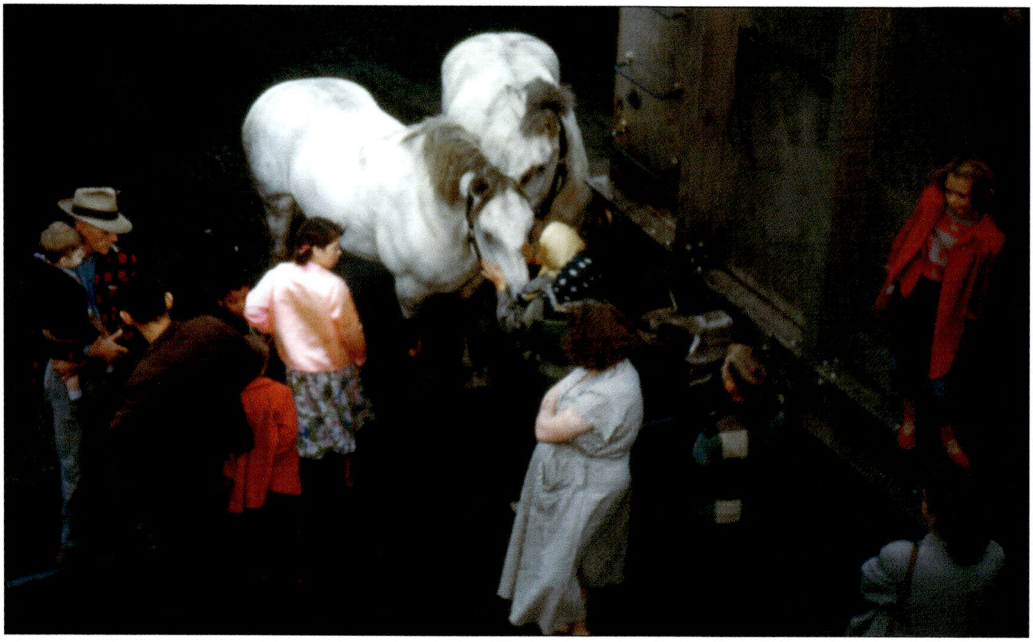

For a small town in the 1950s, the arrival of a circus was nearly as spectacular as the event itself. These photographs show the arrival and setup of the Clyde Beatty Circus, mostly likely taken on August 20, 1953. Above, circus performers mingle with locals just after unloading trick horses from the train. Below, elephant riders set up for the circus parade in downtown Benton Harbor. Later, the elephants will help set up the tents. Local children were also recruited for various odd jobs in exchange for free tickets to the circus. (Both photographs by Leo Spitzke, courtesy of Grant Spitzke.)

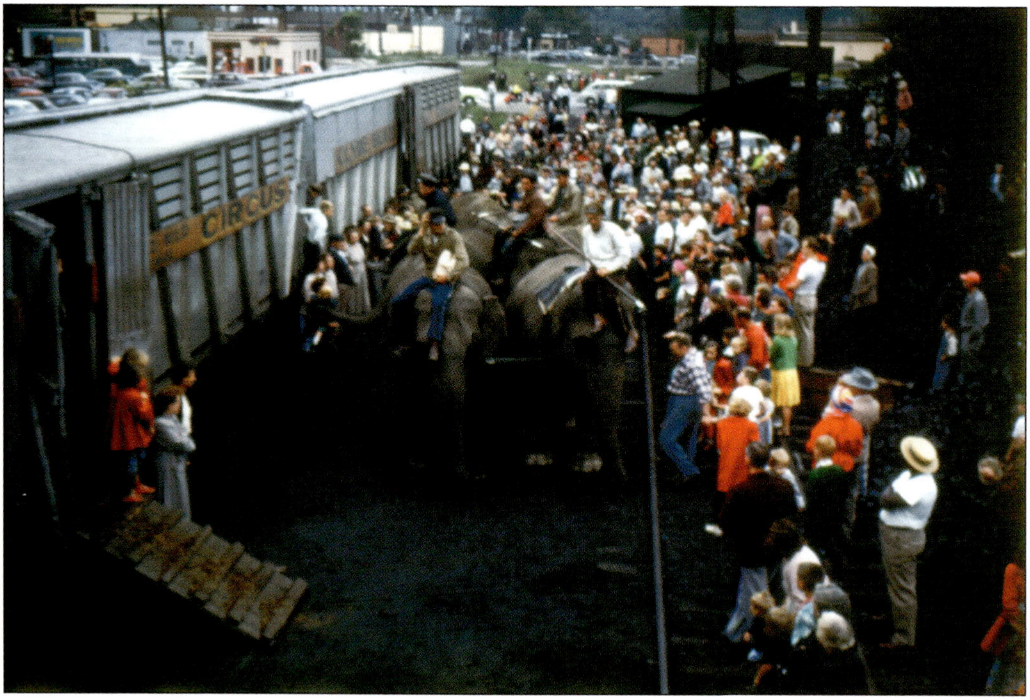

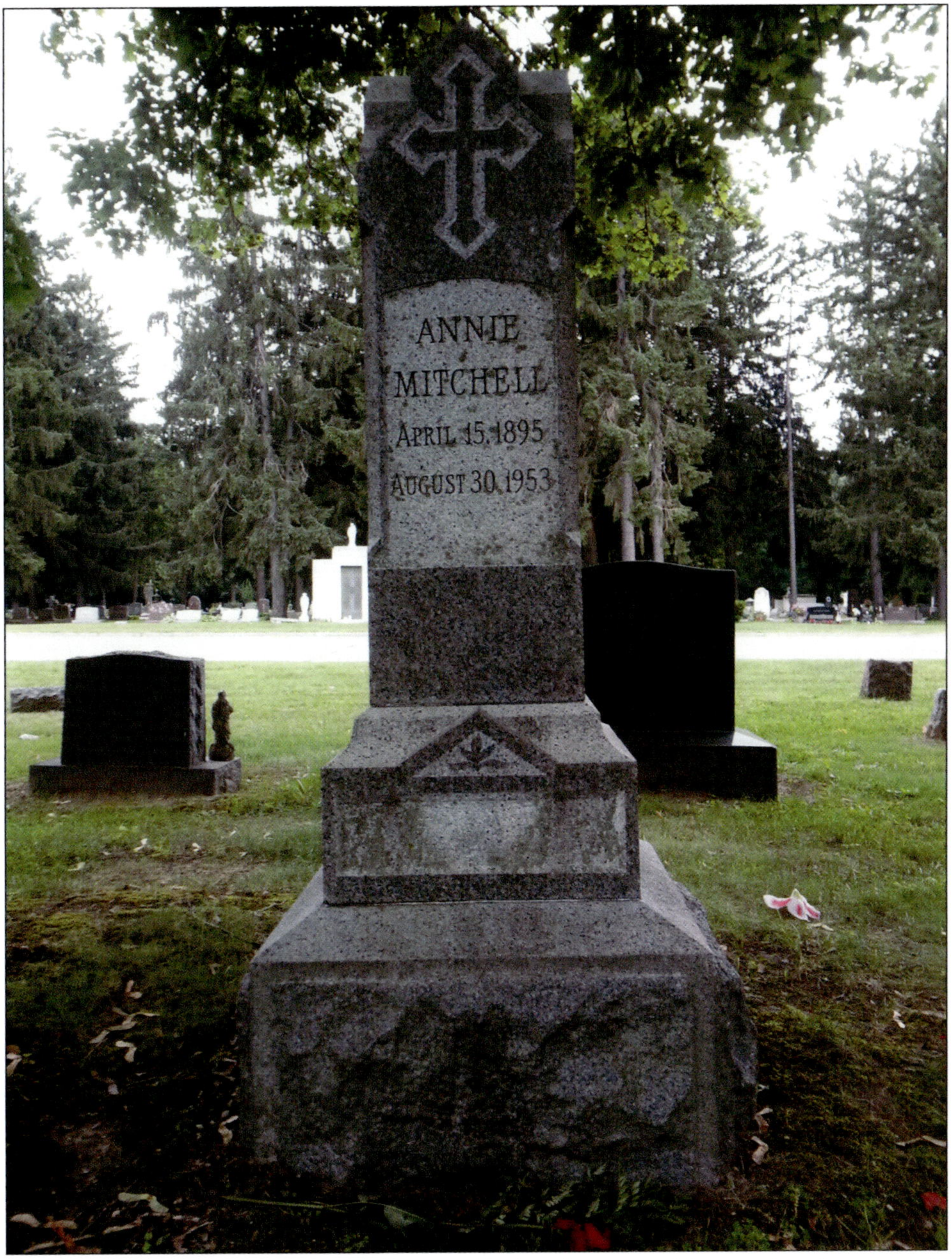

"Fate or circumstances seems to mark Benton Harbor for unusual happenings," wrote a *News-Palladium* reporter on September 2, 1953, when hundreds of Roma people, camping at farms and waysides, came great distances for a month-long vigil at the Mercy Hospital bedside of dying headwoman Annie Mitchell. All month, the *Palladium* published breathless accounts of the colorful visitors and the spectacular funeral. Over 1,500 locals attended her candlelit and flower-covered bier in Florin Funeral Home, while a brass band of local youths played a hymn outside. After a funeral mass at St. John's Catholic Church, family members made graveside libations and farewells, then quietly departed. Only these stories and this serene tree-side gravestone in Crystal Springs Cemetery remain in memory of a powerful woman, a remarkable community, and an extraordinary month. (Author's collection.)

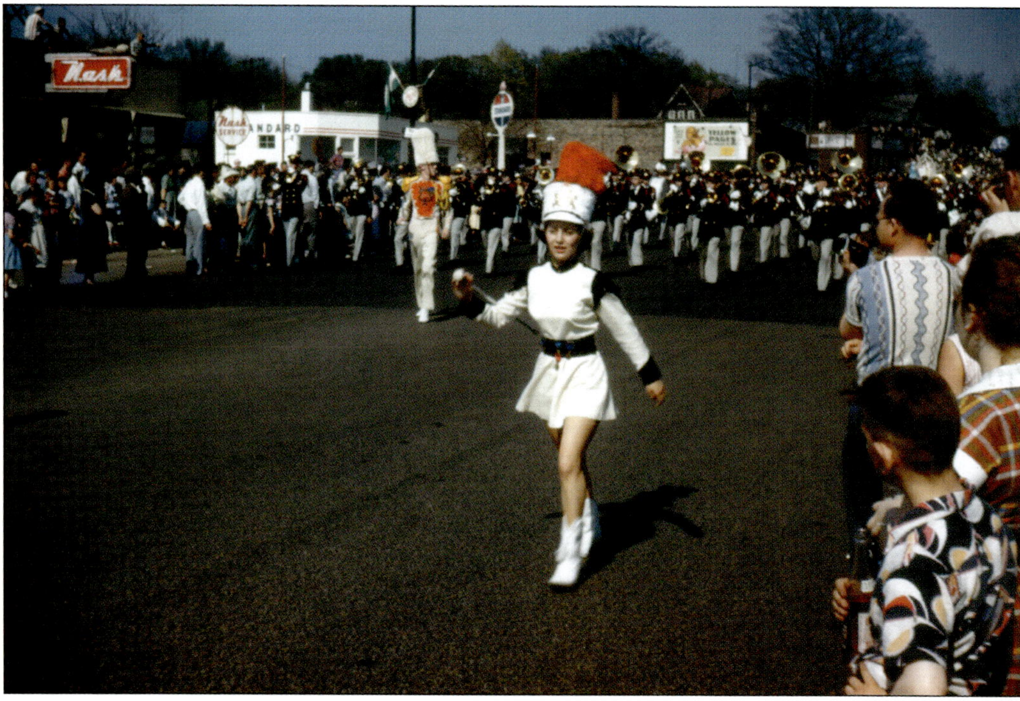

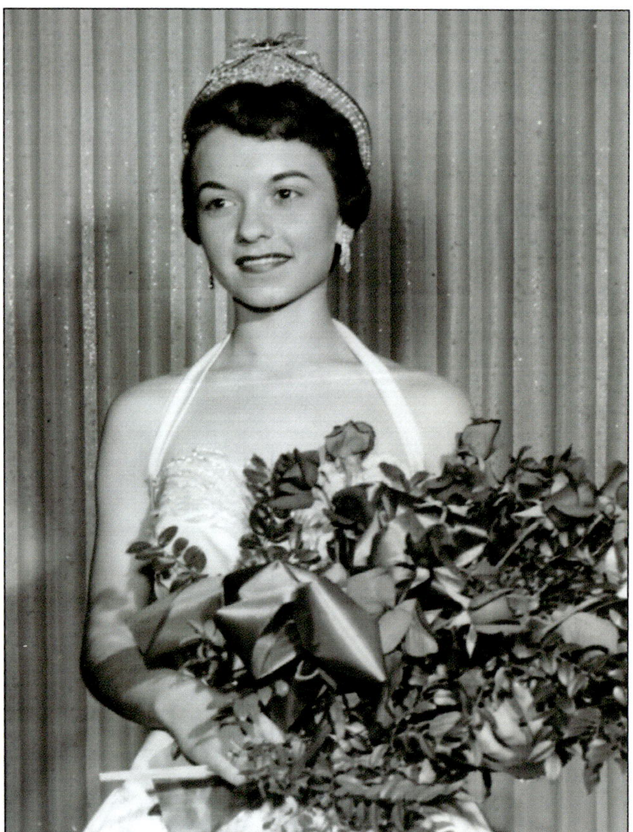

The annual Blossomtime Parade first started in May 1923 to celebrate the flowering of the fruit trees in the local orchards. Held the first Saturday in May, routing between Benton Harbor and St. Joseph, the whole county participates. Local schools, businesses, and professional organizations all build floats, drive cars, or march in the parade. Above is a classic American 1950s parade scene: a high school drum majorette followed by her marching band. The Nash Leuenberger Company was located at 395 East Main Street in Benton Harbor. At left is the 1955 Miss Blossomtime, Patricia Hanley of Dowagiac. (Above, photograph by Leo Spitzke, courtesy of Grant Spitzke; left, courtesy of Brian Ziebart.)

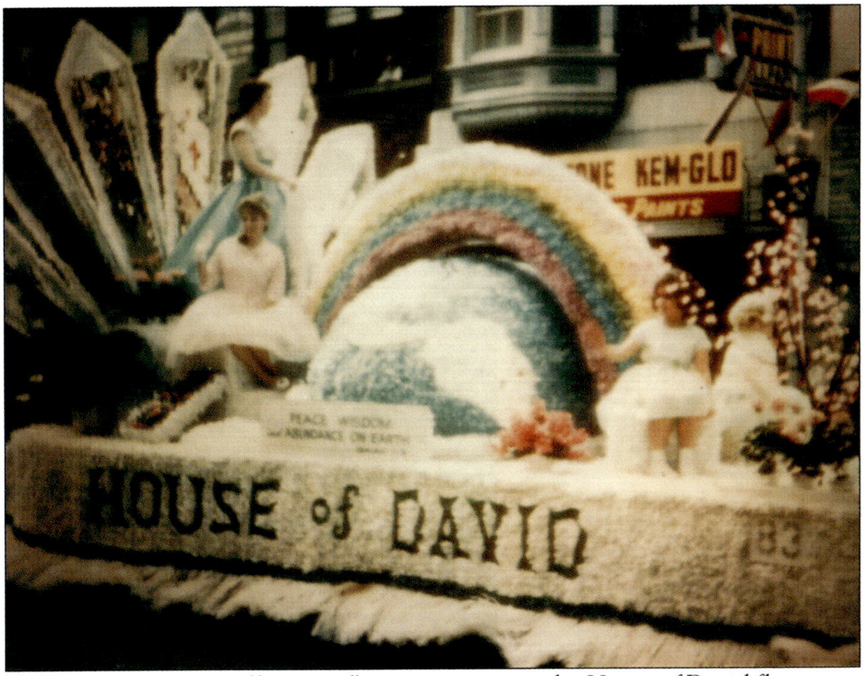

Though all entrants put great effort into float construction, the House of David floats were hard to beat. This one above, from 1962, had flowers and evergreens from colony greenhouses and Emlongs Nursery, live flowering plants and potted fruit trees at both ends, and baskets of fruit from their farms on both sides. Jeanne Marlene Falkenstein, Gale Jeffrey, Lavina Thole, Terry Lyn Martin, and Cheryl Ann Martin rode the float. Some floats also served as whimsical advertisements, such as the float below (from an earlier parade) for Blue Beacon Coal, sold by Consumers Coal Company of 107 Water Street. Consumers Coal is one of the oldest family-owned businesses in Benton Harbor. (Above, courtesy of Hamilton Library; below, courtesy of Jack Kinney.)

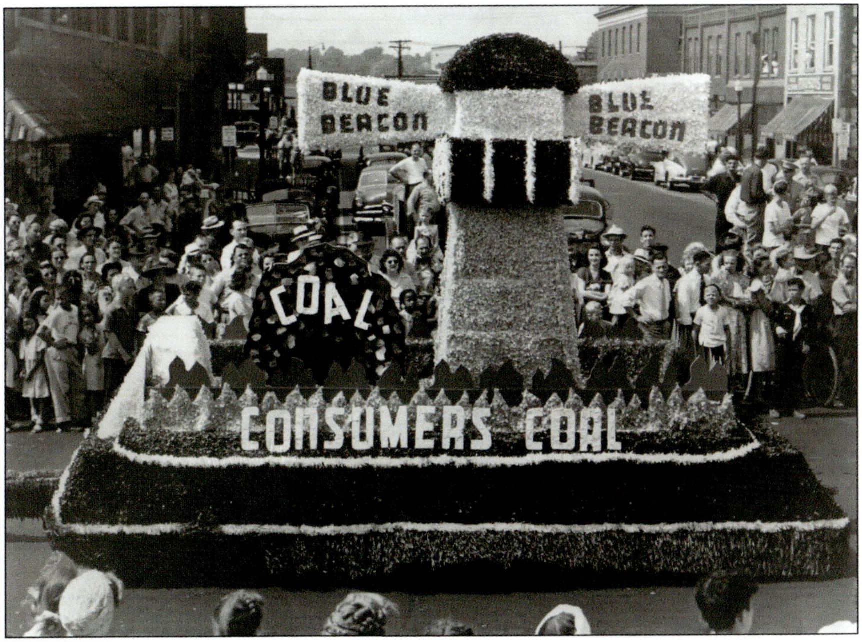

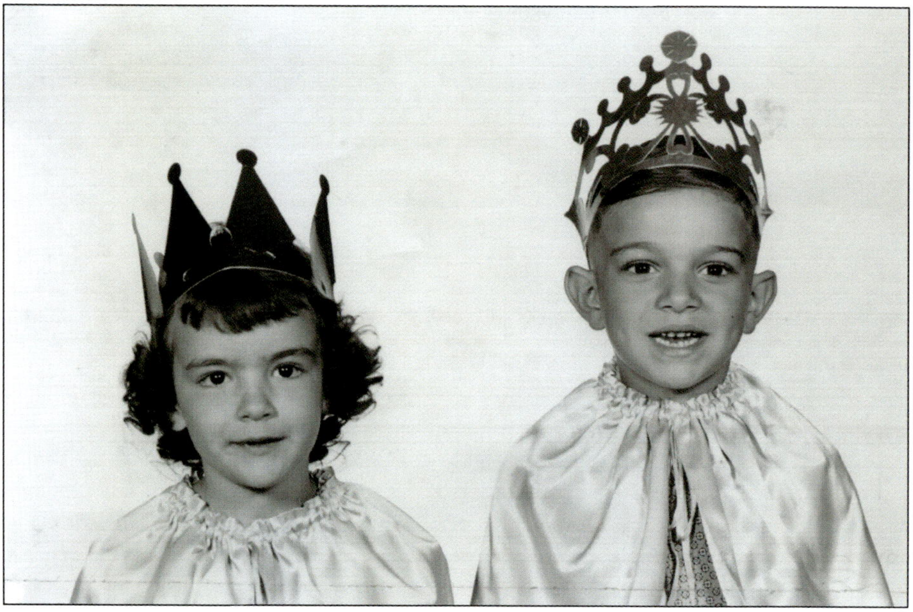

Local children loved the Kiddies' Parade. Schoolchildren, youth bands, 4-H groups, and Scout troops would march, sometimes with decorated bikes or pets on leashes. Every year, a Bud Prince and Princess were selected from a local elementary school. Above are Rebecca Lynn Trux and Sammy Pullano, age five, chosen as the Bud Princess and Prince at Sorter School in Benton Harbor. They won a white ribbon of recognition for the 1955 Blossom Festival Kiddies' Parade. Below is an ethereal fairytale-themed float for another young pair of festival royalty, sponsored by Producers Creamery. (Both, courtesy of Larry Podjan.)

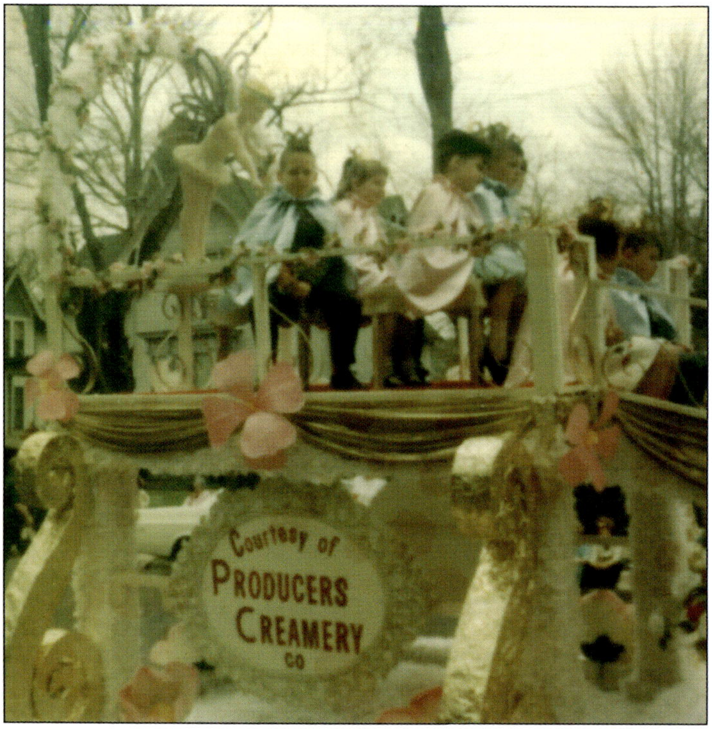

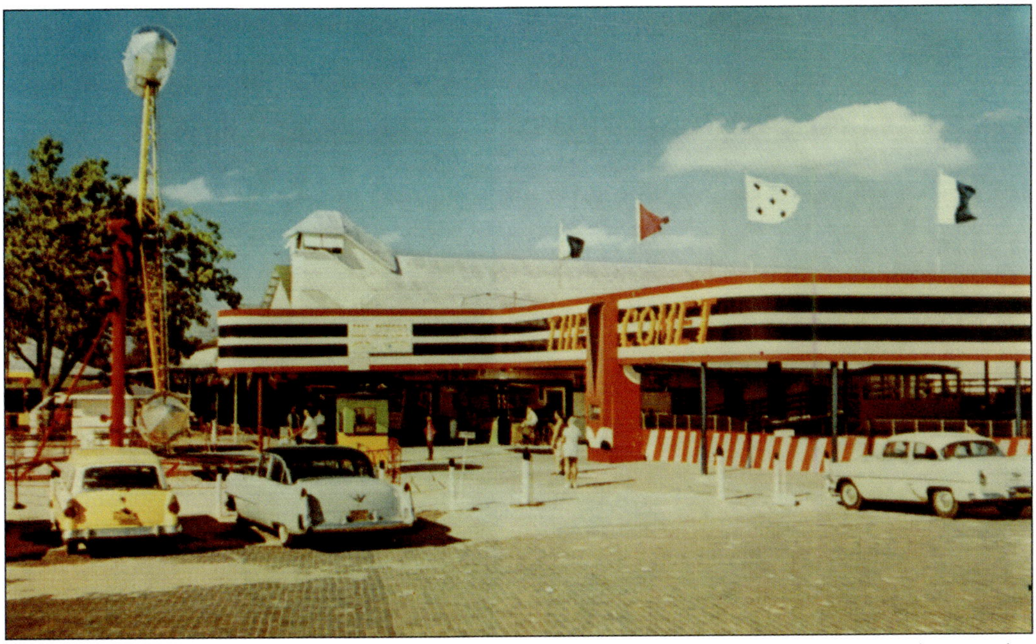

Opened in the 1880s by Logan Drake and Louis D. Wallace, Silver Beach remained a popular attraction for locals and visitors until 1971. Above is the south entry to the midway and The Comet rollercoaster. To the left is the Roll-o-Plane. Below, looking southwest from across the St. Joseph river channel, is a skyline view of The Comet in early evening, in 1962. The camelback-truss swing railroad bridge in the foreground, which turns to accommodate ships entering and leaving the channel, is still in operation. Between the bridge and the amusement parks are factories, waterfront service and manufacturing businesses, the Cooper and Wells stocking factory, Wallace and Sons Lumber, and Skidmore Pumps. (Above, courtesy of the Benton Harbor Public Library; below, courtesy of Larry Podjan.)

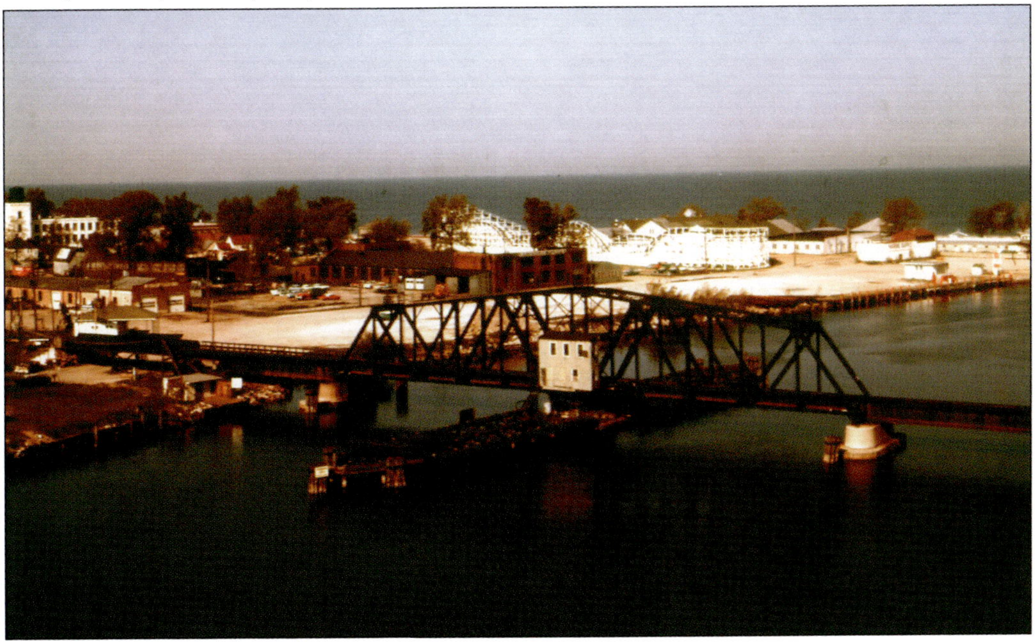

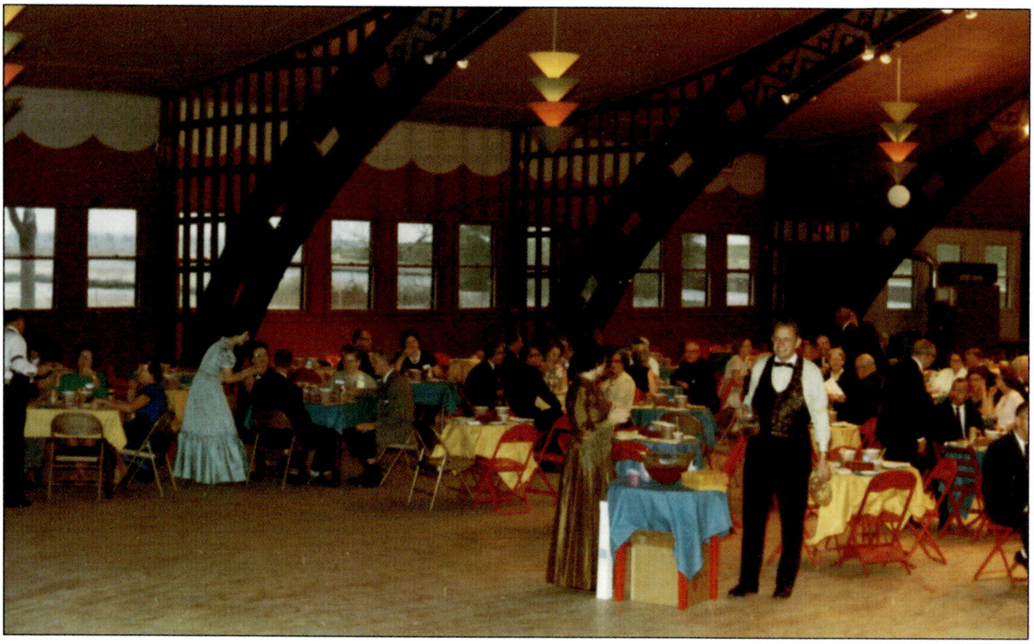

Pictured here is the interior of the Shadowland Ballroom at Silver Beach in 1966. Built in the 1920s, it remained in continuous use until the late 1970s. When large dancehalls fell out of vogue, the ballroom was still used for events such as this "Gay 1890s"–themed party for Auto Specialties employees. (Courtesy of James and Edward Tiscornia.)

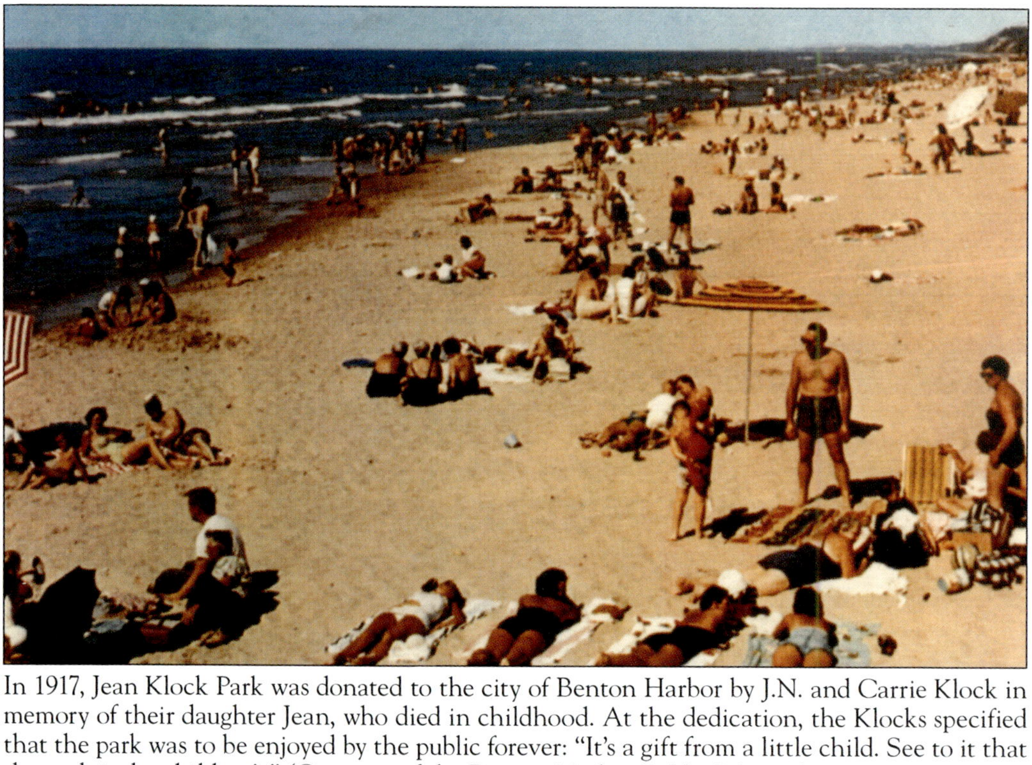

In 1917, Jean Klock Park was donated to the city of Benton Harbor by J.N. and Carrie Klock in memory of their daughter Jean, who died in childhood. At the dedication, the Klocks specified that the park was to be enjoyed by the public forever: "It's a gift from a little child. See to it that the park is the children's." (Courtesy of the Benton Harbor Public Library.)

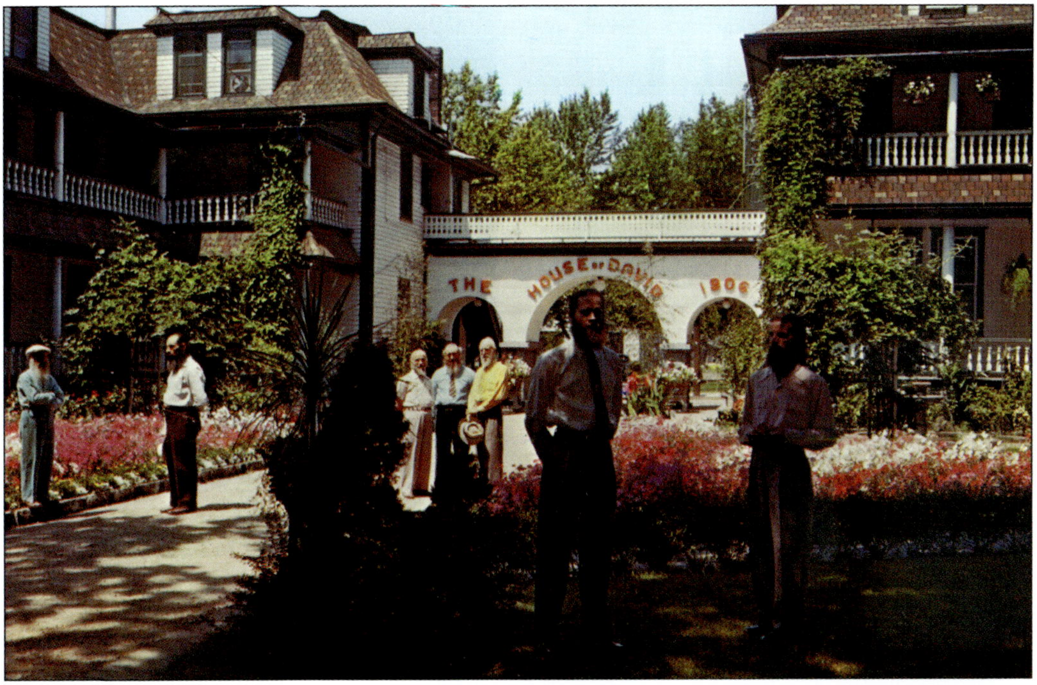

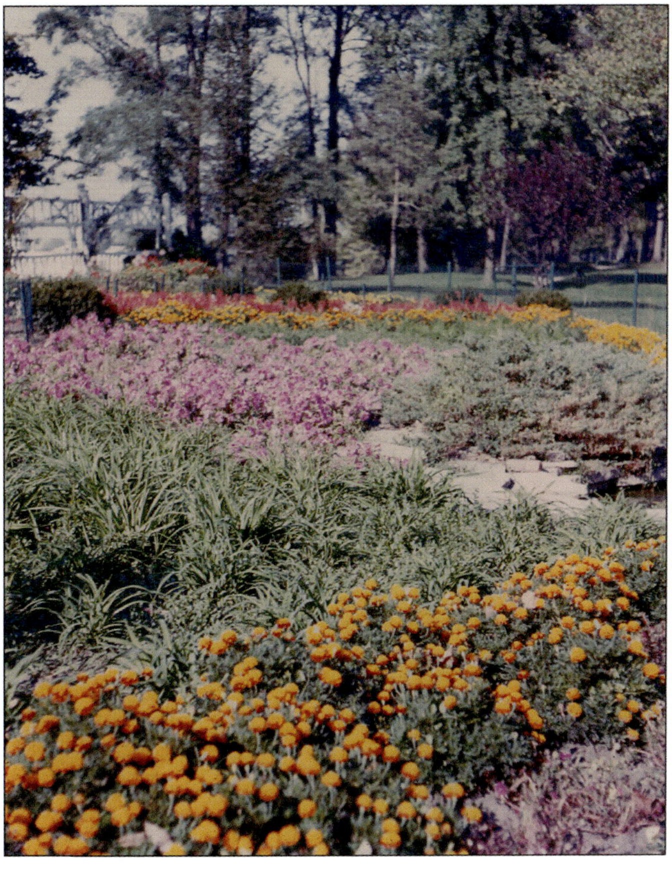

Though aging and dwindling in numbers, the Israelite House of David, founded in 1902 by Benjamin and Mary Purnell, remained a significant presence in Benton Harbor in the 1950s and 1960s. On the far left are Dominick Zittela (left) and Clayton Lowery. Zittela tended the beautiful gardens in the park and around colony property, while Lowery performed various tasks. To the far right are Paul A. Johnson, who had a degree in horticulture, grew apples, and established beehives around the county, and William Robertson (right), who worked in the print shop. The image on the right, of one of the beautiful gardens in Eden Springs Park, serves as an example of Zittela's work. (Above, photograph by John Penrod, courtesy of the Maud Preston Palenske Memorial Library; right, courtesy of Larry Podjan.)

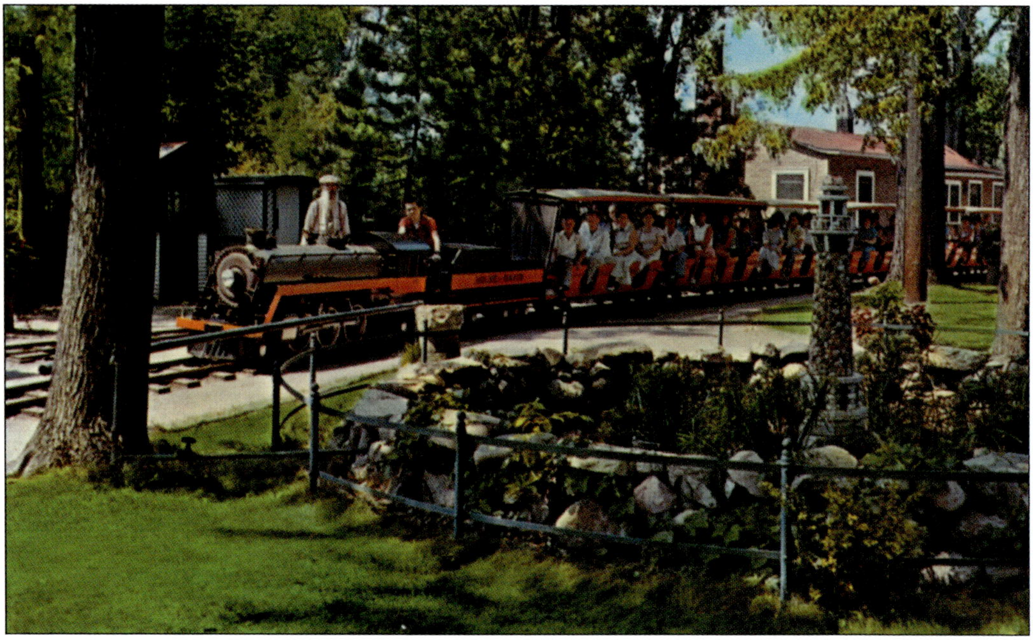

Locals recall days spent at the House of David among their happiest childhood memories. They remember the delicious homemade ice cream, the beautiful park, and most of all, the miniature steam trains—many of which were hand-built by colony members. The stone lighthouse in the image above was built by stonemason John Herron. The colony continued also in many of the various enterprises that sustained the local economy. Below is the House of David greenhouse on Red Arrow Highway, run first by Paul and Albert Falkenstein from Germany, and later purchased by Paul's daughter Jean and her husband, Henry Thole, who eventually renamed it H&J Greenhouse. (Above, photograph by John Penrod, both images courtesy of the Maude Preston Palenske Memorial Library.)

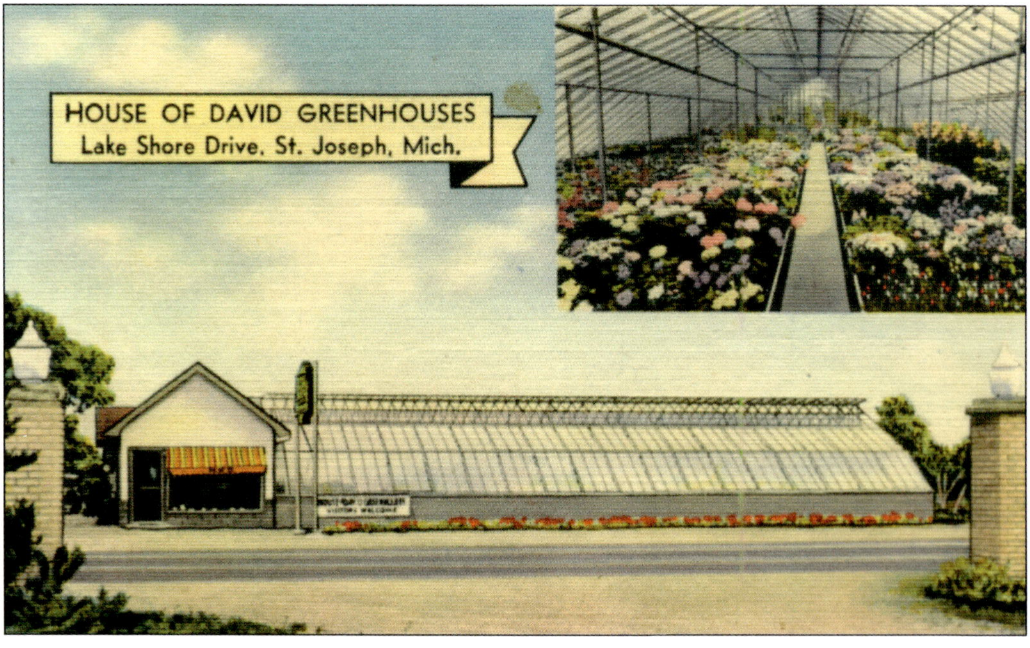

Everyone loved roller skating at the Central Dock. Located on the second floor of the terminal building, the rink was enjoyed by church groups, school groups, and children celebrating birthdays and other occasions. Pictured here are the very stylish Mack (left) and Howard Rodgers of Benton Harbor, about 1955, with an unidentified little girl. (Courtesy of the Benton Harbor Public Library.)

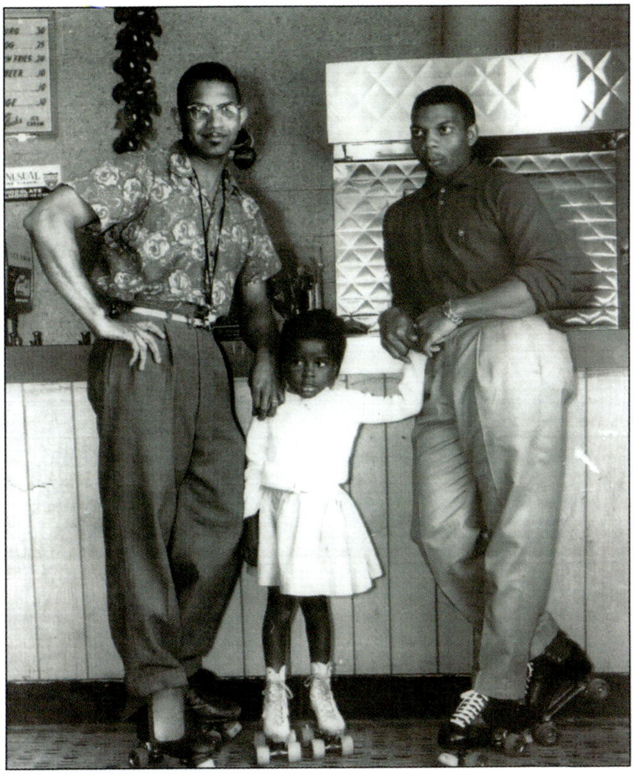

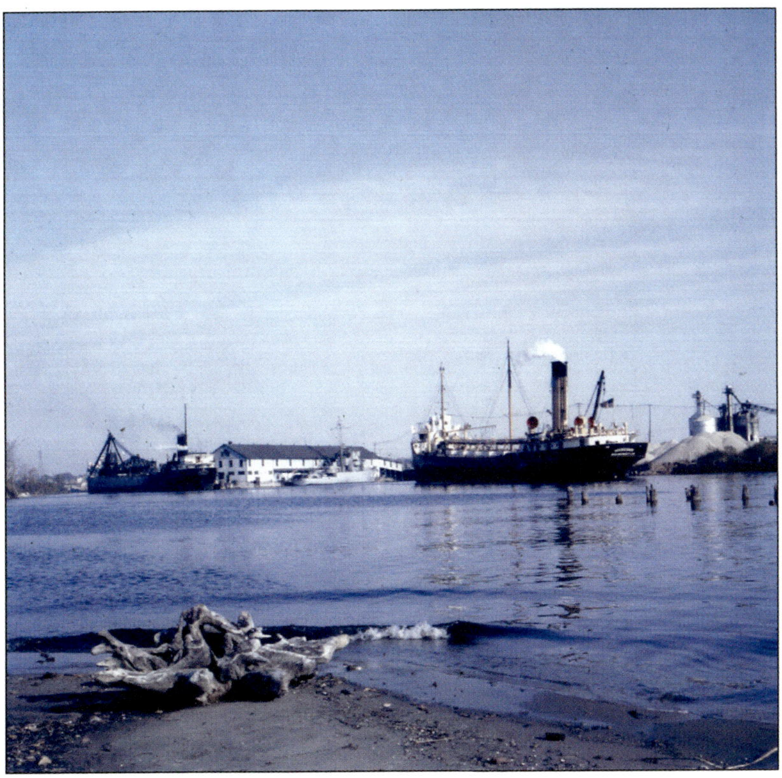

Located where the St. Joseph and Paw Paw Rivers meet, the Central Dock testifies to the region's importance as a Great Lakes port. Here are three different types of working vessels. At left is the *Reise*, unloading for Consumers Coal; at center is the USS *Havre*, a Navy reserve training ship; and at right is the *Mercury*, unloading fuel for the Thiesen Clemings storage tanks. (Courtesy of Larry Podjan.)

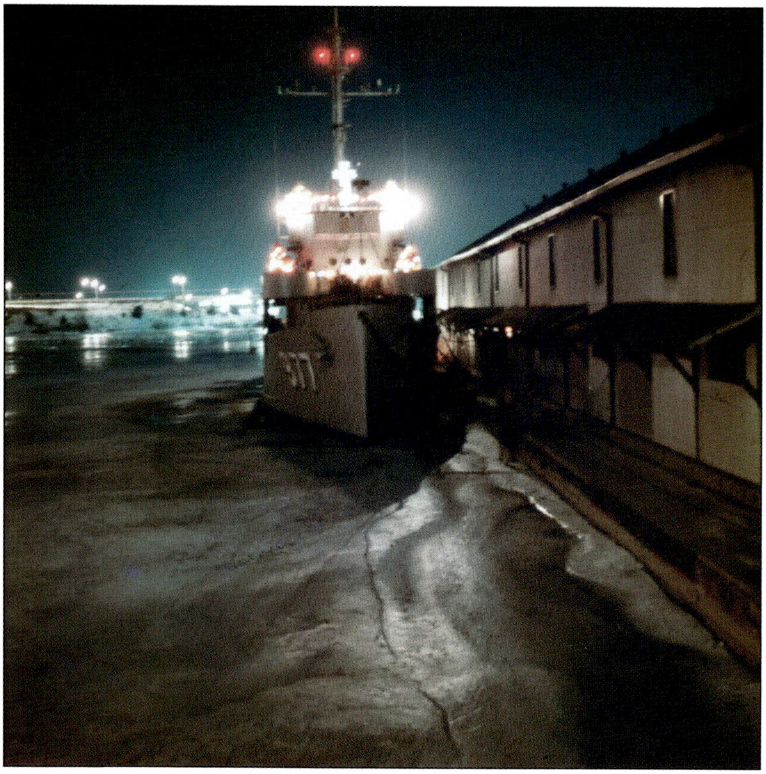

The USS *Havre* is pictured here in port. After service during World War II among the Iwo Jima invasion forces, she sailed the Great Lakes as a Navy reserve ship in the 9th Naval District. When docked in Benton Harbor, her crew welcomed local children on board for tours and decorated her every year for a Christmas party at which they distributed gifts for underprivileged children. (Courtesy of Larry Podjan.)

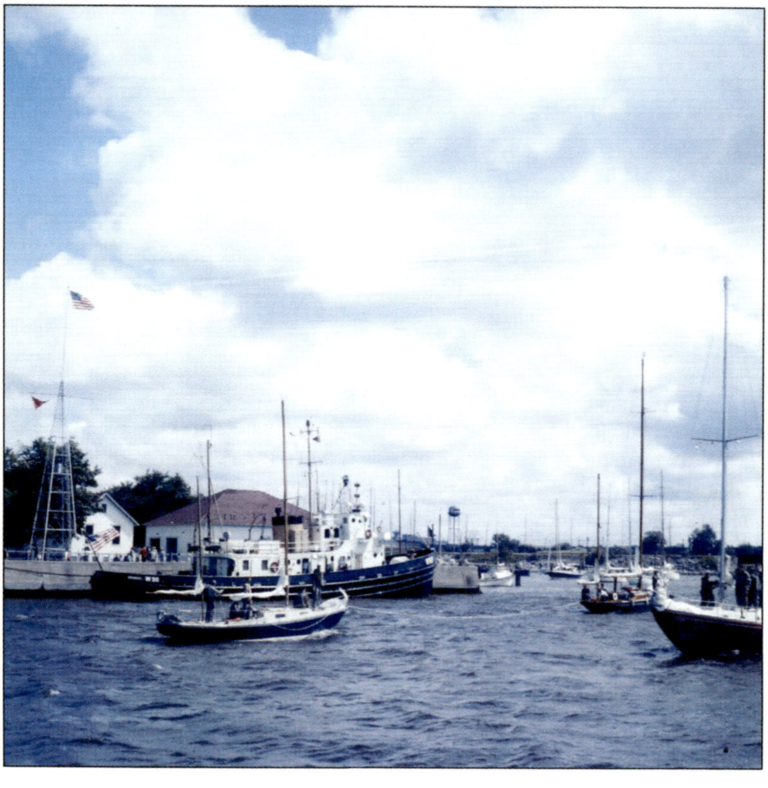

This lovely summer scene depicts the US Coast Guard tug *Arundel* docked alongside the red-roofed Coast Guard station in St. Joseph, with sailboats in the foreground. In a waterfront region serving an international shipping industry, with an economic base founded on manufacturing and tourism, work and play often occur in exactly the same spaces. (Courtesy of Larry Podjan.)

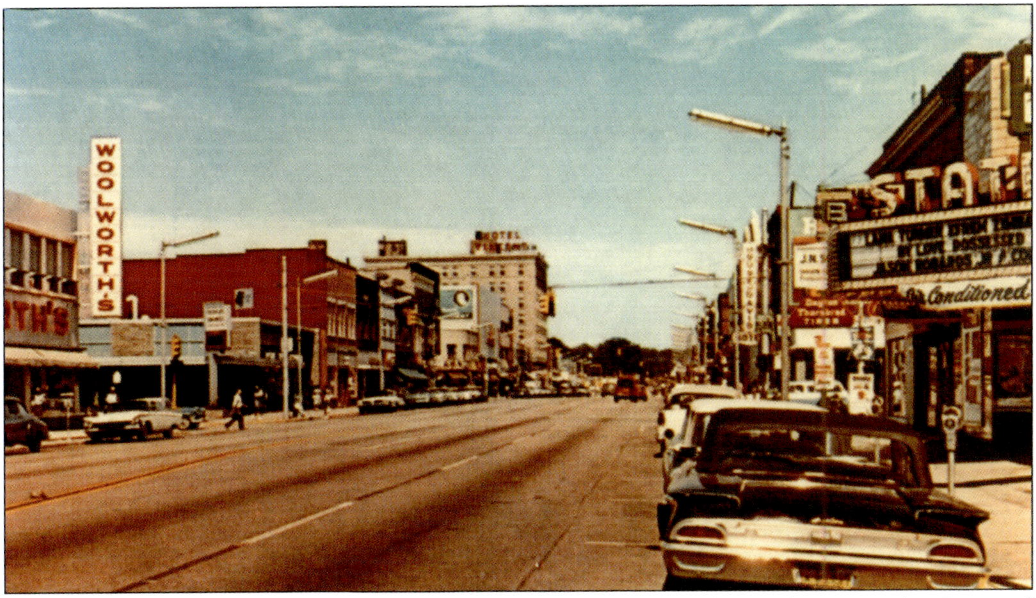

Benton Harbor's Main Street included four movie theaters: the Liberty, the State, the City, and the Lake; national retailers such as Sears and Woolworth's; the locally owned Vincent and the House of David Hotels; and several family shops. Locals remember ice cream at Woolworth's, the old pneumatic tubes running across the ceiling at Penney's, and prime views of the annual Blossom Parade from rooftops. The film advertised on the State Theater marquee in the photograph above, *By Love Possessed*, dates this image to 1961. Below is Holly's Grill, one of a chain of restaurants popular for breakfast and lunch. Next to the restaurant is Gorton's music store. The City Theater is also visible. (Both, courtesy of the Benton Harbor Public Library.)

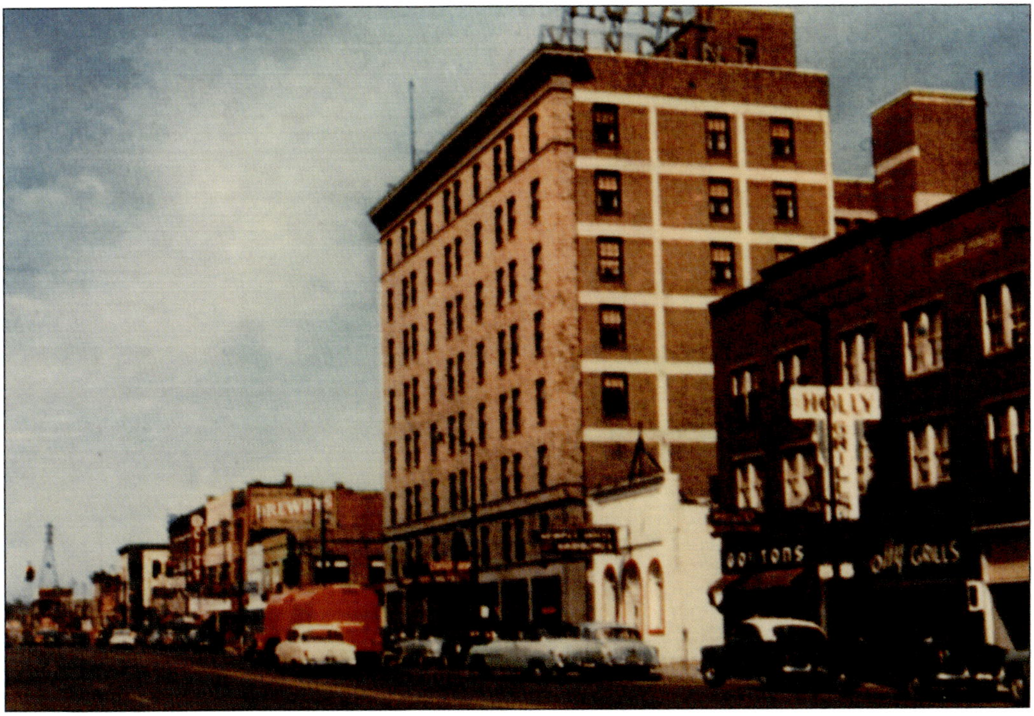

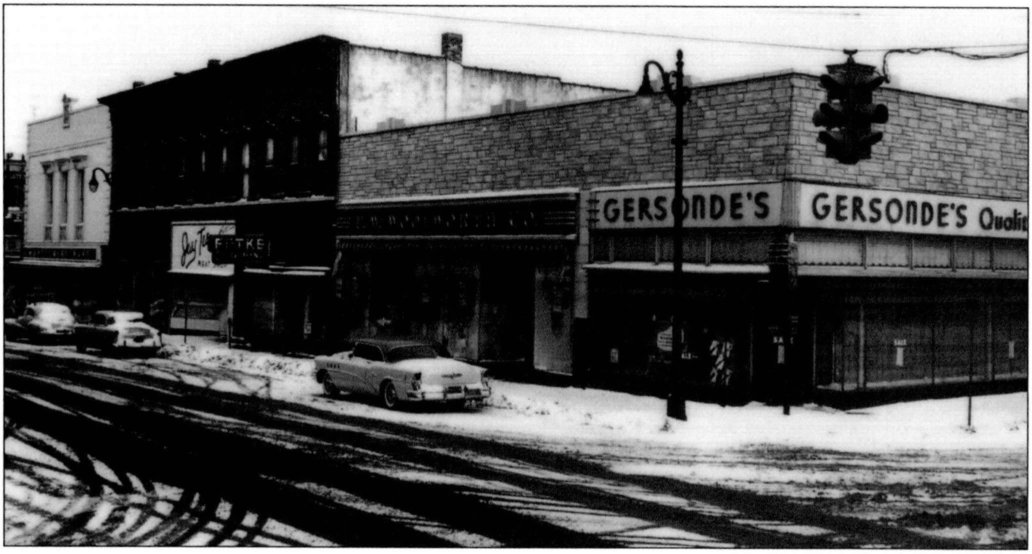

St. Joseph's State Street also had its national chains and family establishments. This view of the corner of Pleasant and State Streets depicts Gersonde's men's clothing store and the ubiquitous Woolworth's, with Fetke's clothing on the other side. Established in 1909, Fetke's was passed down from father to son until closing in 1969. Its slogan was "Everything for dad and lad." (Courtesy of Daryl Schlender.)

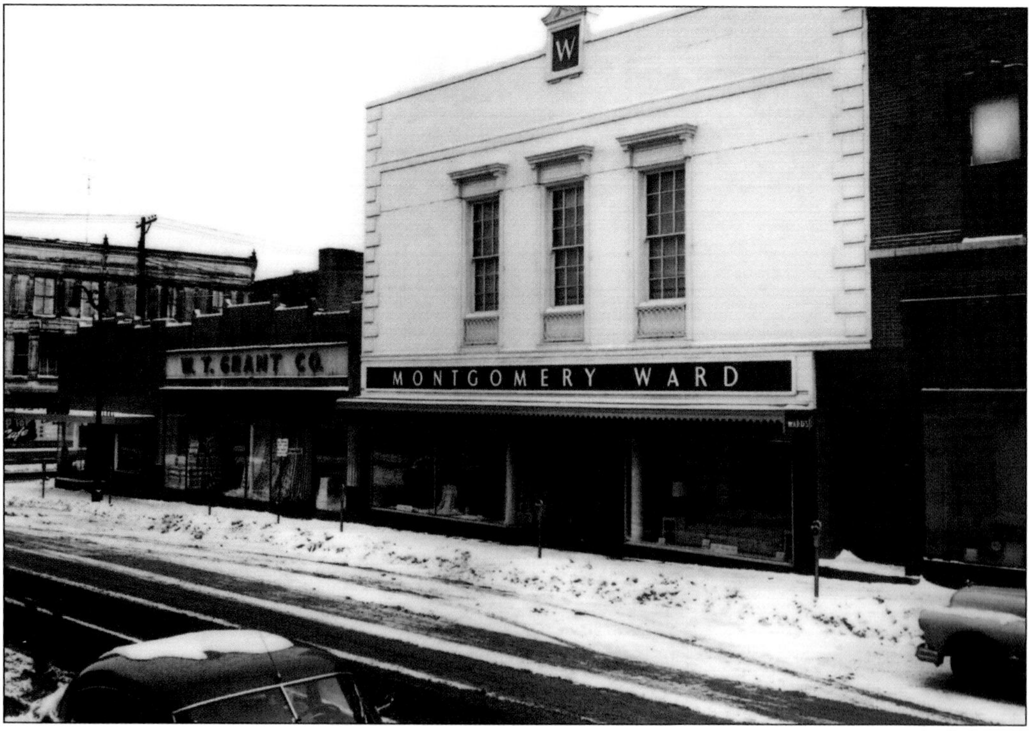

Aaron Montgomery Ward, founder of the famous catalog mail-order business, was once a stock boy at BF King's general store at 15 State Street. This early retail outlet was located between the W.T. Grant store and Jay Tees Meat Market on State Street, between Ship and Pleasant Streets. Young people referred to the business as "Monkey Wards." (Courtesy of Daryl Schlender.)

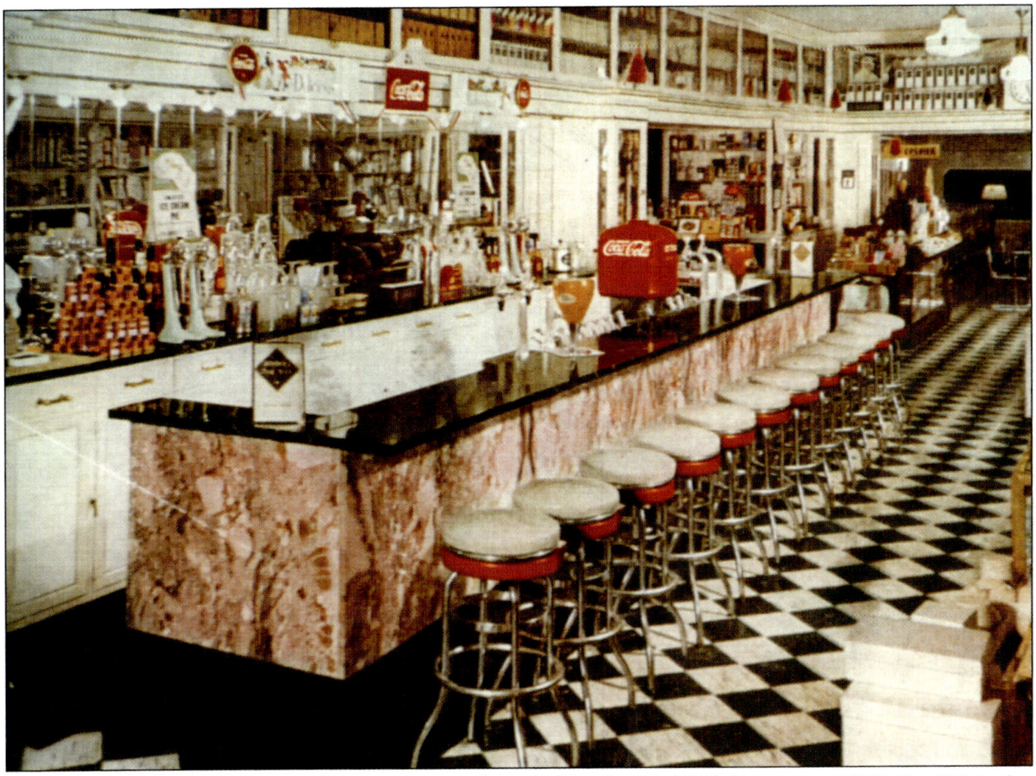

Gillespie's Pharmacy, 220 State Street, was founded by Frank T. Gillespie in 1905. By 1964, the business grew to four locations in the Twin Cities area. This photograph of the original St. Joseph location highlights its beautiful marble soda fountain. Gillespie's malts and milkshakes came with two sugar cookies. Their sodas and banana splits were also popular. (Courtesy of the Heritage Museum and Cultural Center.)

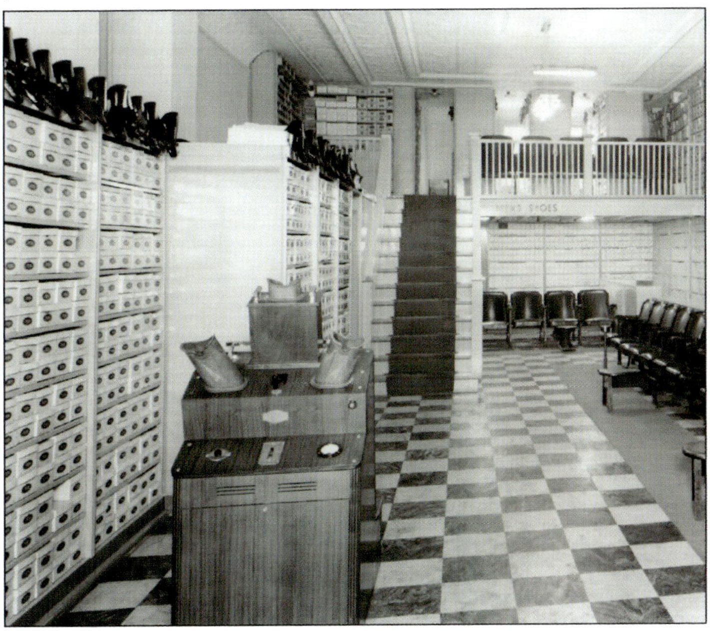

The boxy structure in the left foreground of Don Wynkoops shoe store, 318 South State Street, is a shoe-fitting X-ray fluoroscope machine. Typically used to fit children's shoes, the young patron would insert both feet inside and peer down through a viewing lens at their bones visible inside the shoes. Concerns about radiation exposure eventually rendered such sales gimmicks obsolete. (Courtesy of Daryl Schlender.)

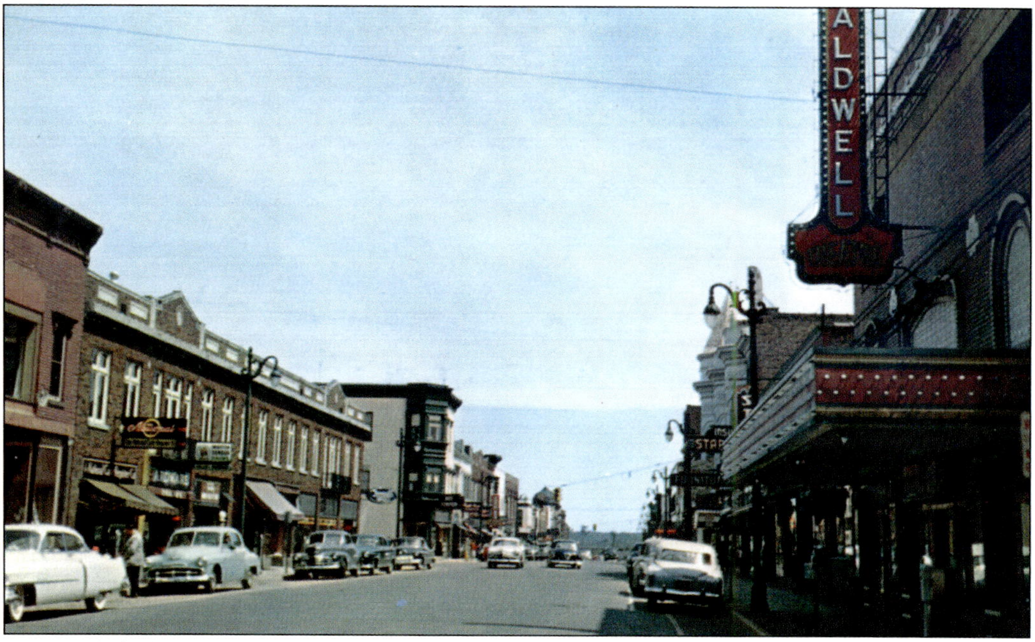

St. Joseph had two movie theaters on State Street. The Harlo at 107 State Street closed about 1951. The venerable Caldwell, at 417 State Street, stayed in business until 1955. Built in 1913 on the site of a derelict livery stable, the Caldwell was once one of the nation's best equipped and furnished movie theaters. Wildly popular during the Depression and the war years, competition from television and drive-in theaters forced many old-style movie theaters out of business. The image below, of the Caldwell building before it was torn down in 1960, features a poster directing patrons to the air-conditioned comfort of the Liberty Theater in Benton Harbor. Both were owned by Butterfield Theaters. (Above, courtesy of Daryl Schlender; below, courtesy of Larry Podjan.)

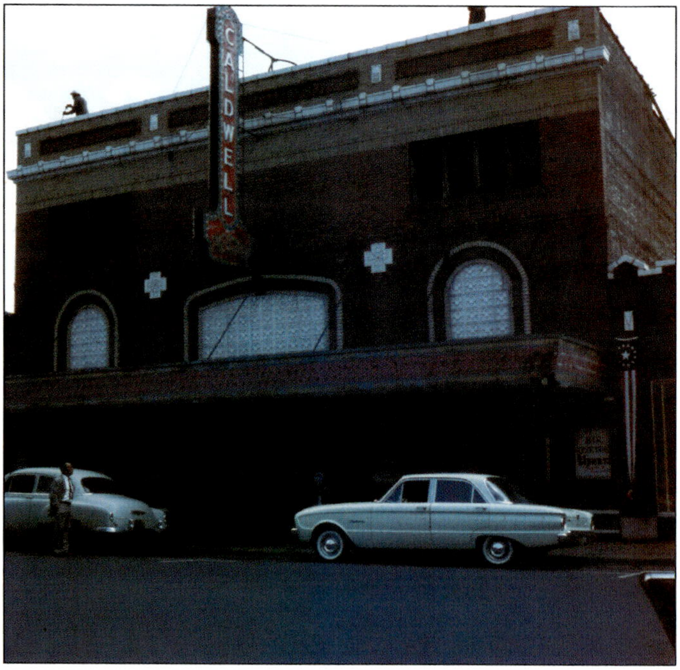

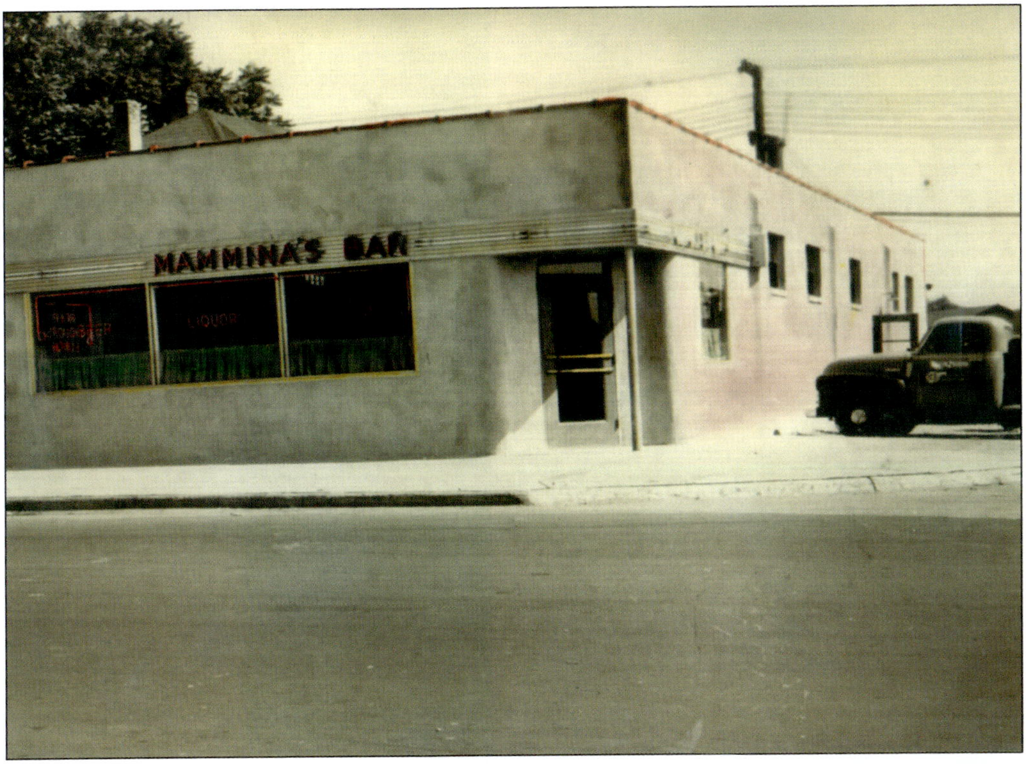

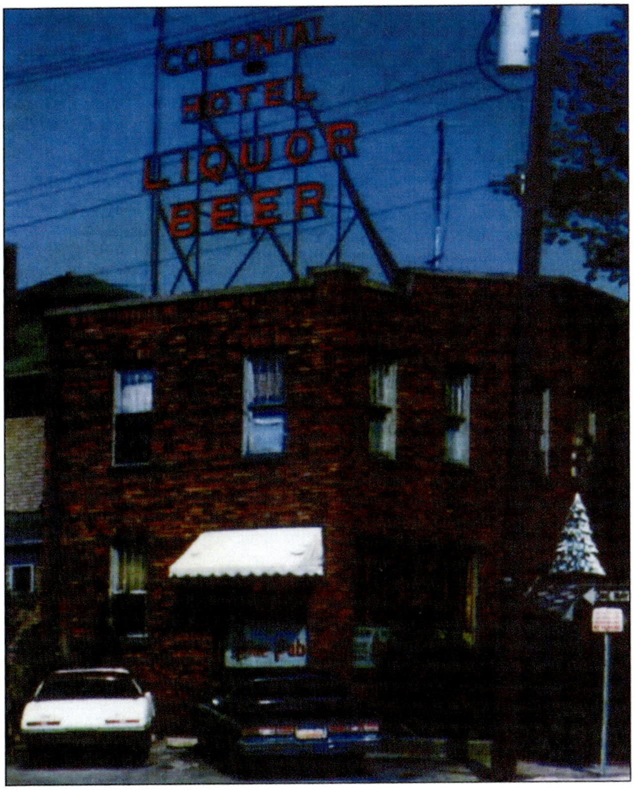

Family-owned restaurant and taverns were the heart and soul of small American towns. They offered strong drinks, good burgers, fried fish, and pizza at affordable prices, unpretentious atmospheres, and a warm welcome to regulars. One such eatery was Mammina's (above) in Benton Harbor, at the corner of Territorial Road and Second Street. Open 24 hours, it was a favorite of third-shift factory workers. Another was the Pine Pub, originally located in the Colonial Hotel at 713 Broad Street in St. Joseph. In 1964, longtime bartender Bob Farnan and his business partner Adam Owca purchased the business, and they eventually moved it next door to 715 Broad Street, where it remained until it was razed in 1979. (Above, courtesy of Ben Mammina; right, courtesy of Joseph Lodyga.)

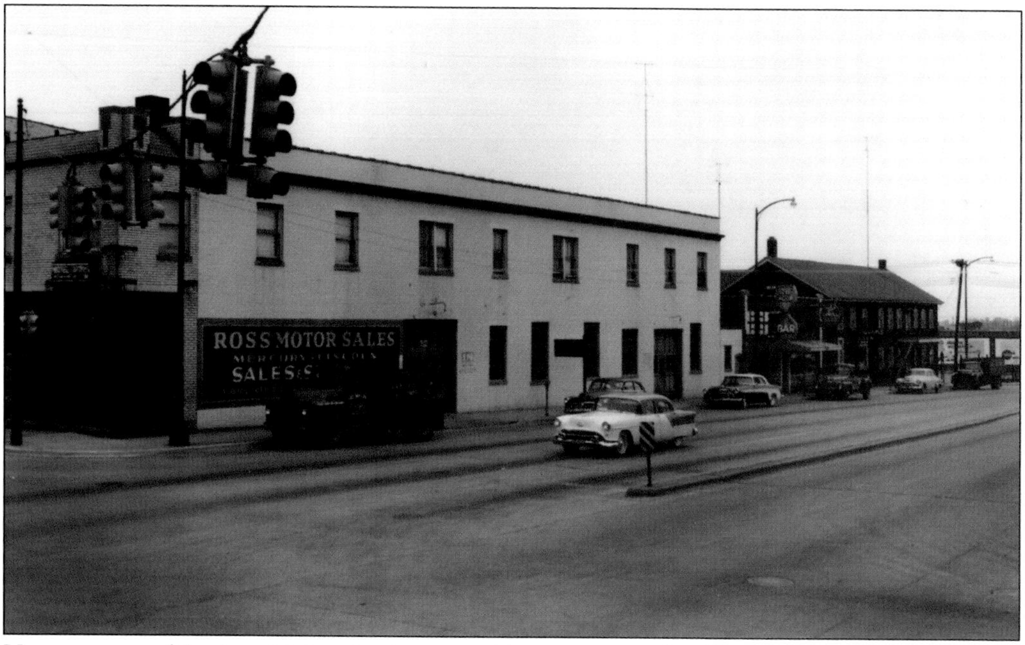

Here are two of St. Joseph's lost institutions. Above, just north of Ross Motor Sales, is the Idle Hour Bar on 110 Main Street, just north of Ship Street. Owned by Raymond and Helen Strasburg, this blue-collar oasis served mostly beer and sandwiches. Below, between Mawhinney's Ice Cream Bar and Kniebes' Music Mart at 416 State Street, is the Silver Dollar Saloon. In the 1960s, the Idle Hour changed ownership, moved to State Street, and became the Pump House Lounge, then H.I.'s Saloon—a favorite spot for young people. The Silver Dollar moved to 412 State Street, the building with the "For Rent" sign in the photograph, where it served burgers, beer, and cocktails to loyal clientele until 2008. (Both, courtesy of Joseph Lodyga.)

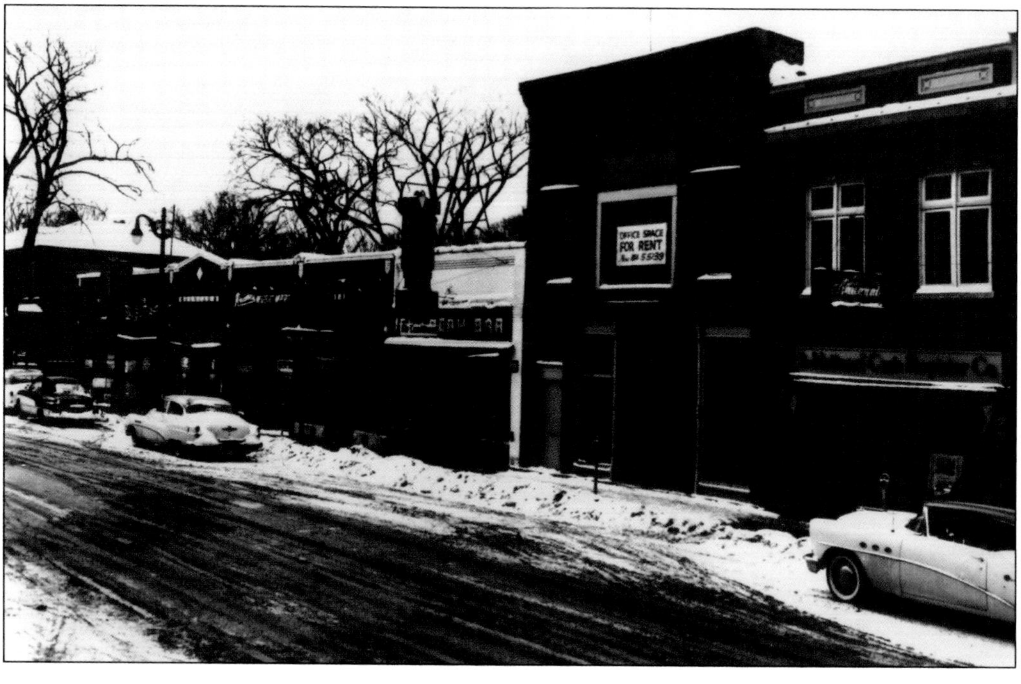

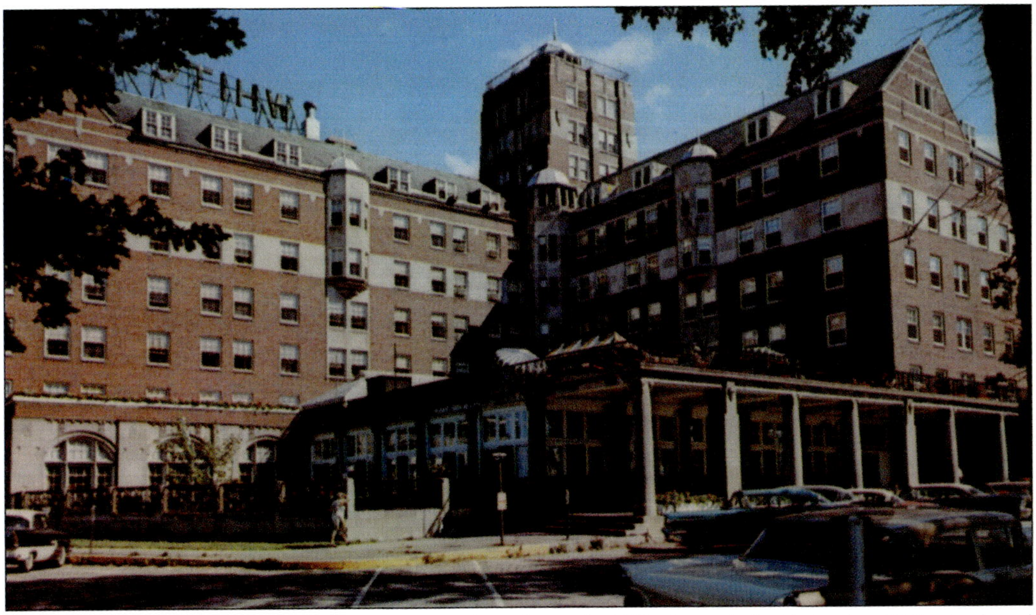

The Whitcomb Hotel still stands as a reminder of grand old St. Joseph. Built in the 1890s, it closed briefly during the Great Depression, opened soon after, and prospered until 1960. In November 1966, when the hotel closed its doors for the last time, Polly, the famous lobby parrot, was adopted by the St. Joseph Fire Station. Lifetime resident Joe Lodyga reports that her remains are interred at the fireman's monument on the bluff. In 1967, Michigan Baptist Homes reopened the Whitcomb as an upscale retirement community. Below is the landmark Maids of the Mist fountain, across from the hotel. After a period of deterioration during the 1960s, it was renovated in 1974 by the city and the Fort Miami Heritage Society. (Both, courtesy of Daryl Schlender.)

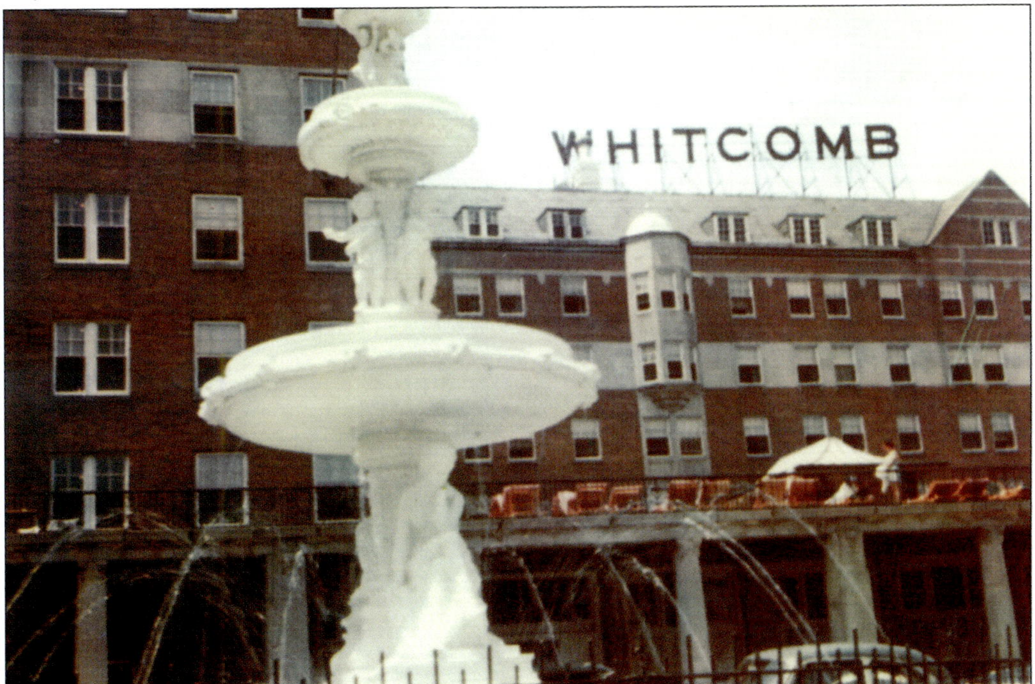

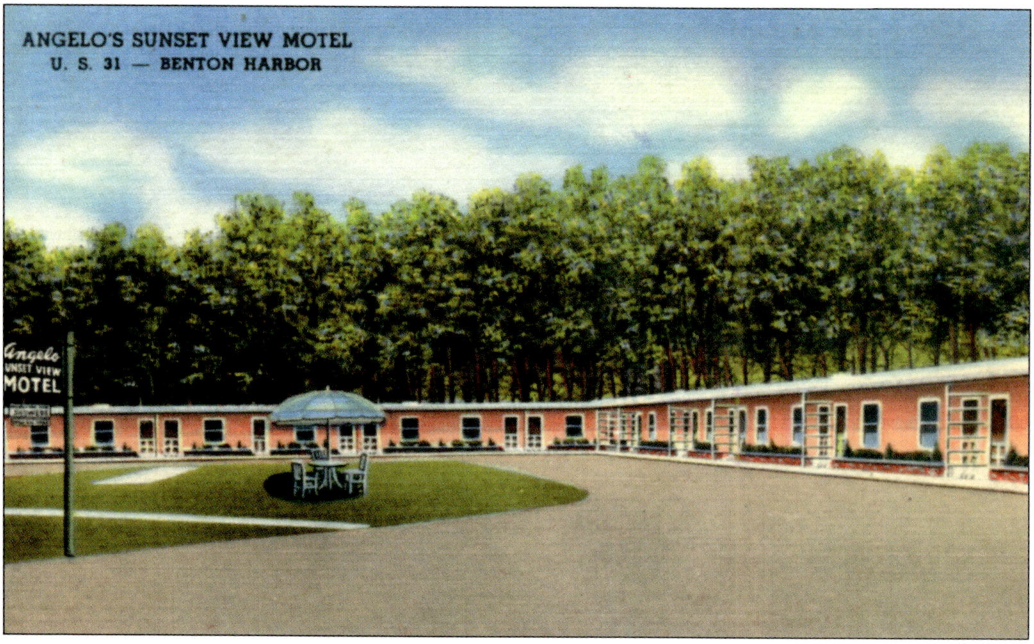

The development of the national highway system in the 1920s, expanded to the interstates of the 1950s, brought a new roadside culture of speed and convenience. Bypassing grand downtown hotels such as the Whitcomb, travelers preferred motor courts such as those depicted here. Located outside of Benton Harbor along the old US Highway 31, now the Blue Star Highway, the Sunset View Motel was owned and run by Tony and Theresa Angelo. Below is the Lake Breeze Motor Court on US Highway 12 outside of St. Joseph. It advertised individual cottages, each equipped with hot water and outdoor lounge chairs, a restaurant on the premises, and an adjacent bowling alley. (Above, courtesy of Theresa Angelo-Immoos; below, courtesy of Daryl Schlender.)

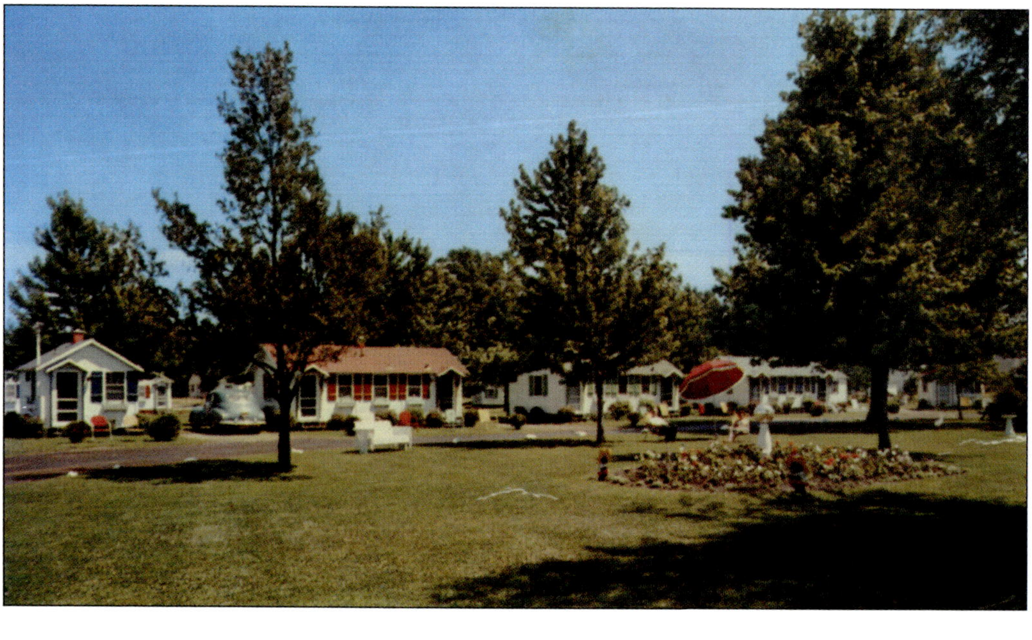

Two

Modern Times

The twin cities of Benton Harbor and St. Joseph were centers of farming, shipping, and manufacturing. Waterfront St. Joseph was a Great Lakes shipping port. With the county's abundant orchards and fruit farms, the fruit market in downtown Benton Harbor, the nation's largest wholesale supplier, was another crucial economic anchor. The Israelite House of David, with its produce and dairy farming, picture framing, commercial greenhouses, cold storage, restaurants, hotels, entertainment, and auto repair industries, further sustained the local economy.

After the long Depression and World War II, the nation was as intent on rebuilding its mood as its economy. Industries largely devoted to war manufacturing retooled for civilian ends—specifically focusing on consumer goods such as electronics, convenience items, and automobiles. Heathkit, one of the earliest contenders in what eventually became the personal computer industry, sold electronic hobby kits comprised of repurposed electronics parts from World War II airplanes. Auto Specialties, which manufactured artillery shell casings during the war, quickly retooled for automotive parts. Whirlpool Corporation, which established its headquarters in Benton Harbor in 1956, became one of the world's largest manufacturers and suppliers of major home appliances.

Urban renewal, the other great force of modernization, brought drastic changes and mixed blessings. Several blocks in downtown St. Joseph were flattened, compelling local establishments to relocate. Although historic State Street was left largely intact, business owners were left with decaying buildings and diminishing retail activity.

Benton Harbor was hit harder. The demolition in the mid-1960s of the lower-income, ethnically mixed, and peaceful Flats community displaced nearly 200 families. Most of the white families relocated outside the city to Fairplain, St. Joseph, or the surrounding rural areas, where blacks, in an era of widespread discrimination, found themselves unwelcome. The frustration of disruption, overcrowding, lack of adequate housing, and diminishing economic opportunities, particularly when the civil rights movement was gaining momentum, eventually erupted into a series of street riots. Increasingly alarmed, Benton Harbor's white population began its exodus, thus beginning an era of racial tension and social division.

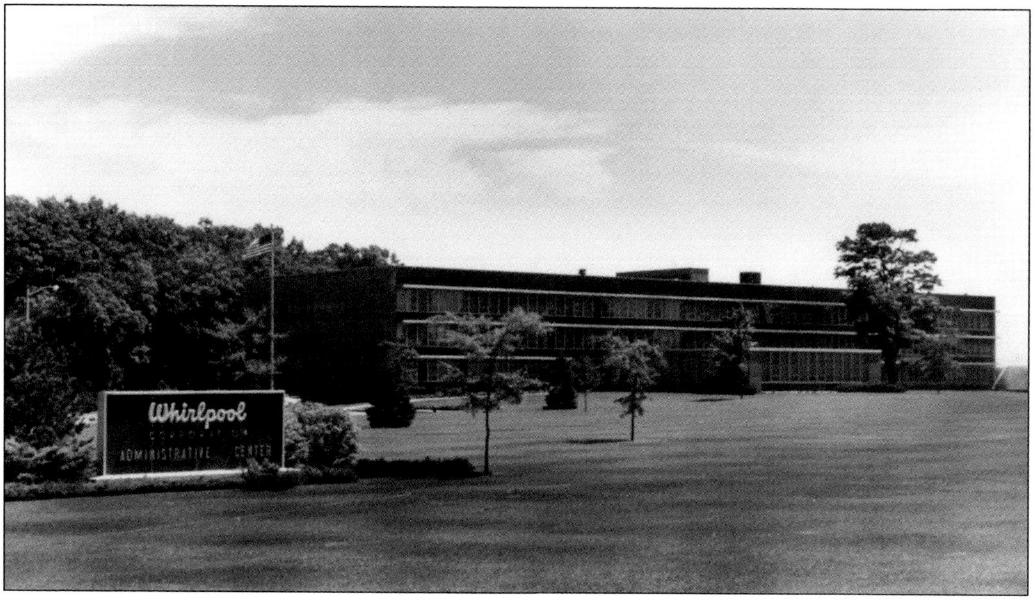

Founded in 1911 by Louis and Emory Upton, Whirlpool Corporation, a multinational manufacturer of home appliances, remains crucial to Benton Harbor's industrial economy. In 1956, the company opened its 100-acre administrative center, pictured above, in Benton Harbor. The image below shows workers assembling washing machines in one of its manufacturing plants. (Both, courtesy of the Maude Preston-Palenske Memorial Library).

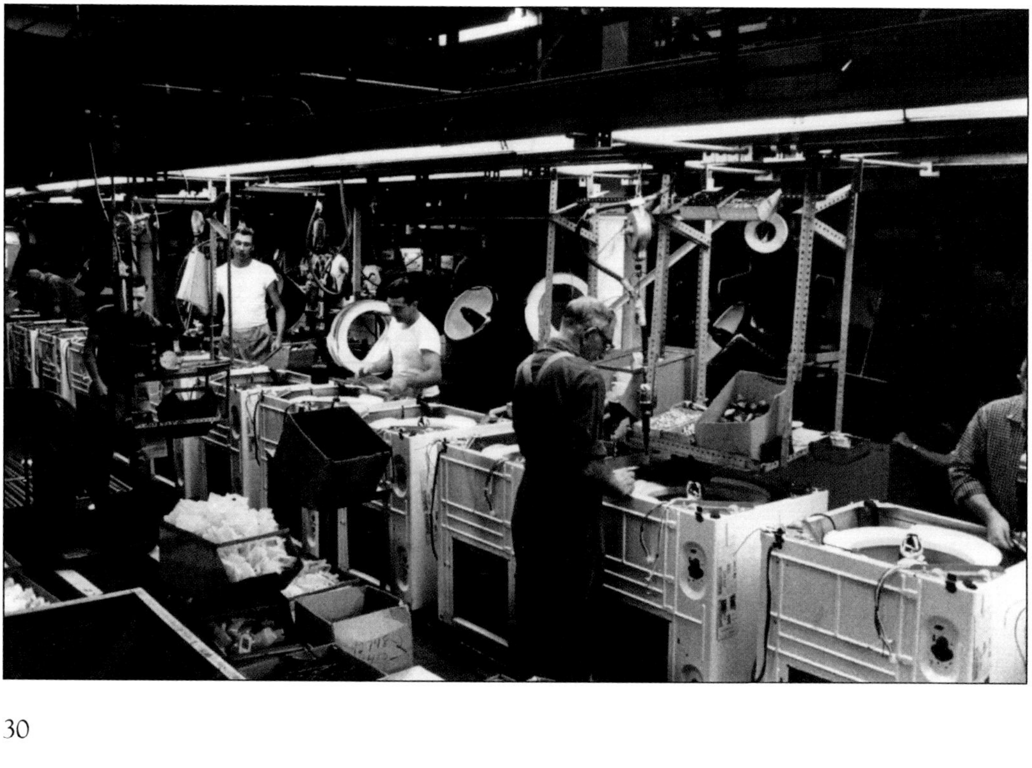

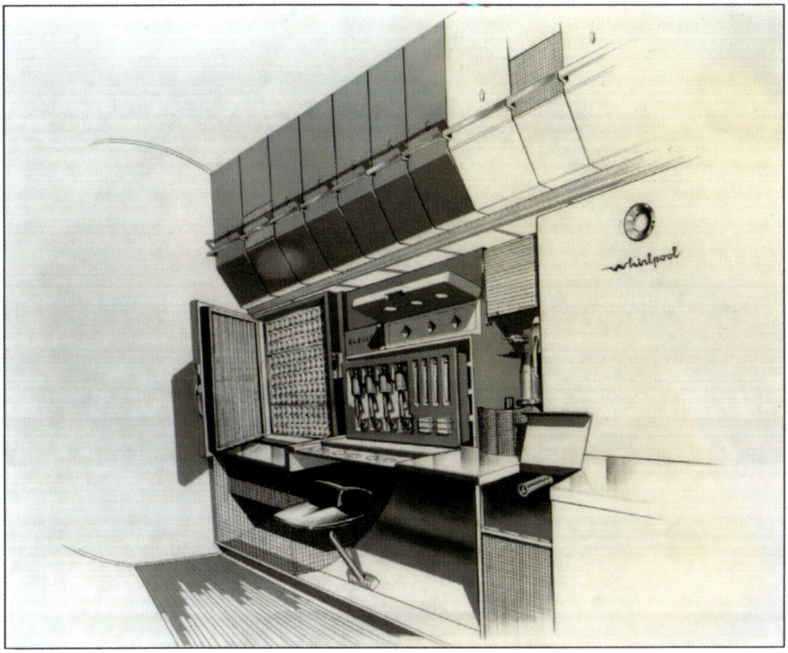

America's optimistic midcentury fascination with the idea of a better future was visualized as an expansion into space; this time was called the space age. In 1960, Whirlpool Corporation received a NASA contract to build an experimental space kitchen, depicted above. As described on the company website, "the kitchen included a miniature thermoelectric refrigerator, freezer, three-cavity oven, self-heated water system," and storage and disposal for food and waste. The appliance engineers had to consider issues of zero gravity in kitchen design. Below is an example of a heated space meal. Note the packets of freeze-dried food cubes displayed around the tray. Children of Whirlpool employees at that time remember parents bringing home such packets to try. They were not particularly palatable. (Both, courtesy of Whirlpool Corporation.)

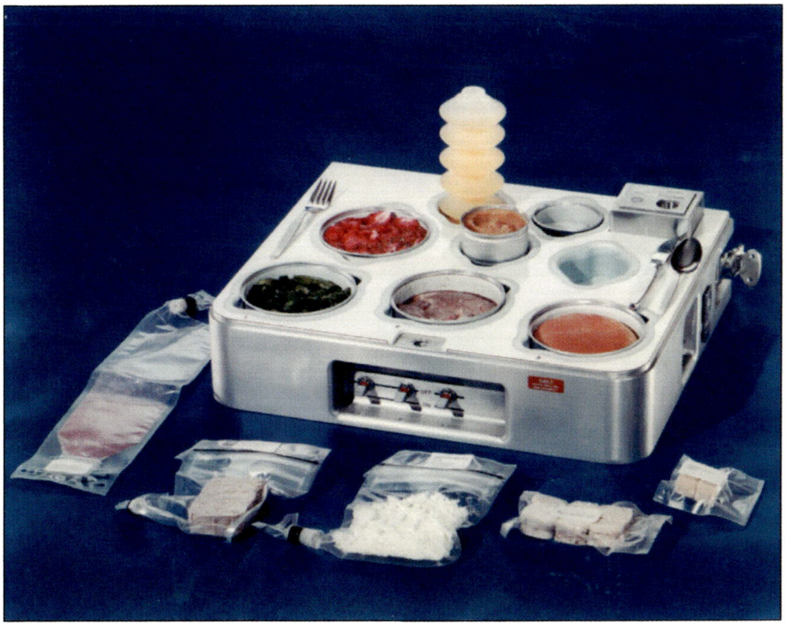

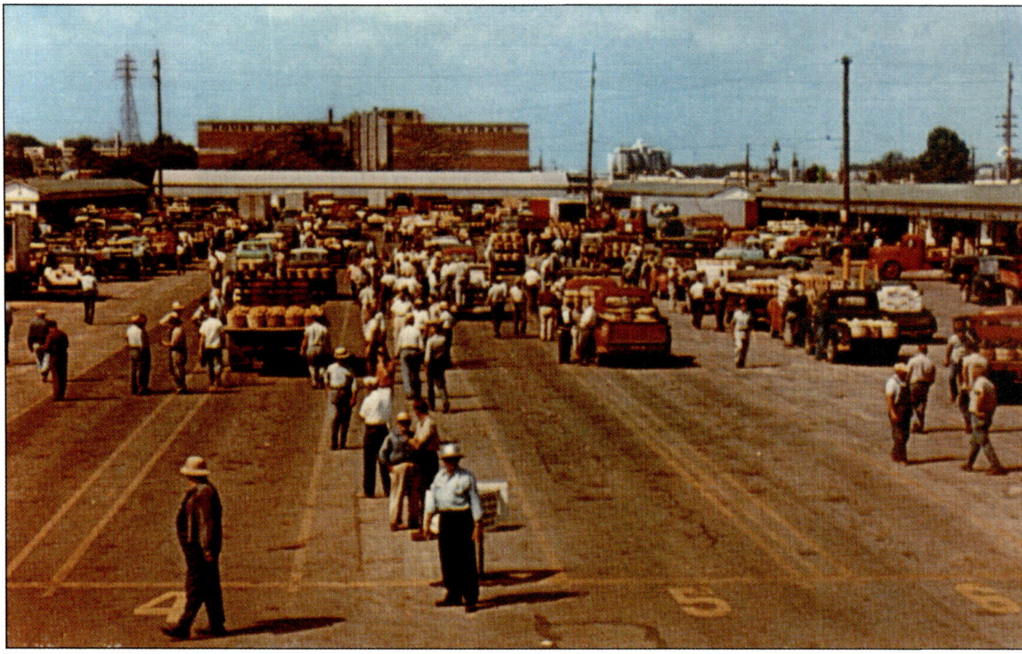

Established in 1860, the Benton Harbor Fruit Market was once the largest cash-to-grower produce market in the world. Local farm families remember the excitement of going to the market, helping out for pocket change, and enjoying lunches such as fried-egg sandwiches dressed with cheese and mayonnaise at nearby diners. Although the market was downtown Benton Harbor's economic anchor, concerns about traffic congestion and competing demands for commercial usage led to its relocation to Territorial Road on the far outskirts of town. Many cite this move out of the downtown retail sector as a major factor in the town's subsequent decline. The House of David cold storage building visible in the background above attests to the economic interdependence of local industries. (Both, courtesy of the Benton Harbor Public Library.)

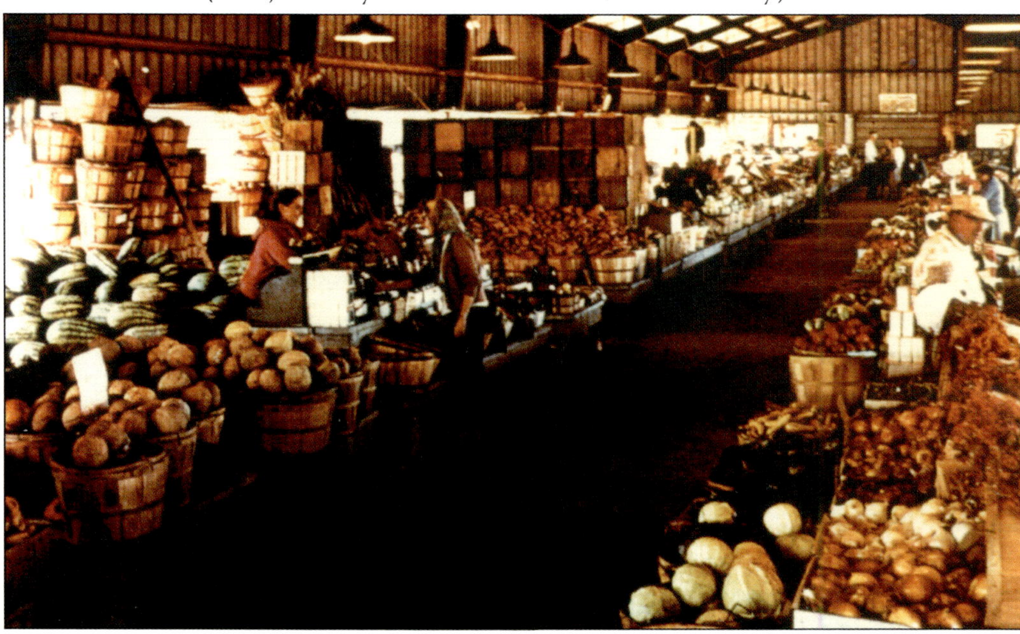

Founded in 1926 by Edward Bayard Heath, the Heath Company originally sold light aircraft kits for assembly. After Heath died during a 1931 test flight, Howard Anthony bought the company. After World War II, by collecting and selling off a huge stock of wartime surplus electronics parts, Anthony recreated Heath as an electronics hobby kit supply company. Heathkit Company manufactured and sold highly popular assembly kits from which enthusiasts built radios, televisions, and even computers. Successful engineers cite their Heathkit hobby as foundational training. At right, a technician welds a B-5 Battery Eliminator. Below, another wires a circuit from a diagram. Heathkits were also known for excellent technical documentation and accurate instructions. (Both, courtesy of the Maude Preston Palenske Memorial Library.)

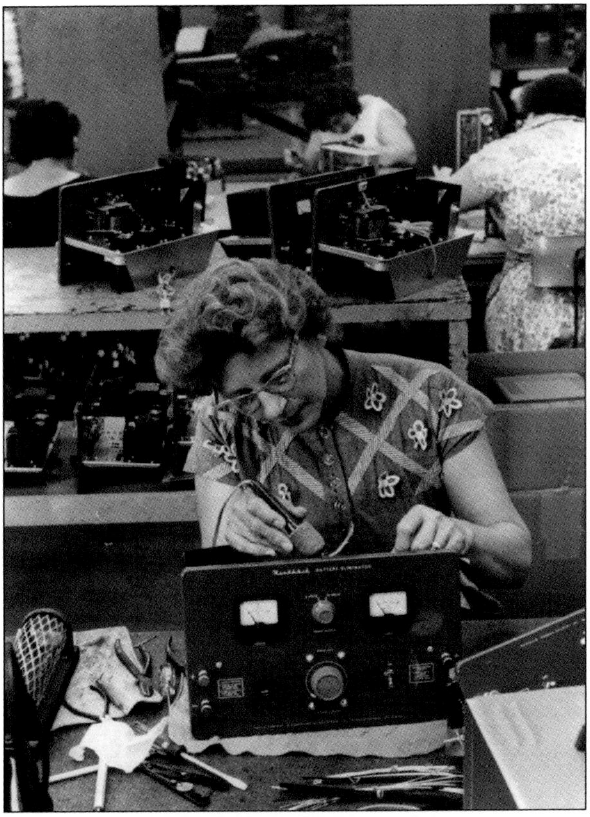

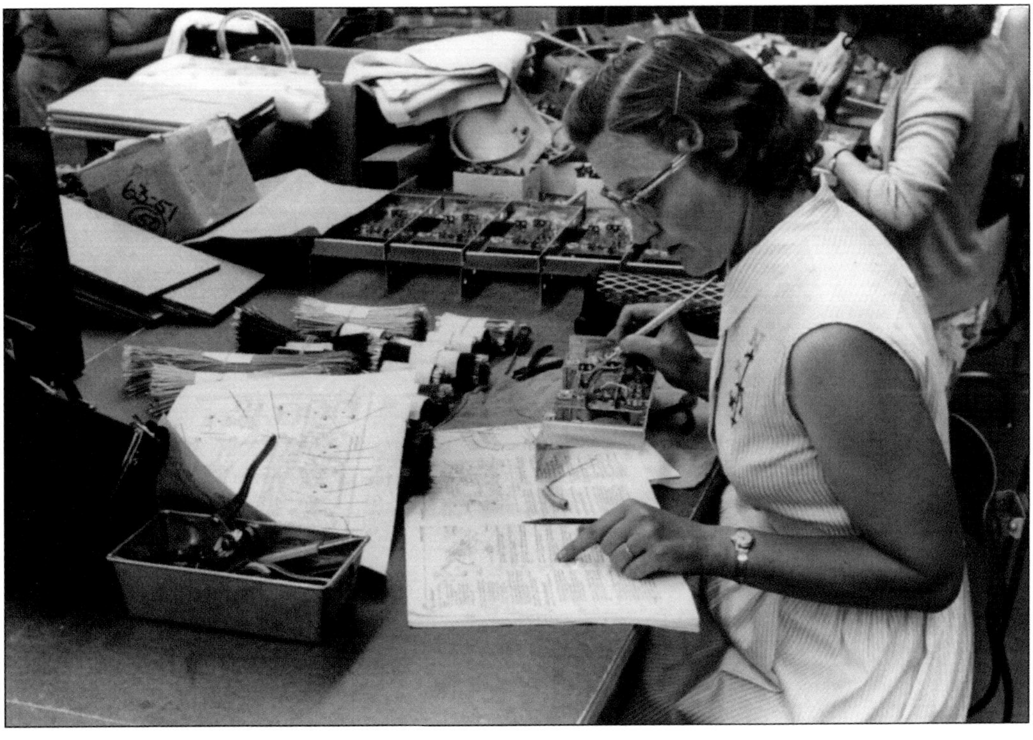

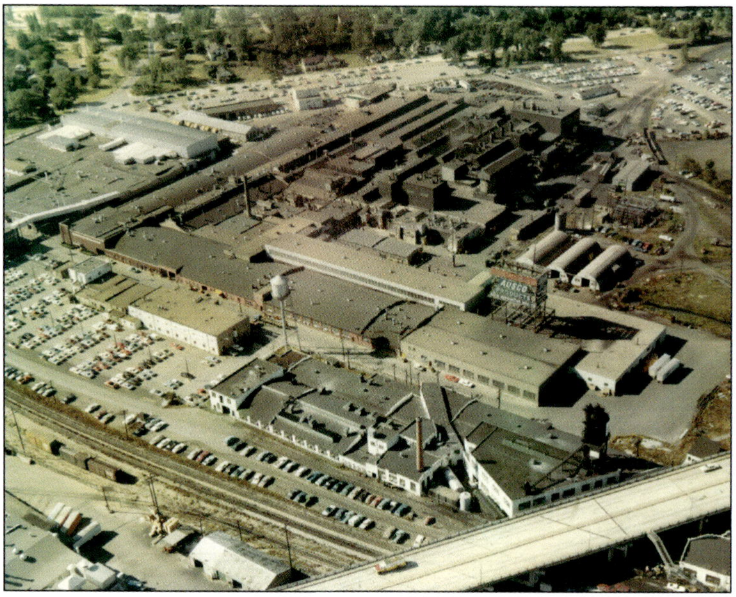

Founded in Joliet, Illinois, in 1908 by James W. Tiscornia and Clarence Bair and soon relocated to St. Joseph, Auto Specialties Manufacturing Company (AUSCO) poured its first casting in 1917. Rapidly growing with the new automobile industry, AUSCO specialized in parts such as hydraulic jacks, disc brakes, and crankshafts. Above is the original Edgewater Plant in St. Joseph. The "time and temperature" sign at center right was a local landmark. During World War II, the Defense Plant Corporation, a federal subsidiary chartered by Congress to expand wartime manufacturing, built the Riverside plant below. Designed by the Detroit architecture firm Giffels and Rossetti and operated by Auto Specialties, it was used for munitions manufacturing until purchased by the Tiscornia family in 1951. After a short postwar run making cast-steel crankshafts for automobiles, this plant was renovated and reopened in 1965 to produce larger malleable-iron castings. Its foundry and machine shop areas totaled over 200,000 square feet. (Both, courtesy of James and Edward Tiscornia.)

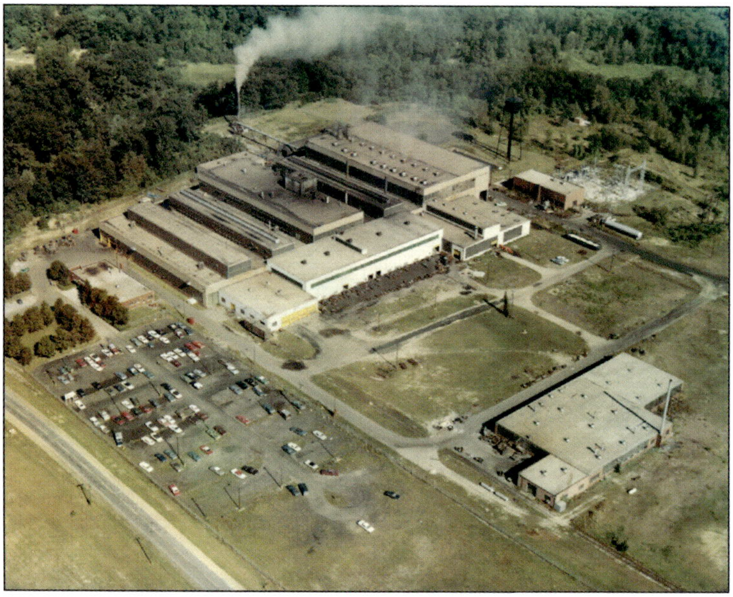

A family operation, AUSCO was part of the community. Waldo Tiscornia, cofounder of the St. Joseph plant with brother James, was mayor of St. Joseph from 1943 to 1955 and beloved for bringing high-caliber minor league and semipro baseball to St. Joseph. In 1940, he built Edgewater Park and started the AUSCOS, who continued their legendary reign until 1957. Tiscornia (left) is pictured here at a commemorative occasion with Carl Kennedy, an AUSCOS player who also golfed for the company team. When minor league baseball dwindled, AUSCO Management Club gifted Tiscornia with Boys Field, to host baseball games for boys in the community in 1957. Pictured below are the AUSCO Tigers, 1966 Babe Ruth Champs. (Right, courtesy of Brian Ziebart; below, courtesy of James and Edward Tiscornia.)

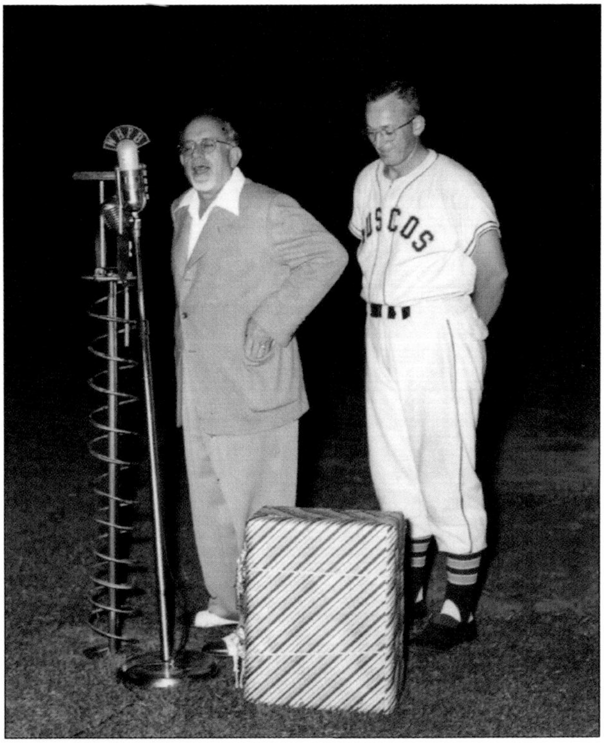

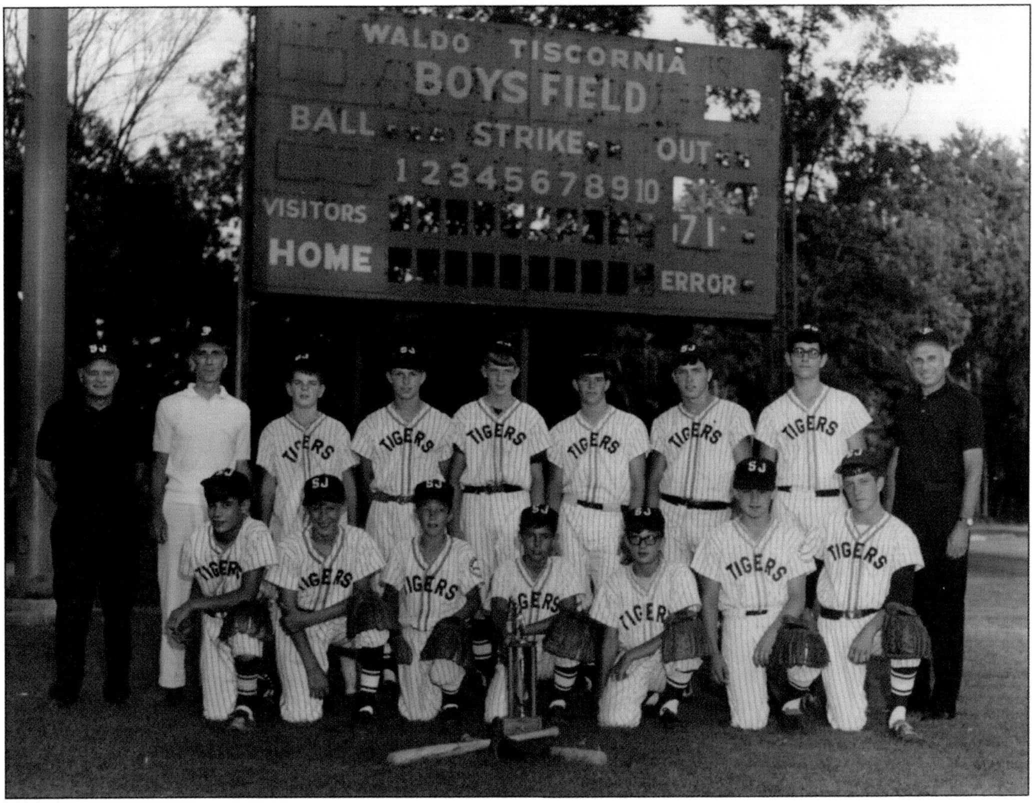

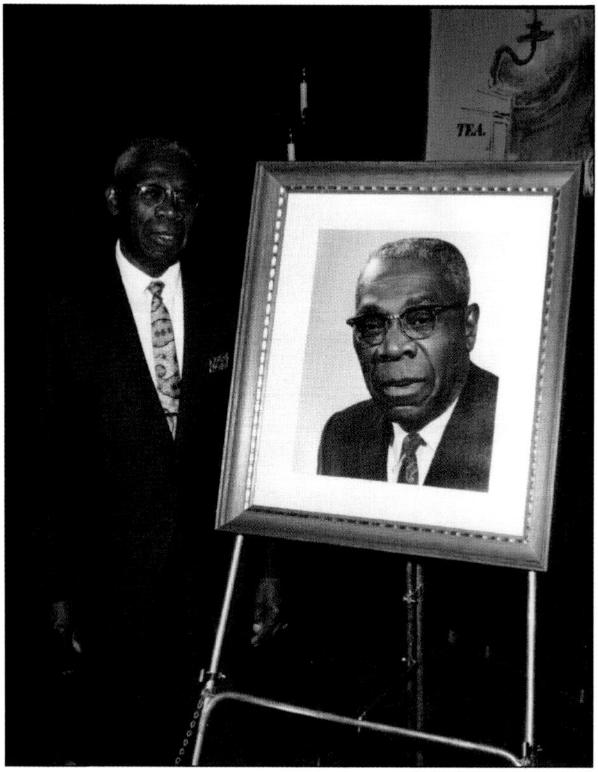

Once, companies typically offered rewards and incentives to workers for lifetime service. Beginning in 1946, AUSCO honored employees who had been with the company 25 years with an annual 25 Year Club dinner, at which they received gold watches and scrolls. At left is Ralph Herndon, honored in 1967 with a portrait of himself for 50 years with AUSCO. He started in 1917, when the company had 200 employees, and worked in production until promotion in 1924 to shipping room foreman. The Tiscornia Foundation, AUSCO's philanthropic branch, also awarded annual college scholarships to children of employees or other eligible local high school students. Below are 1969 scholarship recipients Bruce Martens and Eunice Fay Thomas with their parents. Each was awarded a $3,000 scholarship for high academic achievement. (Both, courtesy of James and Edward Tiscornia.)

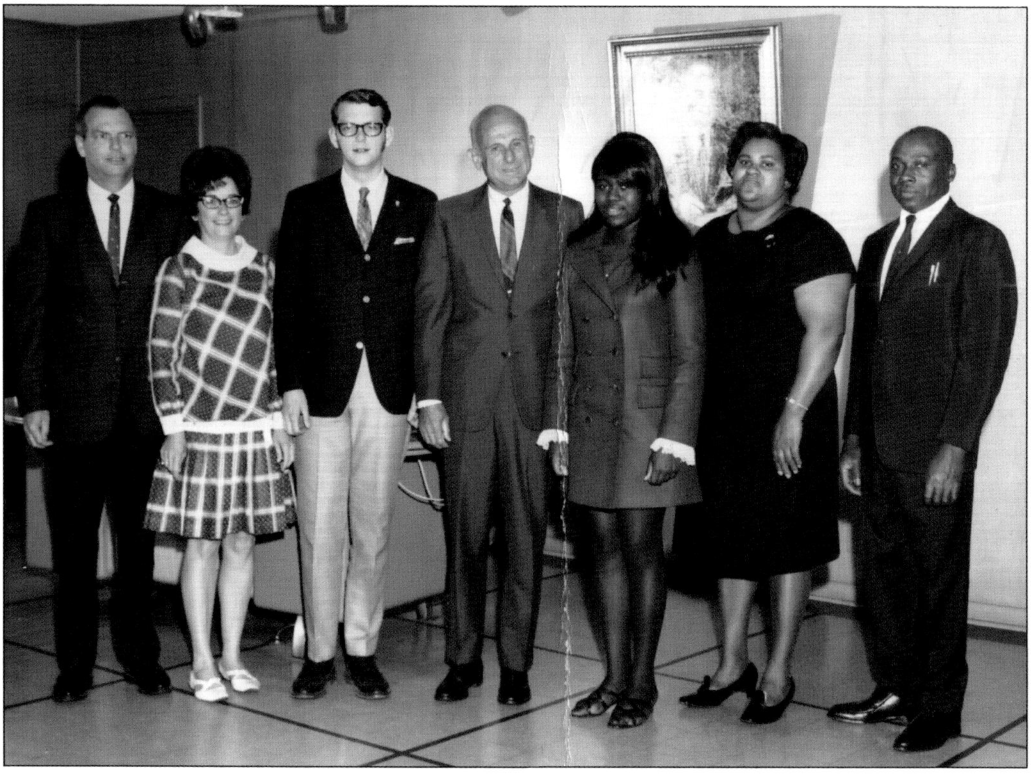

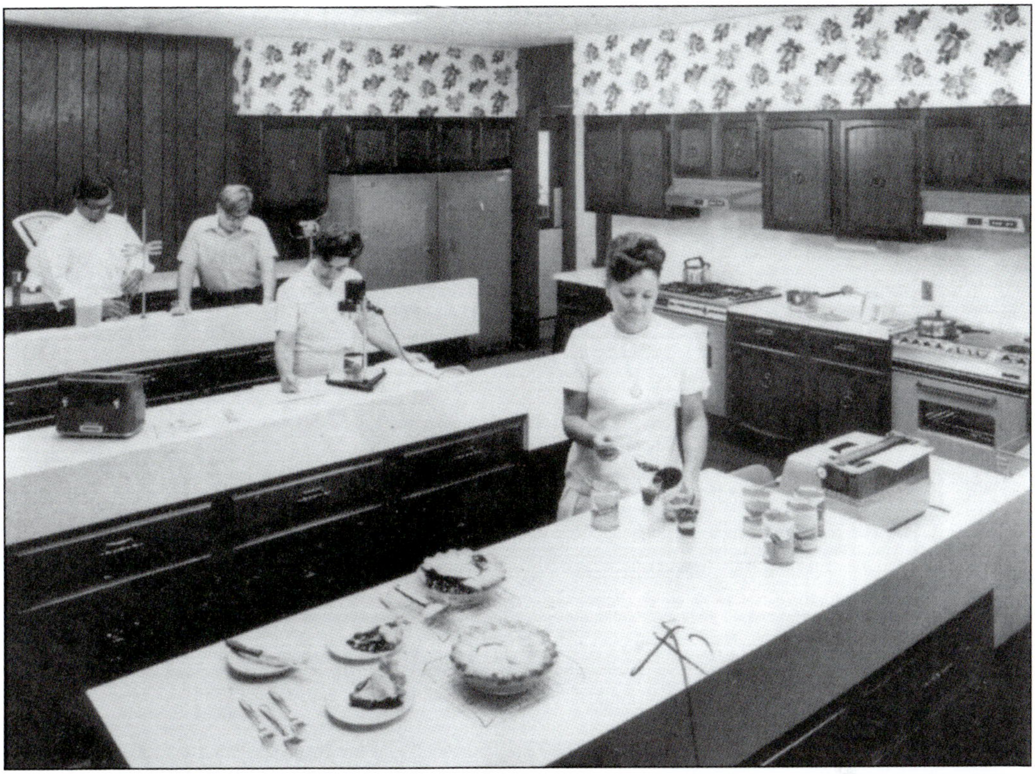

Formed in 1927, Michigan Fruit Canners in Benton Harbor was the largest such company in the Midwest. In the 1930s, it began marketing items such as spiced pears, apples, and peaches under the Thank You brand and introduced canned puddings in 1966. In the midcentury food industry, modernization meant prepackaged convenience foods but also scientific approaches to production and marketing. One such approach was the test kitchen, where trained researchers such as Mary Eppelheimer, pictured above in the foreground, developed recipes and methodically tested them for taste, texture, and durability. Another was food design—arranging and presenting food for commercial photography and advertising. Pictured on the right are some of Eppelheimer's layouts on a commercial brochure advertising ready-to-serve canned pudding for Michigan Fruit Canners. (Both, courtesy of Mary Eppelheimer.)

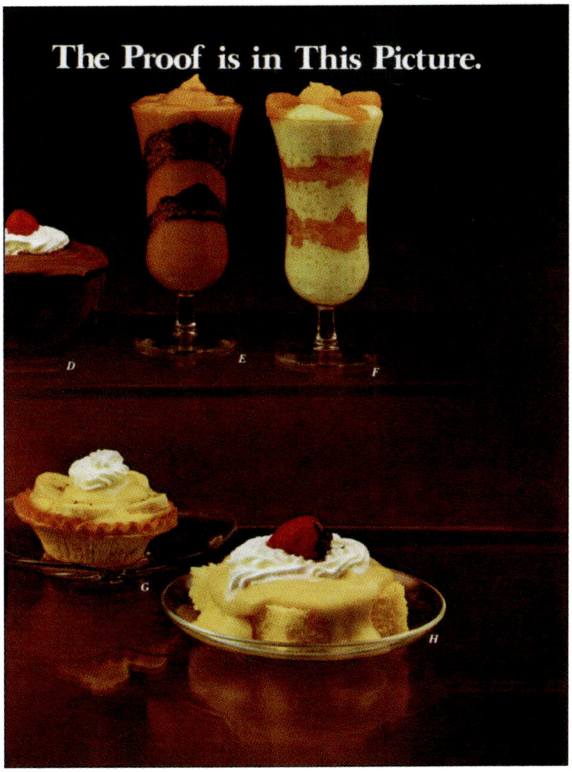

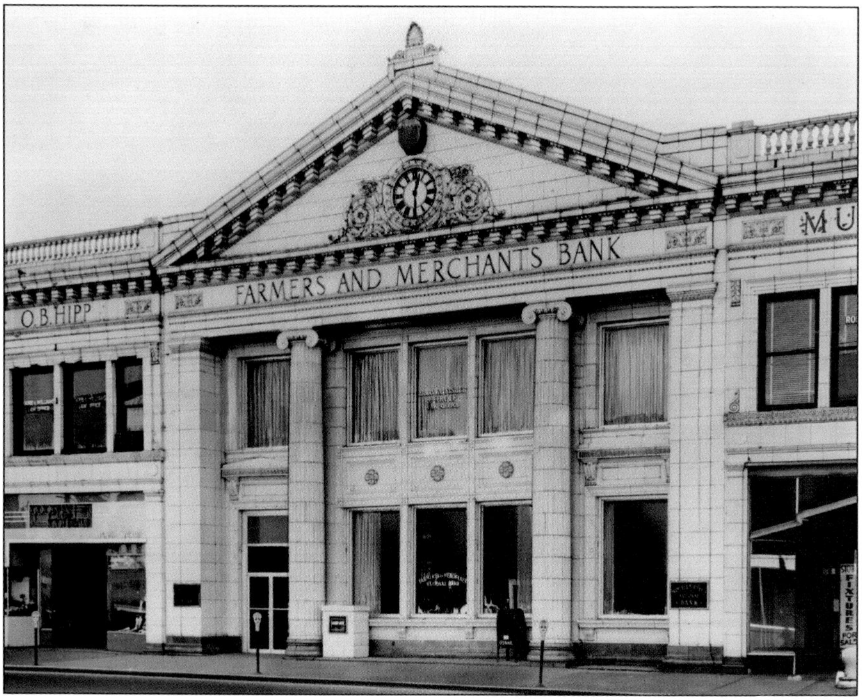

First opened in 1888, this is the Farmers and Merchants Bank, at 94 West Main Street in Benton Harbor, as it appeared in 1953. Above is its lovely Neoclassical exterior, one of the few 19th-century downtown buildings still standing today. Having weathered temporary closure during the Depression, the F&M Bank steadily increased its assets through the 1940s and early 1950s. Below is the bank lobby. Note the tile floor, high ceilings, abundance of polished wood, and Grecian-style columns. The mix of laborers, professionals, and everyday people gives a good glimpse of Benton Harbor's economic and racial demographics at the time. (Both, courtesy of Jim Willard.)

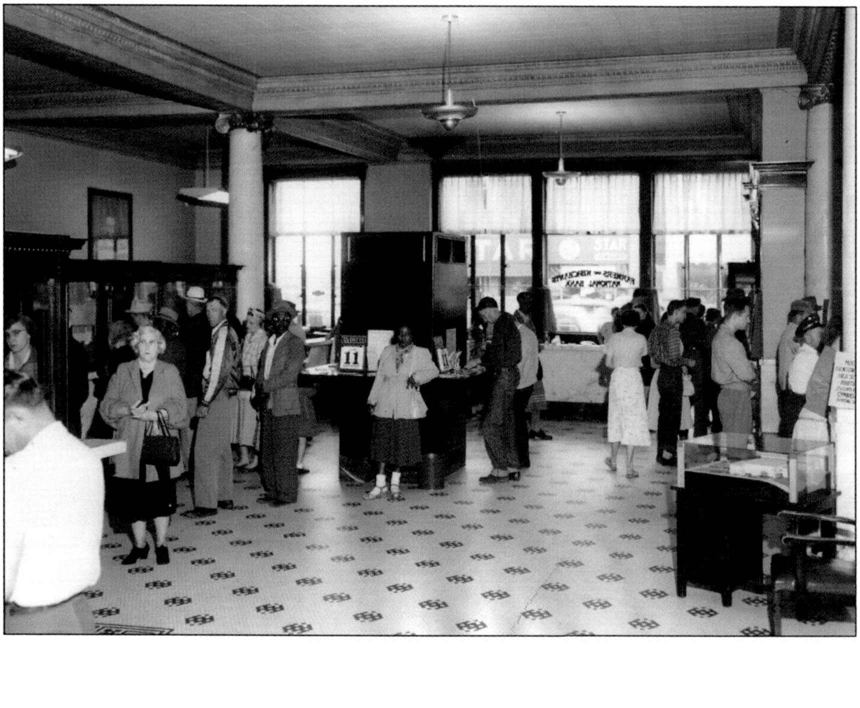

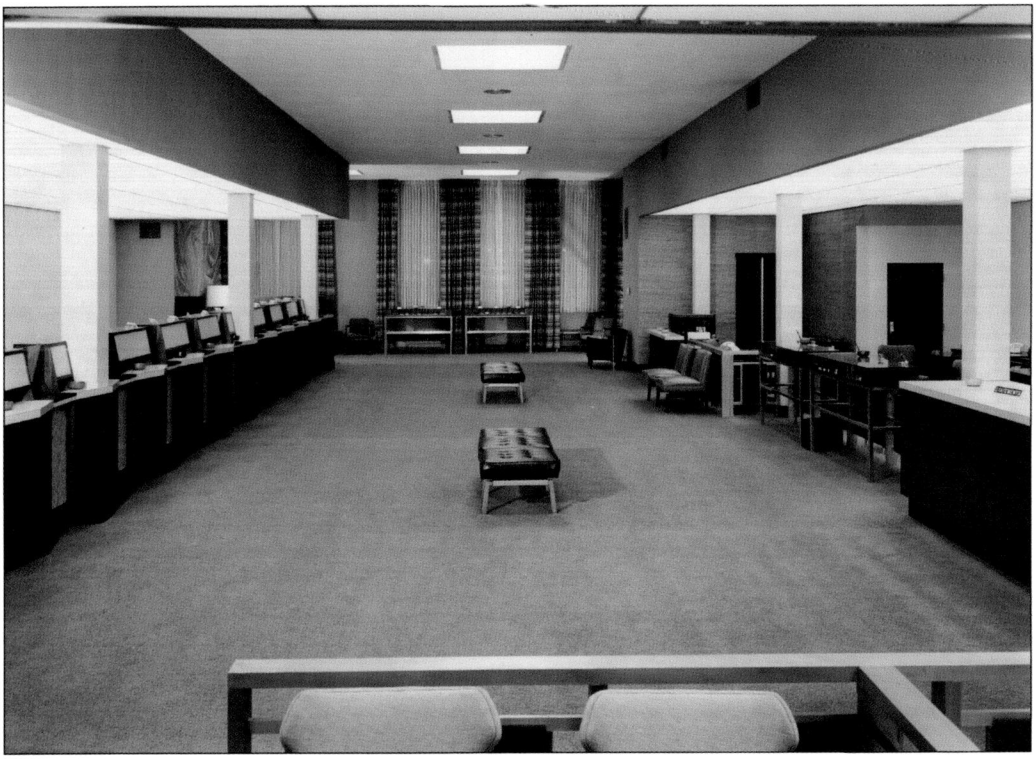

Farmers and Merchants modernized the bank's interior. The open floor plan, minimalism, and stark geometry are all characteristic of midcentury design, aimed toward efficiency and eliminating what was then regarded as the outdated clutter of the more ornate styles of public buildings of the previous century. (Courtesy of Jim Willard.).

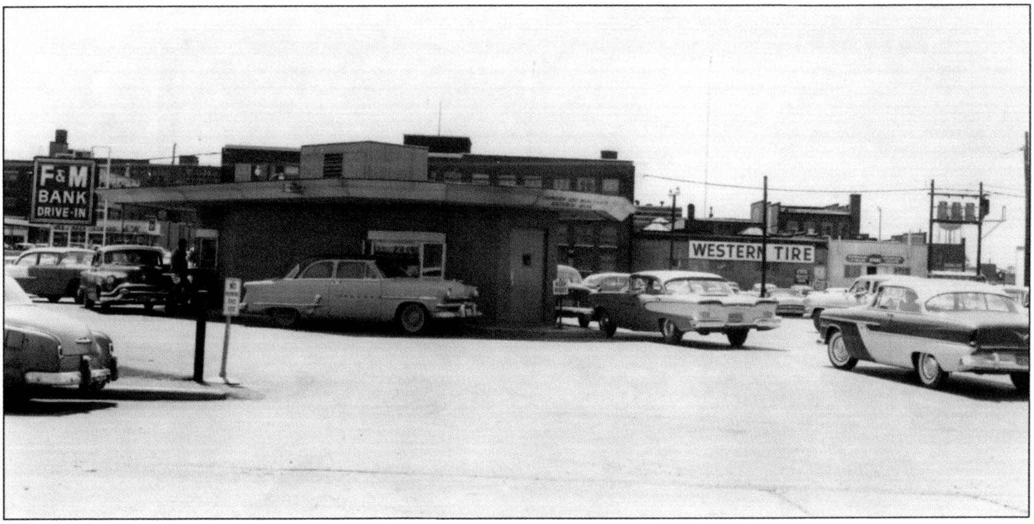

Drive-in branch banks served the new automobile culture demanding efficiency and convenience. The diamond configuration of this new F&M drive-in on the corner of Colfax Avenue and Hinkley Street in Benton Harbor allowed four teller windows at once. Jim Willard, son of then-vice president of F&M, recalls that this branch stayed open late on Christmas Eve so Whirlpool employees could cash their annual bonus checks. (Courtesy of Jim Willard.)

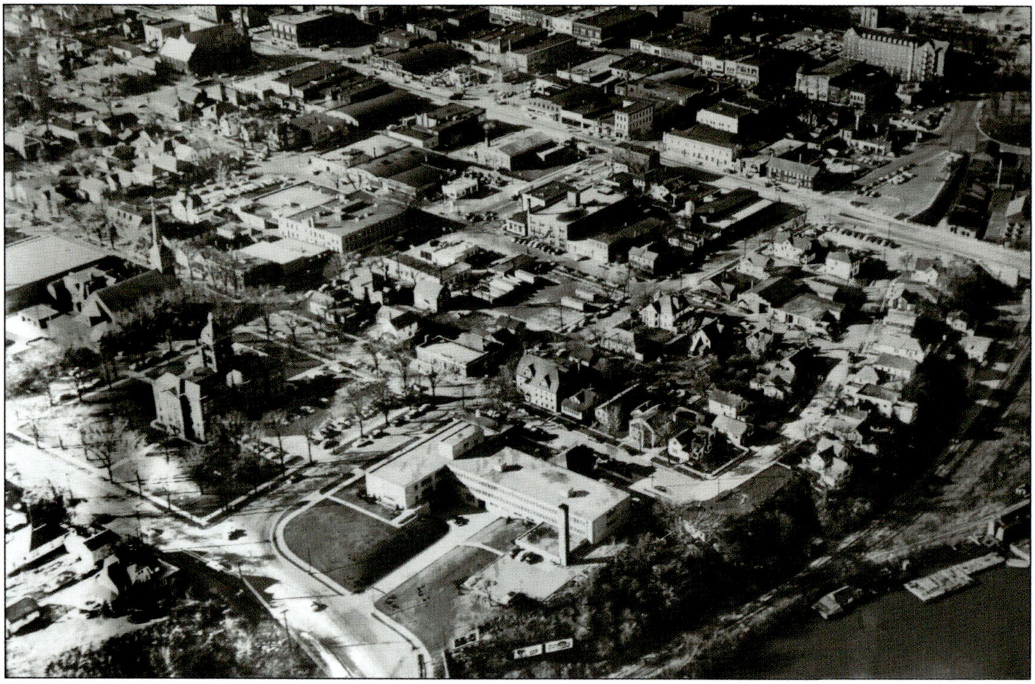

The aerial shot above shows pre-renewal St. Joseph in the late 1950s. The domed structure in the left center foreground is the old courthouse. The long, low L-shaped building is the county jail. At upper right is the silhouette of Whitcomb Tower. Designated highest priority, fundraising for the new courthouse began in 1962. Most of the $2.7 million set aside for this program came from federal aid. A city block just west of the jail was leveled for the new construction. The holiday card from Burch Printers below depicts the new Greek Revival courthouse just behind the old one, which was finally leveled in 1968. (Above, courtesy of Joseph Lodyga; below, courtesy of the Maude Preston Palenske Memorial Library.)

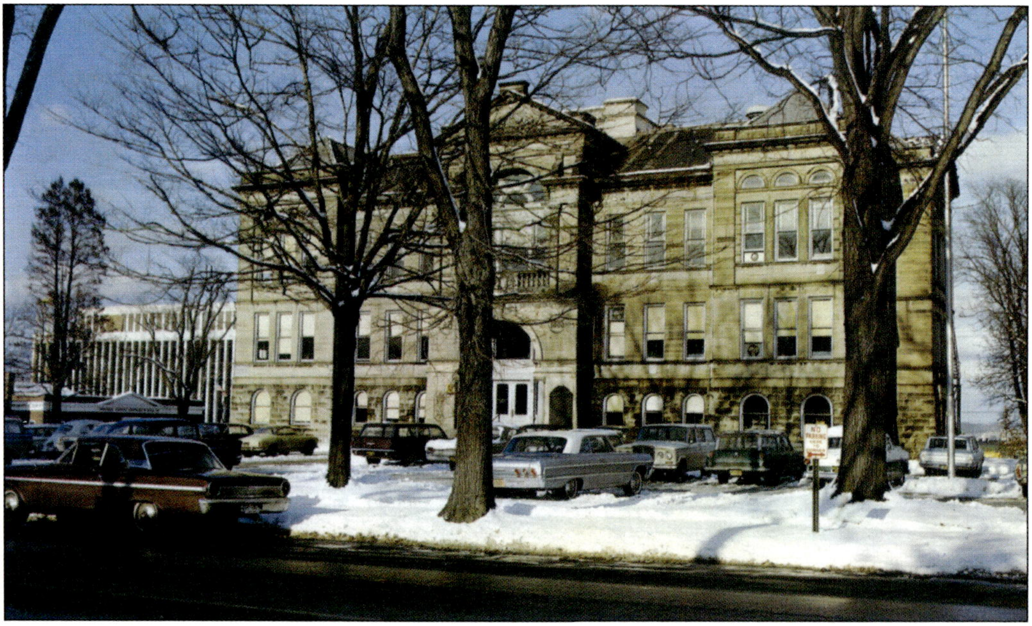

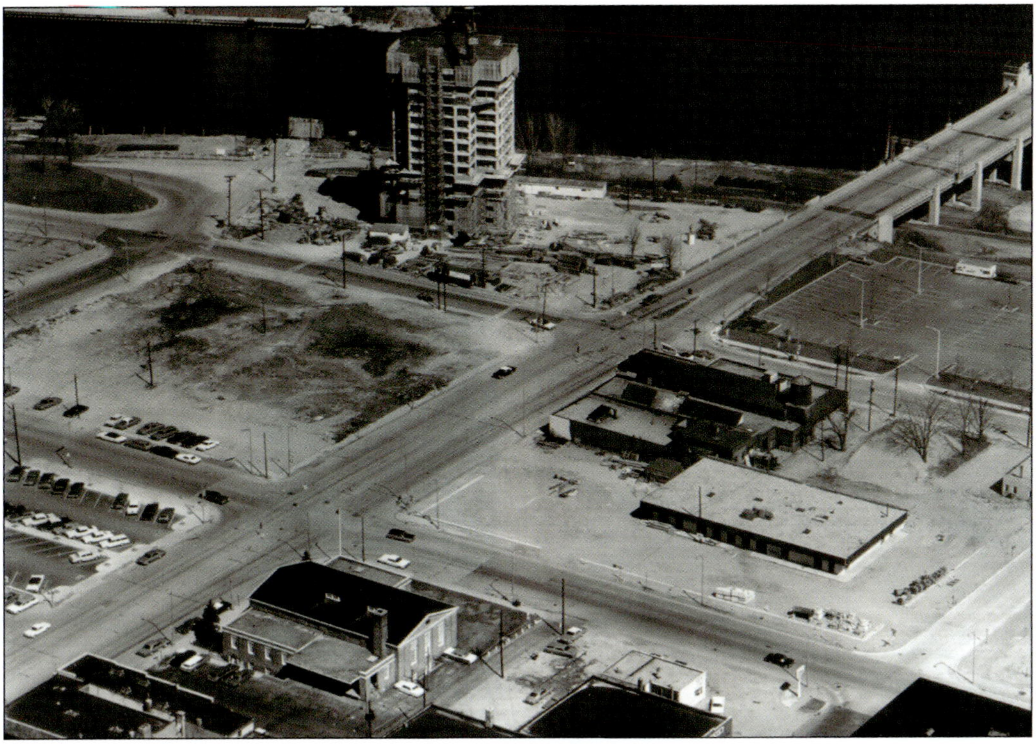

St Joseph's renewal zone comprised 32 acres bordered by Wayne Street, the river on the north, and the C&O Railroad bridge up Water Street, State Street, and Ship Street, as shown above. Newspaper accounts from 1964 anticipated "the city of the future." The high-rise under construction is Lake View Terrace, partly subsidized senior housing. The postcard image on the right depicts Lake View Terrace and the courthouse, St. Joseph's highest-priority new constructions. The focus on senior housing signified another modern trend—independent living for the elderly outside the care of extended family. (Above, courtesy of Joseph Lodyga; right, courtesy of the Maude Preston Palenske Memorial Library.)

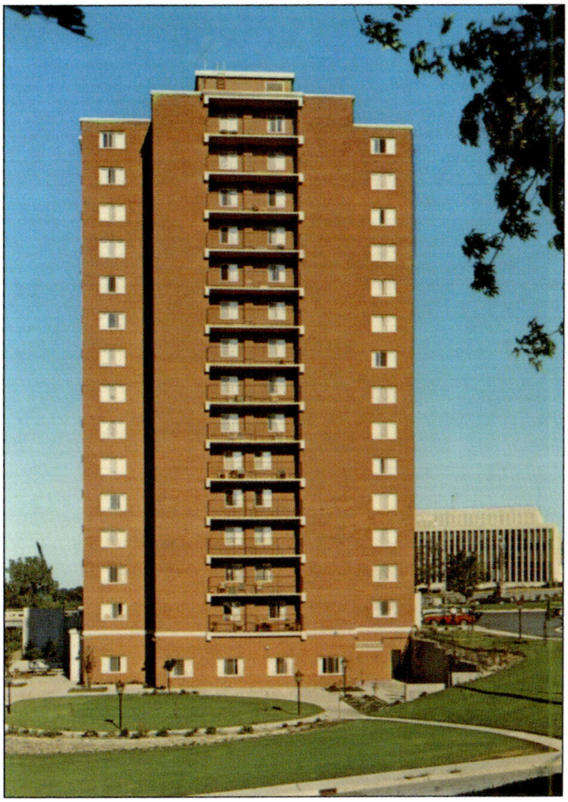

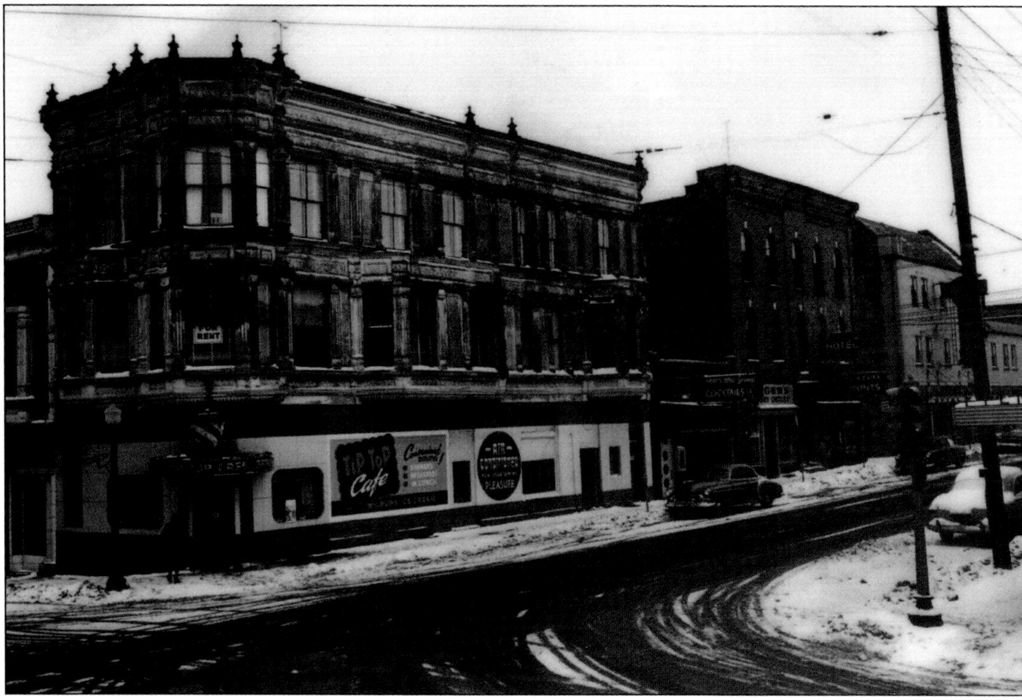

The lovely building housing the Tip Top Café, on the corner of Ship and State Streets, was one of the last holdouts against urban renewal. Its owners, Bill "Corky" and Marguerite Connors, were reluctant to give up their business. Opened in 1936, the café was a favorite gathering spot for high school students. Local business owners regularly met for lunch there, then reconvened for drinks after work at the L-shaped Brass Rail bar around the corner on Ship Street. A dance studio was once located on the second floor. The café finally closed in 1966. Below is the new Holiday Inn, in 1970, built behind where the Tip Top once stood. (Above, courtesy of Daryl Schlender; below, courtesy of James and Edward Tiscornia.)

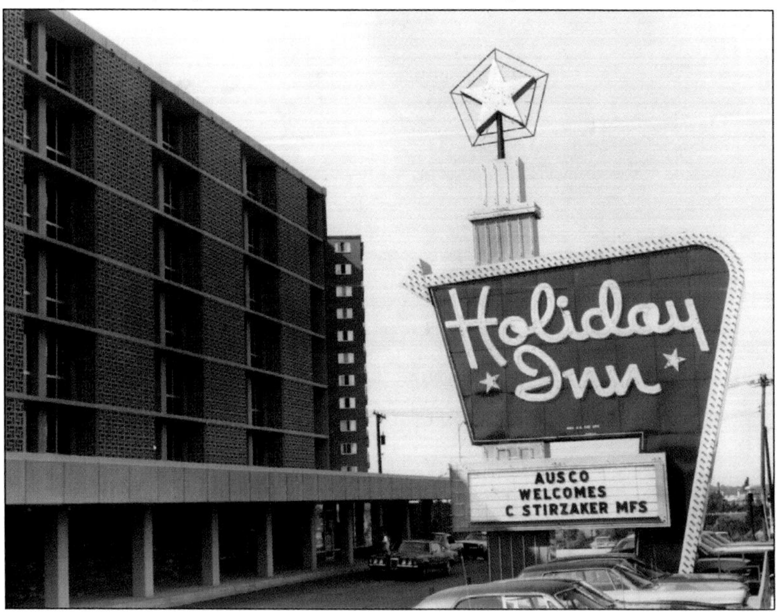

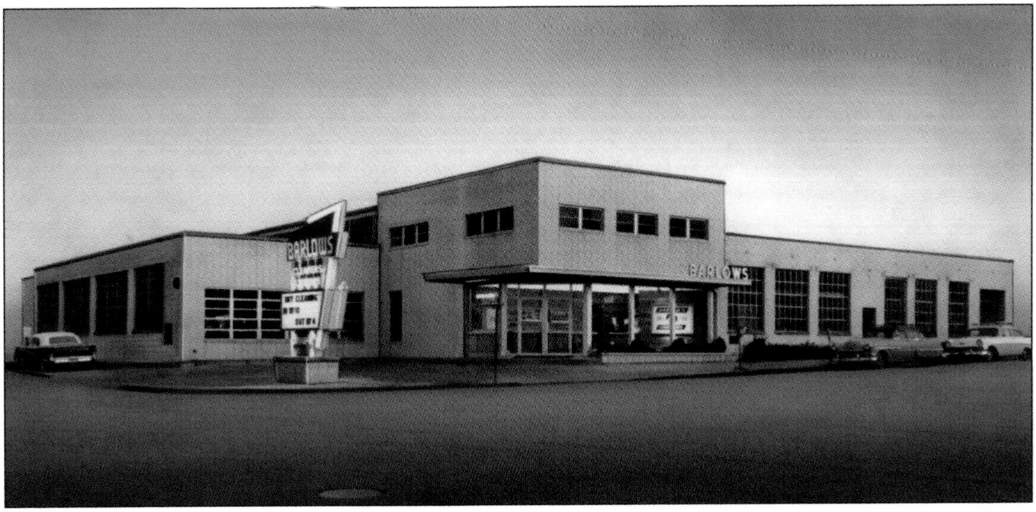

Urban renewal plans paradoxically involved relocating businesses from city centers to outlying areas, but some business owners simply expanded. When Barlows Laundry and Dry Cleaner was razed, the Barlows bought the entire block bounded by Ship, Port, Court and Main Streets for $50,000 to redevelop as a shopping center, and built this sleek new facility in south St. Joseph at 3298 Cleveland Avenue. (Courtesy of Brian Ziebart.)

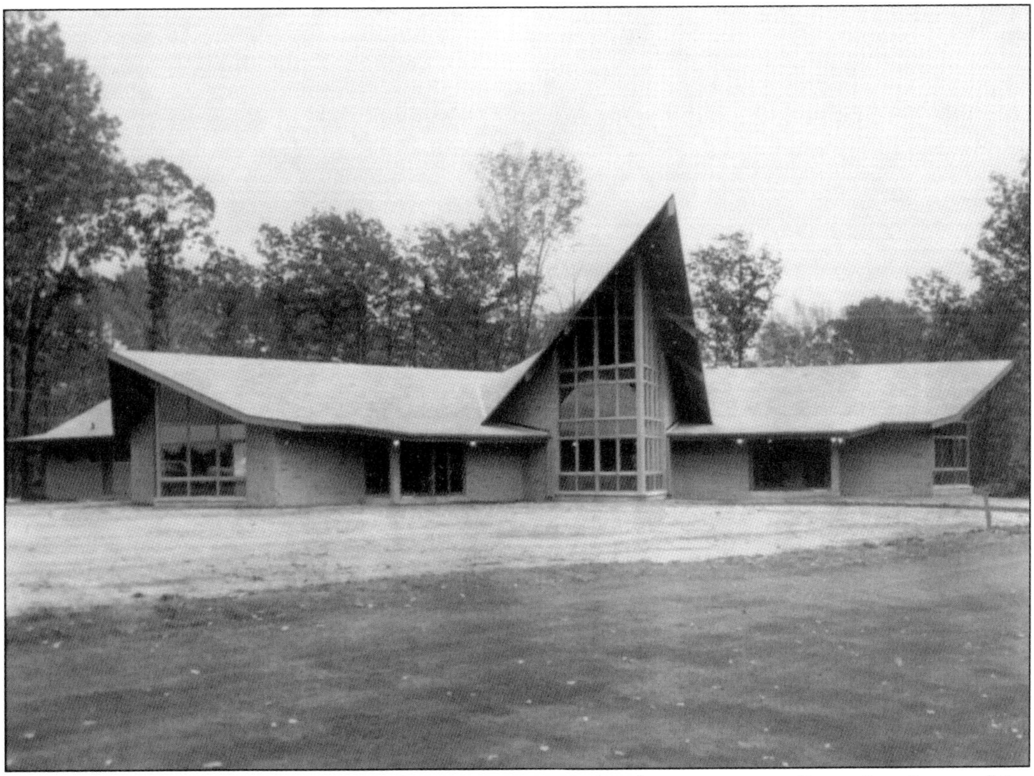

The trend to the ultramodern in architecture extended to leisure spaces. Considered one of the best in the nation, the then-new Point o' Woods Golf Course built this clubhouse in 1959. A cocktail lounge and dining room were built in the wings, and the main lounge boasted a massive copper fireplace—all state-of-the-art at the time. (Courtesy of Brian Ziebart.)

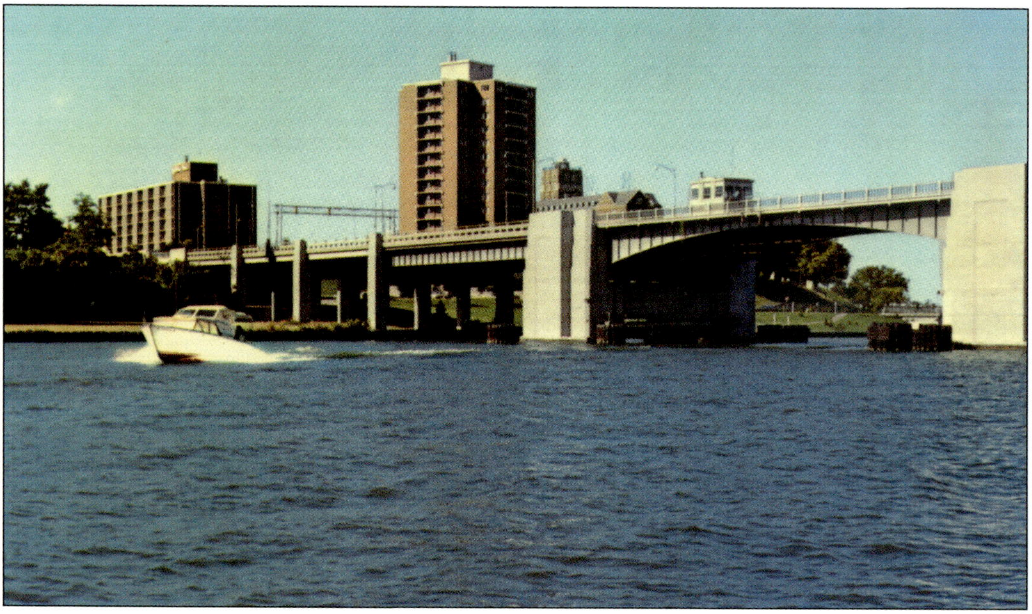

Renewal also aimed to improve traffic flow through cities increasingly dominated by automobiles, and bridge renovations were key to that effort. Above is the Blossomland Bridge, the main crossing between Benton Harbor and St. Joseph, after renovations were completed in 1966. This historic bascule bridge can be raised on either side to accommodate boat traffic. Visible in the background are the Holiday Inn and Lake View Terrace—prominent features in the newly-modernized St. Joseph skyline. Below is the Napier Avenue Bridge, which spans the St. Joseph in Fairplain. Locals who recall the terror of driving over the long, narrow, and aging span for driver's education classes were particularly grateful for the 1966 remodel, shown below in its beginning stages. (Above, photograph by John Penrod, courtesy of the Maude Preston Palenske Memorial Library; below, courtesy of the Heritage Museum and Cultural Center.)

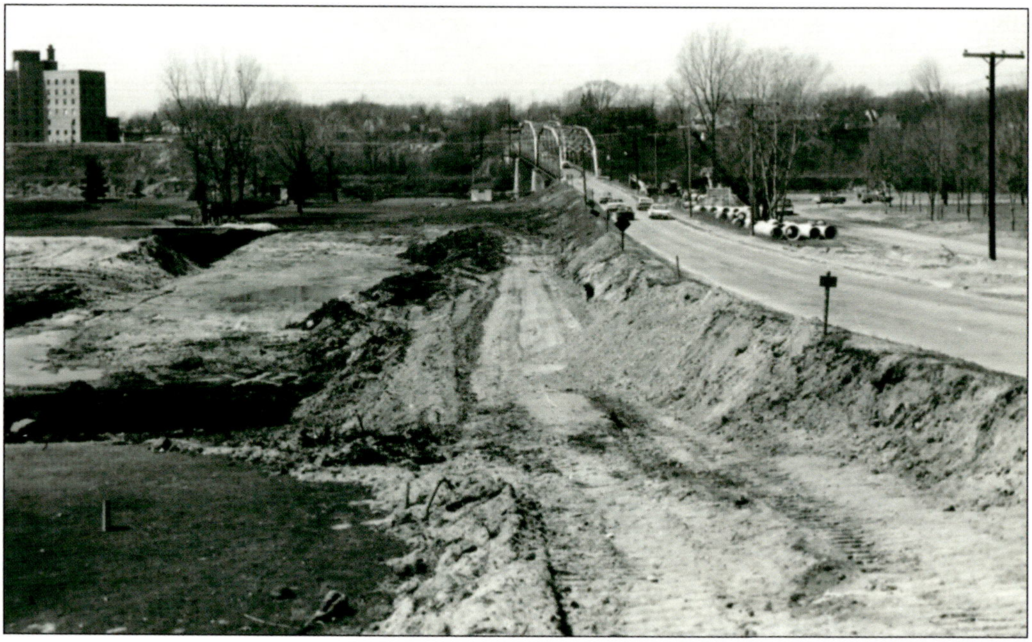

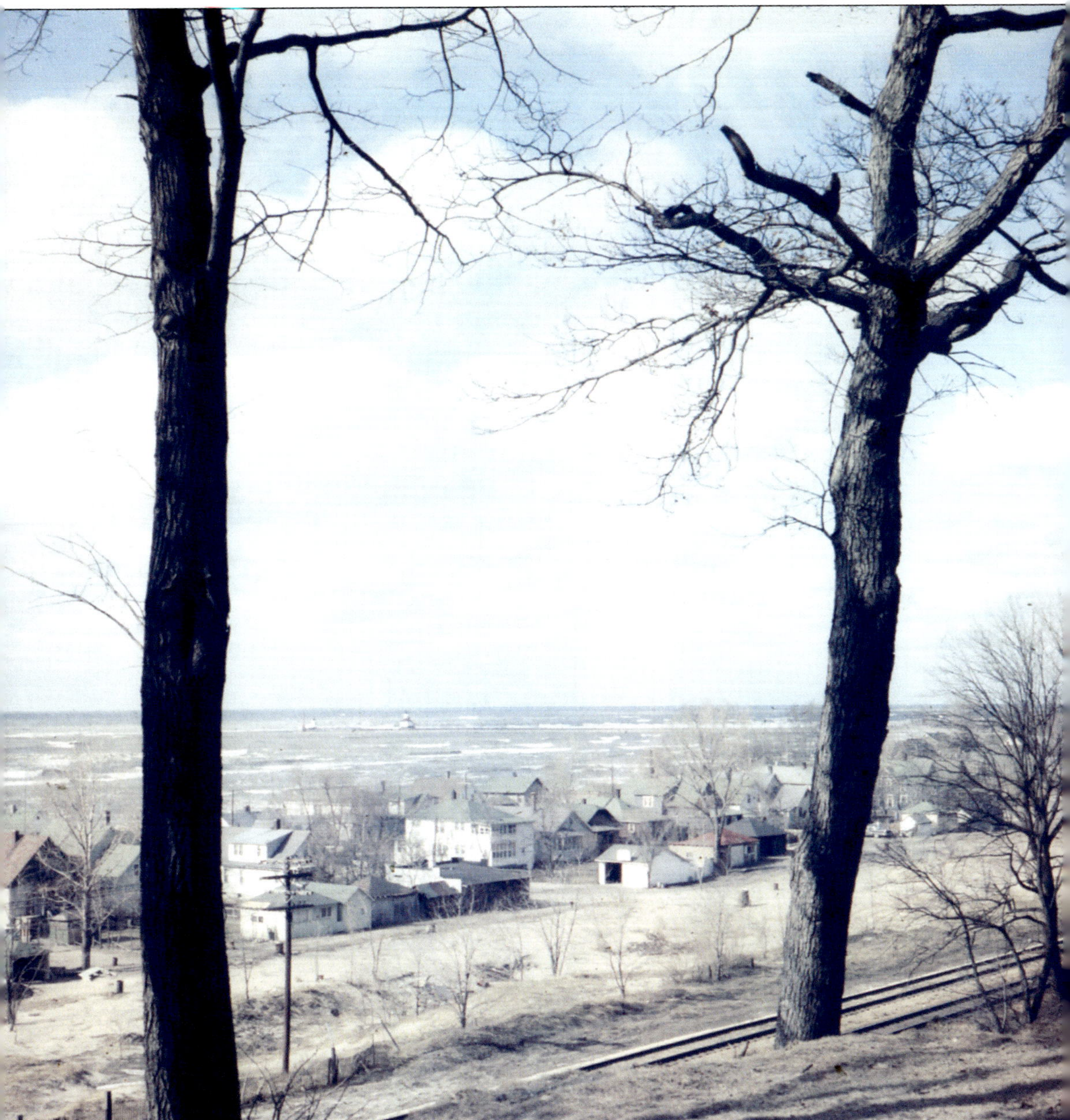

One St. Joseph neighborhood changed very little. Residents in this row of houses along the lake front between Pine Street (now Lions Park Dive) and Silver Beach, mostly recent German immigrant factory workers, were generally poor. Wealthier residents who lived uphill called them "sand rabbits," a name some hardworking denizens claimed with pride. Other residents of this neighborhood were Silver Beach employees, including the George family, who were Roma, called gypsies at the time. Those who grew up here recall idyllic childhoods. In the 1970s, after some of the original residents died or moved away, this became one of St. Joseph's rougher neighborhoods. Now, these waterfront cottages command some of the highest real estate prices in the area. (Courtesy of Larry Podjan.)

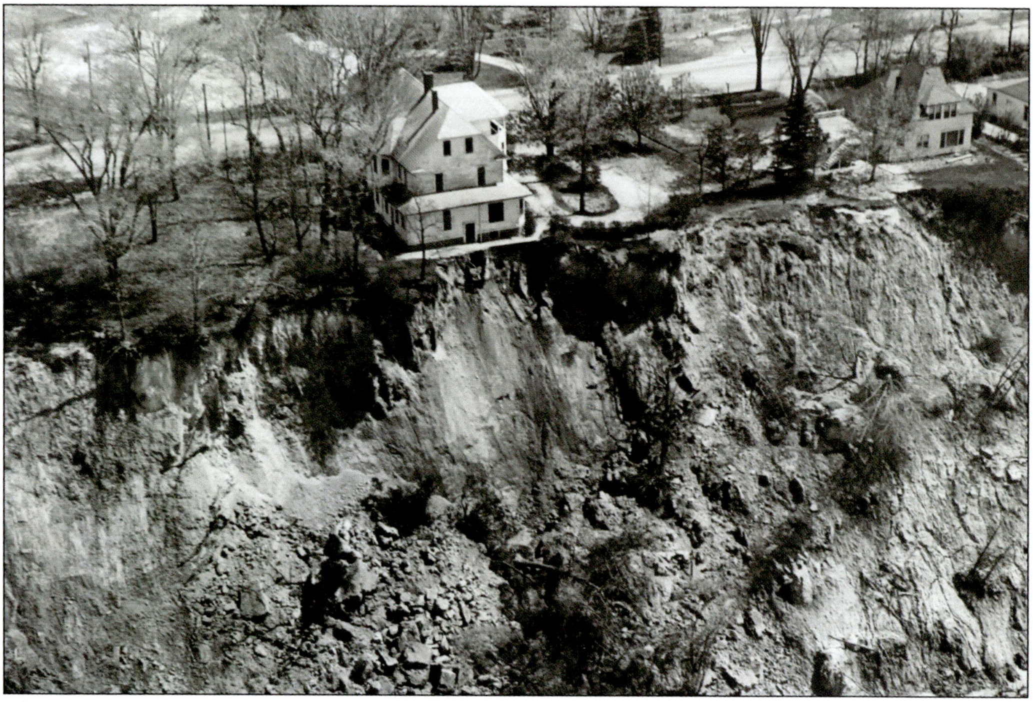

The more upscale lakeside neighborhood along Lakeshore Drive just south of St. Joseph had other issues. The image above from June 1954 shows shoreline erosion, ultimately caused by improper angling of the two piers that comprised the St. Joseph Channel. In October 1954, a series of catastrophic earth and mudslides threatened 13 homes. Six of them fell over the bluff, four were successfully relocated, and one was destroyed during the move. The Eppelheimer home below, at its new address of 24 Lakeshore Drive, survived the move. Don and Mary Eppelheimer and their three sons vividly remember the summer of 1961 when house-moving day came. Moving houses required closing off Lakeshore Drive, which at that time was US Highway 12. (Above, courtesy of Brian Ziebart; below, courtesy of Mary Eppelheimer.)

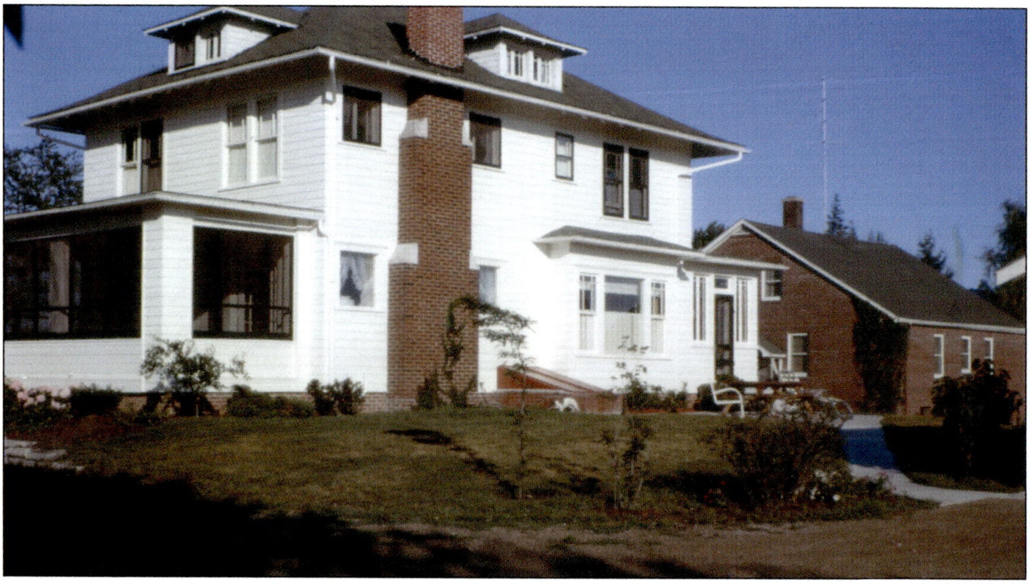

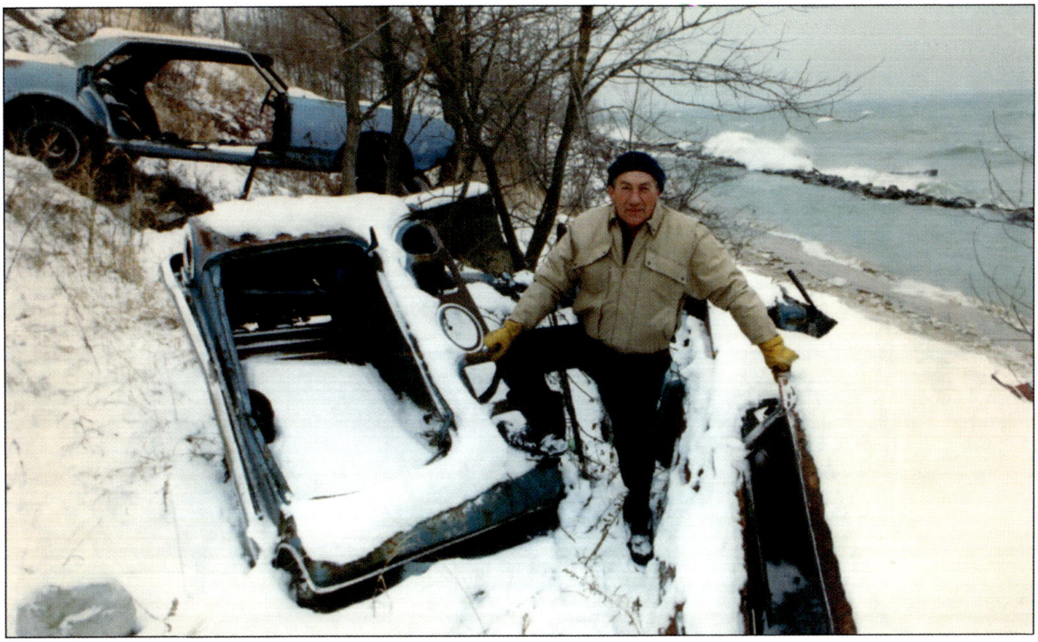

When erosion persisted, alarmed homeowners grew increasingly inventive in their attempted solutions. Above is Carl Kuyat of 28 East Lakeshore Drive in December 1968, standing by the junked cars he dumped down the bank to protect the bluff—much to the disapproval of his neighbors. Others tried rubble from the recently-demolished courthouse. Below is engineer George Morren of Spiedel Foundation and Marine of St. Joseph in April 1973, inspecting a zigzag retaining wall built by his firm as an anti-erosion measure south of St. Joseph. (Both, courtesy of Brian Ziebart.)

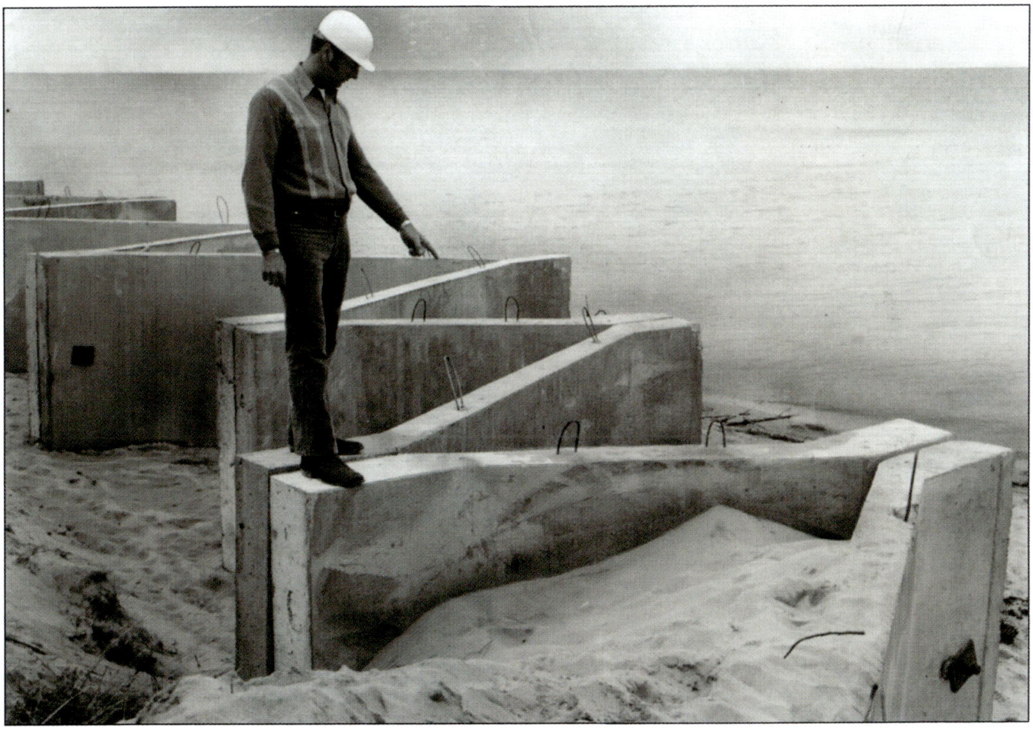

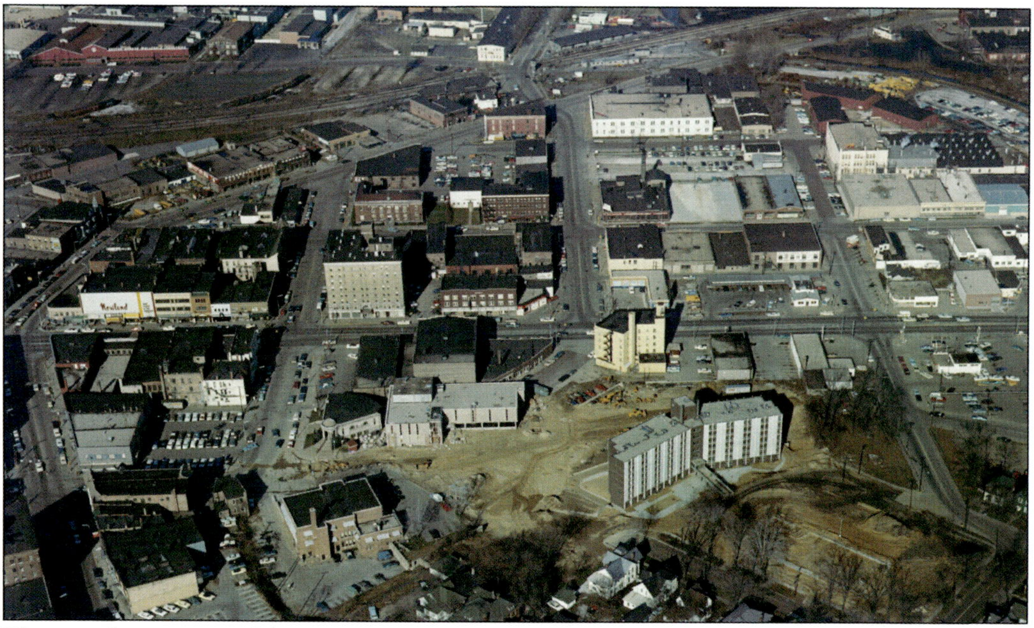

This aerial panorama of downtown Benton Harbor in 1967 shows the city-wide scale of renewal. At lower right are the River Terrace Apartments; senior housing was prioritized, as it was in St. Joseph. Malleable Industries is at upper-left. The small wedge-shaped building in the mid-left foreground is the old Carnegie Library, razed after the completion of the new public library to its right. (Photograph by Don Ames, courtesy of Ken Ankli.)

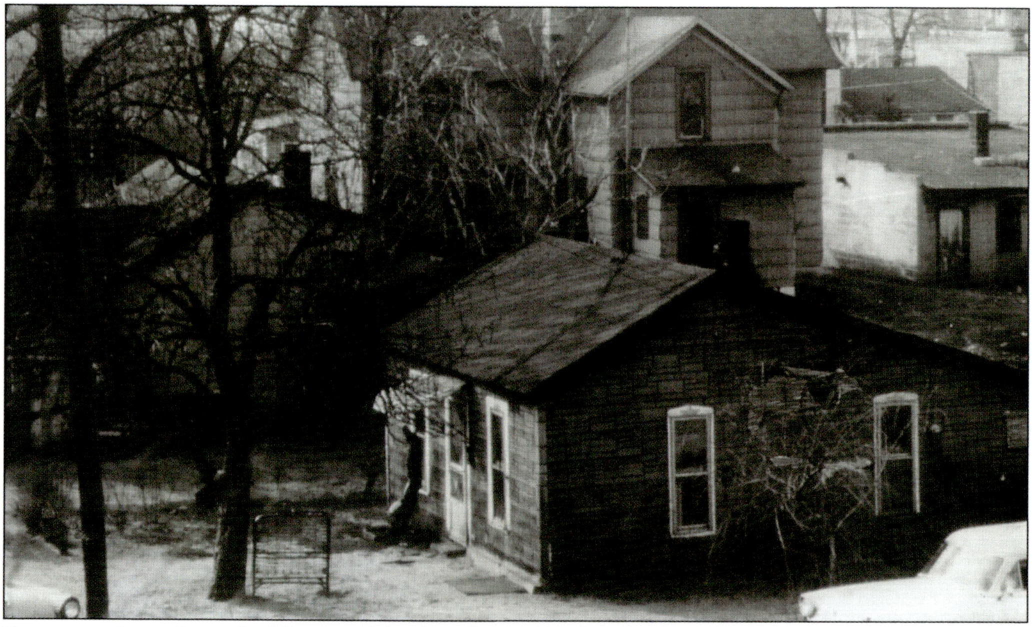

Designated as a slum, the Flats neighborhood was slated first for demolition. This home, 181 Lions Street, was among those leveled in 1964. Urban renewal was touted as the chance for Benton Harbor to be a "city of tomorrow." However, the dispersal of community and displacement of its poorest citizens created new problems, particularly for African American families. (Courtesy of the Benton Harbor Public Library.)

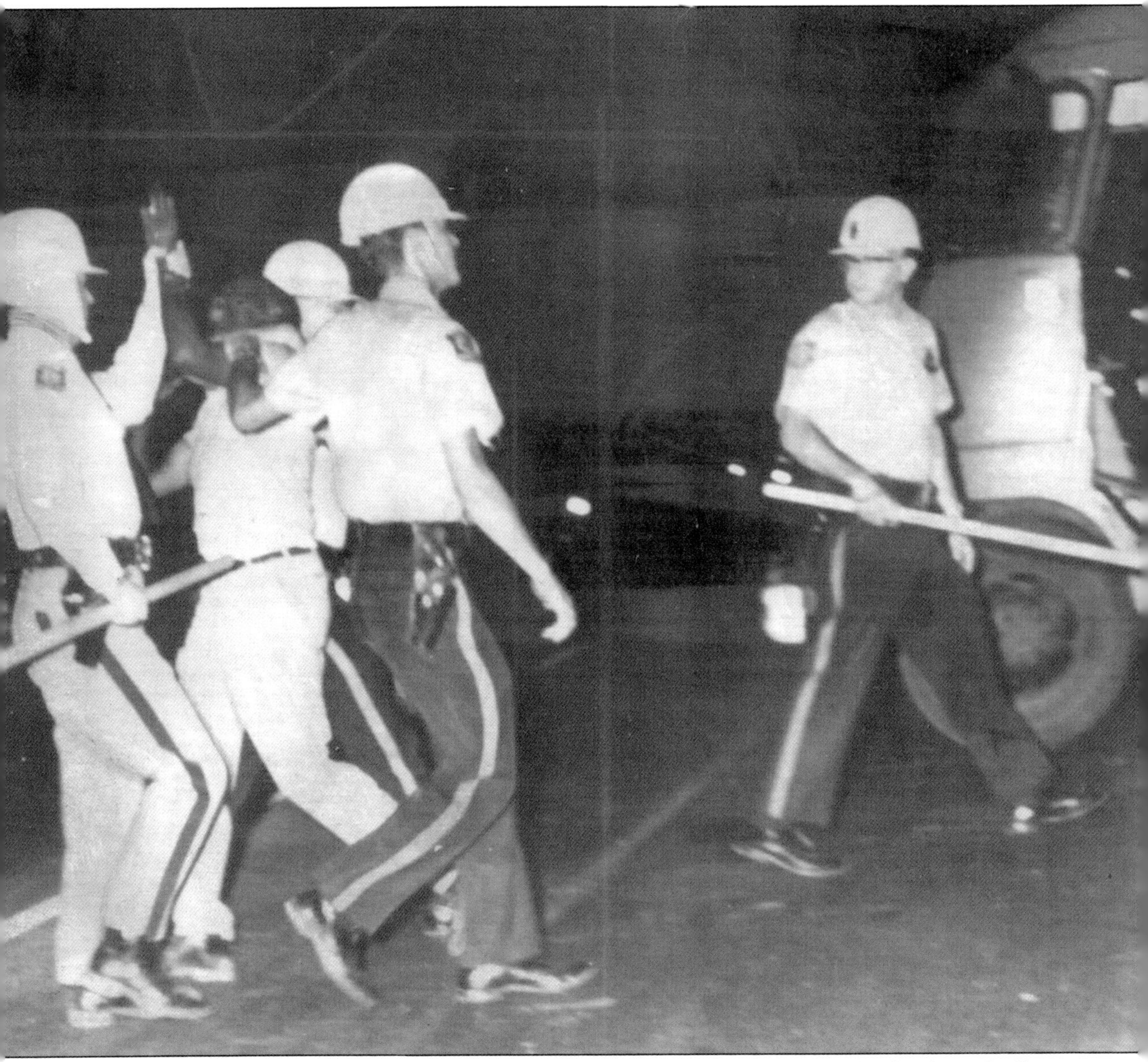

On August 29, 1966, a disturbance involving some 300 black youths outside Sheehey's Roller Rink on 543 Highland Avenue in Benton Harbor became a three-day riot. Reports cited the immediate cause as disrespectful policing, inadequate housing, limited employment, and lack of recreational spaces. Although Gov. George Romney alerted the National Guard, they were never sent to the scene. A heavy deployment of state troopers assisted local police, while members of the Michigan Civil Rights Commission and black leaders calmed the crowd. Despite the dramatic depiction in this photograph, only eight arrests were made. Few injuries were sustained until on the third night, 18-year-old Cecil Hunt was killed by a gunshot from a passing car. The night before, three white youths were arrested in a car near the scene for possessing a shotgun. A fourth man was arrested for Hunt's murder but released for lack of evidence. The killer was never found. (Courtesy of Brian Ziebart.)

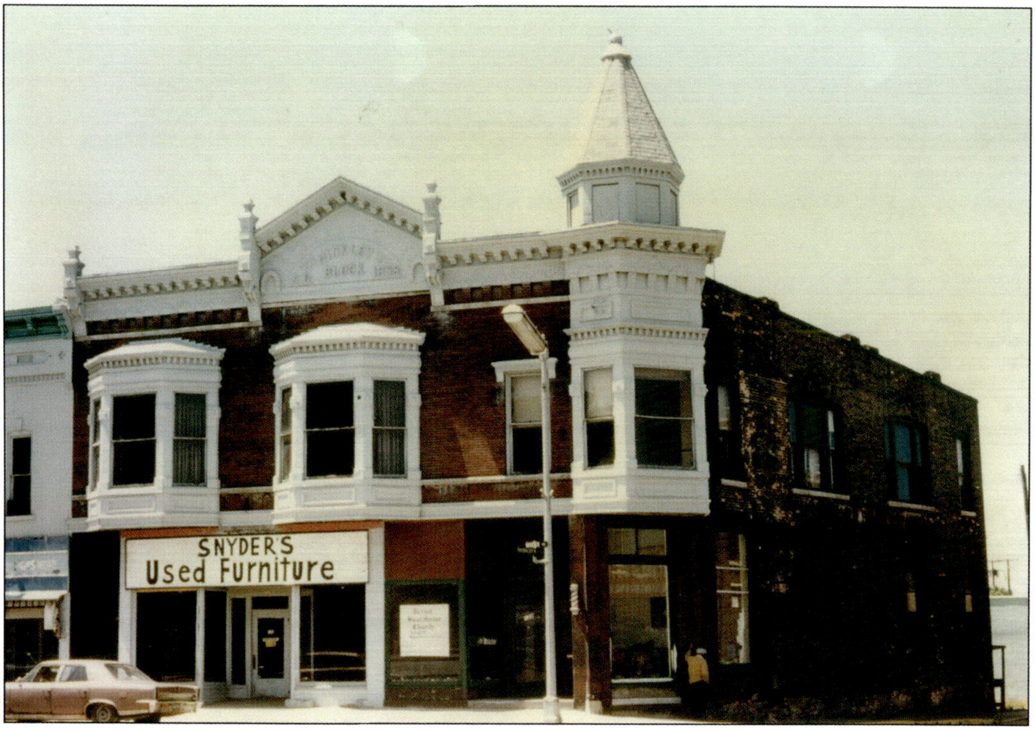

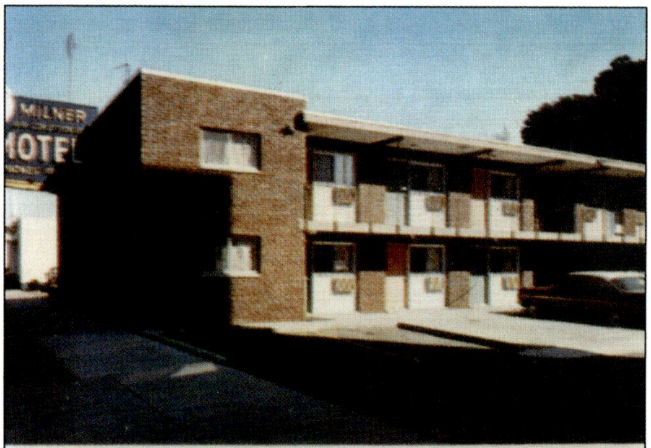

White families and white-owned businesses fled downtown Benton Harbor to Fairplain, St. Joseph, or other nearby towns, leaving Benton Harbor mostly poor and black. This 1976 image of the Hinkley Building, 132 Water Street, shows the changed demographics. Storefront churches such as the Bethel Soul Harbor Church, common during this time, became important worship and community centers in lower-income neighborhoods. (Photograph by Harold Atwood, courtesy of Kathy Catania.)

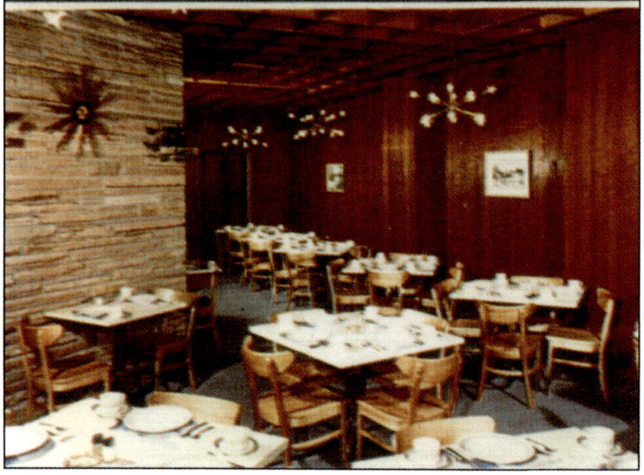

On June 1, 1973, the *News Palladium* published an open letter from the president of Milner Hotels to city and state officials, citing poor government, high taxes, and crime for the failure of the 250 East Main Street facility. After serving as housing for seniors, veterans, and finally convicts on work release, the Milner finally closed down in August 1978. (Courtesy of the Benton Harbor Public Library.)

Three

Everything Old is New Again

The 1970s were an uneasy time. National issues of declining industrial production, wildly fluctuating energy prices, an unstable economy, suburbanization, and the new impersonality of interstates and strip malls drastically impacted the Twin Cities. Faced with scarred cityscapes, increasing violence, and economic uncertainty, many felt the good times were over. When increasing gang violence led to the permanent closure of Silver Beach in 1972 and the beloved amusement park was completely torn down in 1975, St. Joseph mourned for months afterward. Benton Harbor's House of David was gone too—its members had grown too old and were too few in number to run the parks and tend the gardens and the shops. There was little to do in downtown St. Joseph. Downtown Benton Harbor was a shell of what it had been. Then, one by one, in the 1980s, the factories closed.

But, life went on. Young people found plenty to do. If not much was happening downtown, there was shopping or cruising around in cars on Saturday nights at the Fairplain Plaza. If Silver Beach was closed, the boarded-up midway remained, delightfully haunted with the ghost of the laughing clown, and rock bands held concerts in the still-beloved if now decrepit Shadowland. Both cities had excellent, well-stocked libraries where children could read or listen to the latest records for free. There were baseball games, high school football matches, beach parties, lessons at the art center, and music on the radio.

Benton Harbor was not yet in a good position to improve matters. In the late 1970s, however, the citizens of St. Joseph took a hard look, and realized that the heart and soul of a city is its downtown. St. Joseph had once been a pretty little lakeside resort with a true hometown feel. It was time, they realized, to bring that back. And so, in the 1980s, they began.

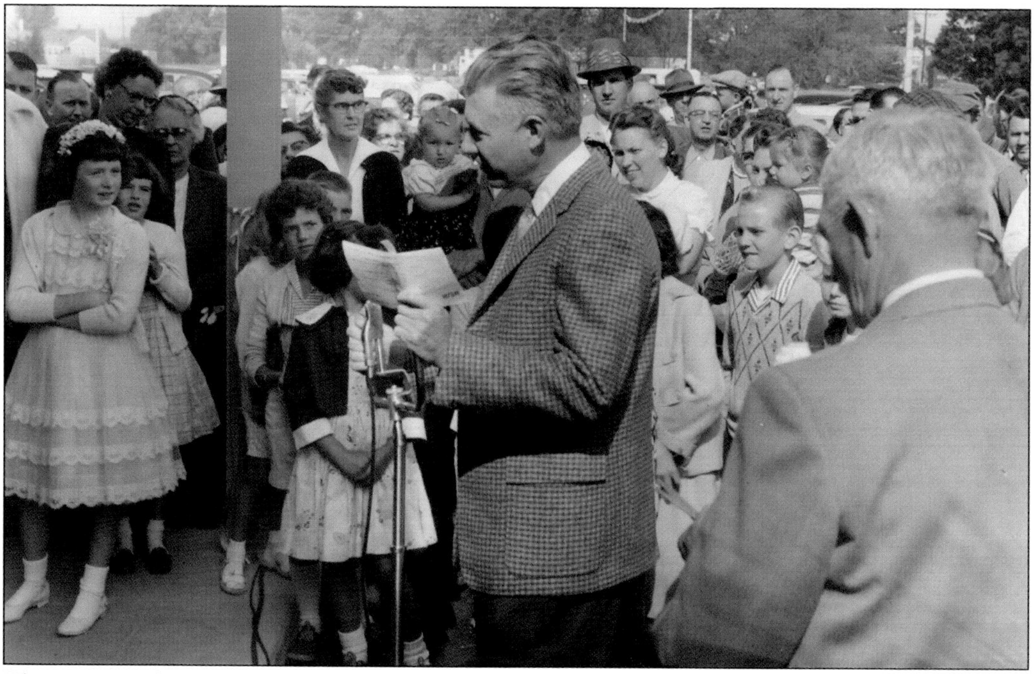

The nationwide postwar trend of suburbanization saw homes and retail centers expanding outside cities. With new emphasis on high-volume automobile traffic, new shopping centers were built near interstate exits and featured huge parking lots. When the Fairplain Plaza opened on June 18, 1958, on the corner of M-139 and Napier Avenue, one of its main advertised features was parking for almost 2,000 cars. Purchased in 1955 by Joseph Angelo as a way to expand his Benton Harbor grocery business, the plaza included boutiques, a department store, restaurants, and offices. Above is Mark East, project manager, speaking to a crowd on opening day. Below are Angelos Supermarket employees standing in front of their newly built plaza supermarket. (Both, courtesy of Theresa Angelo-Immoos.)

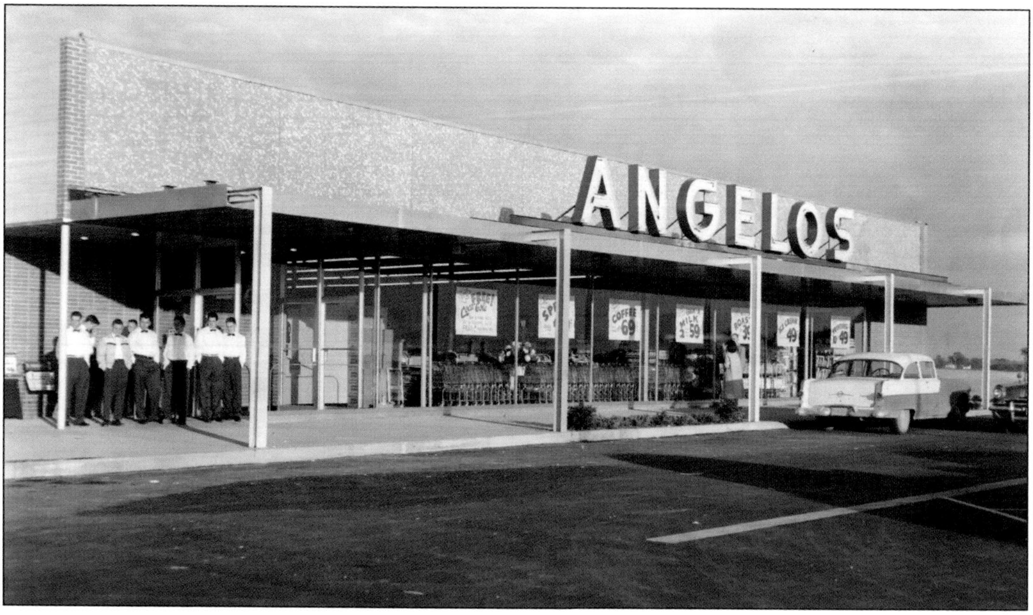

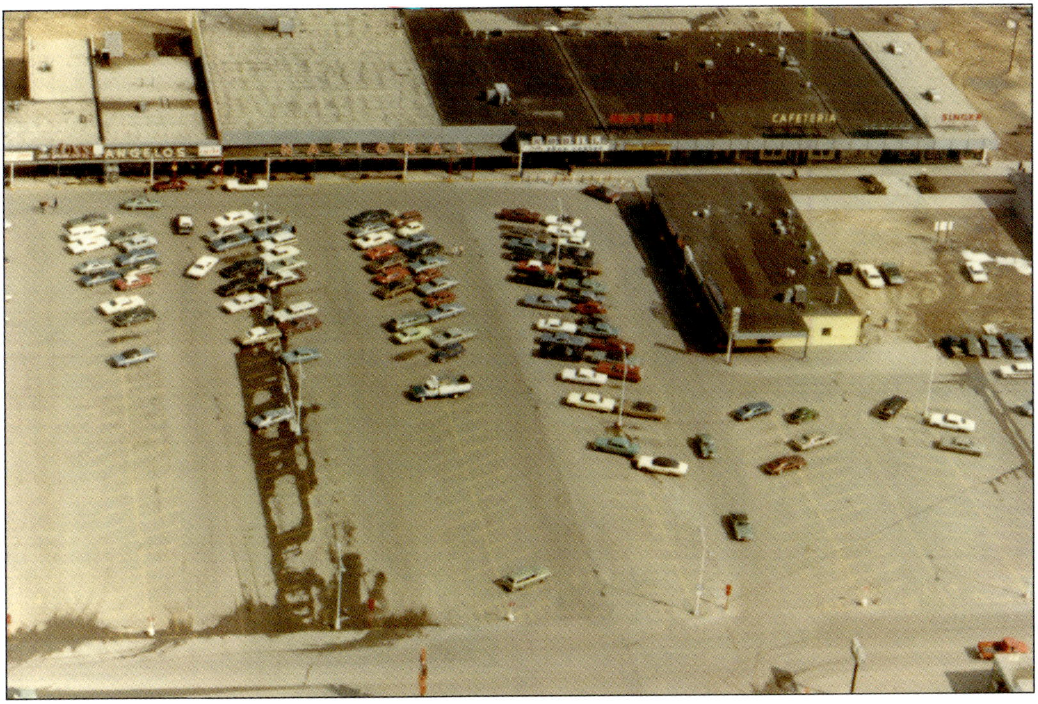

The new car culture had far-reaching social effects. Teenagers old enough to drive began to spend weekends cruising in cars. The Fairplain Plaza, with its vast parking lot and relative safety, became a favorite cruising destination for teens in the 1960s and 1970s. Young people from all around would drive around the parking lot for hours on Saturday evenings, eating fast food, greeting friends, and showing off muscle cars. Above is the south end of the plaza in 1971. On the right is a young woman in 1977, posing on a 1973 Gold Duster in a then-stylish Gunne Sax maxi dress, checking in with friends in St. Joseph before an evening of plaza cruising. (Above, courtesy of Theresa Angelo-Immoos; right, courtesy of Fran McCauley.)

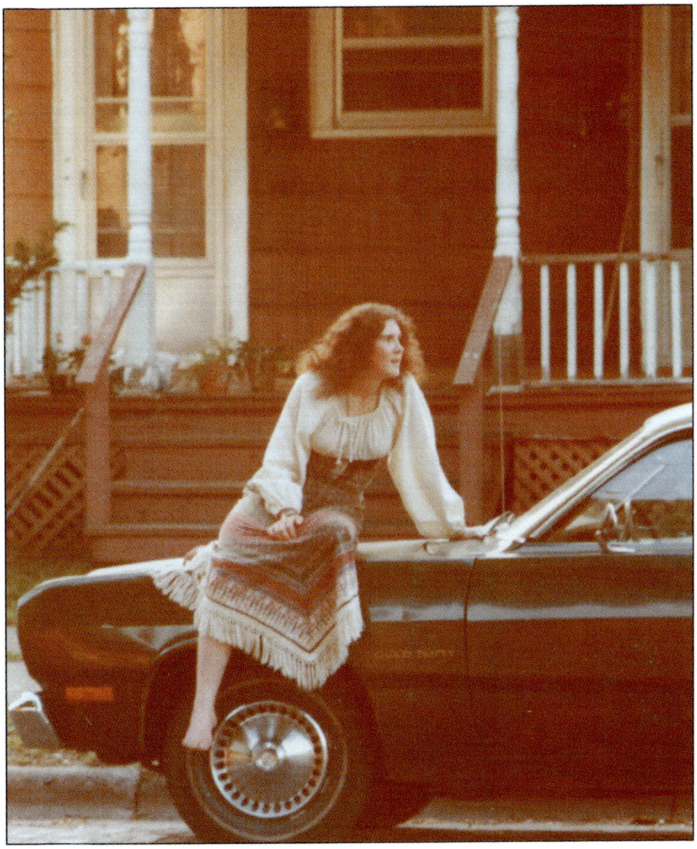

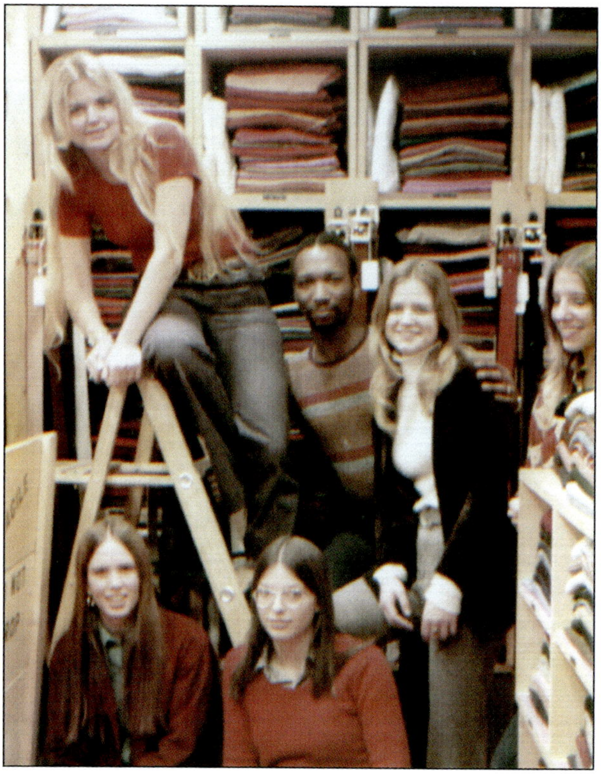

Two youth-oriented plaza shops offered stylish selections. The Man Alive sold jeans. Bell bottoms, high-rise, and low-rise Levis and Wranglers were shelved in stacked wooden crates, with leather belts hung between. There was a pink cash register and shag carpet. In the image on the left, the young staff models the store's latest styles. From left to right are (first row) Jenna Betz and Lynda Hoffman (Ficca); (second row) Sue Bublick, Larry Phillips, Karen Dorsey, and Lynn Krolzick (Riccioni). The shop was founded by brothers Norbert "Norby" and Ronald Bublick in 1971. Below is a coupon advertisement from 1974 for the Hang Up, started by a third brother, Mandell Bublick, in 1972. Specifically for young women, it featured brands such as Gunne Sax, Jodi T, and Hang Ten. They also sold incense, candles, jewelry, and gift items. (Left, courtesy of Debra Anderson; below, author's collection.)

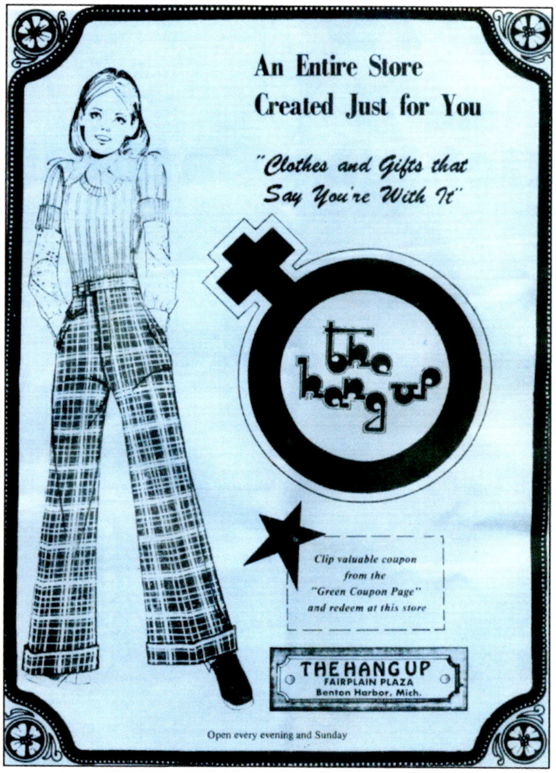

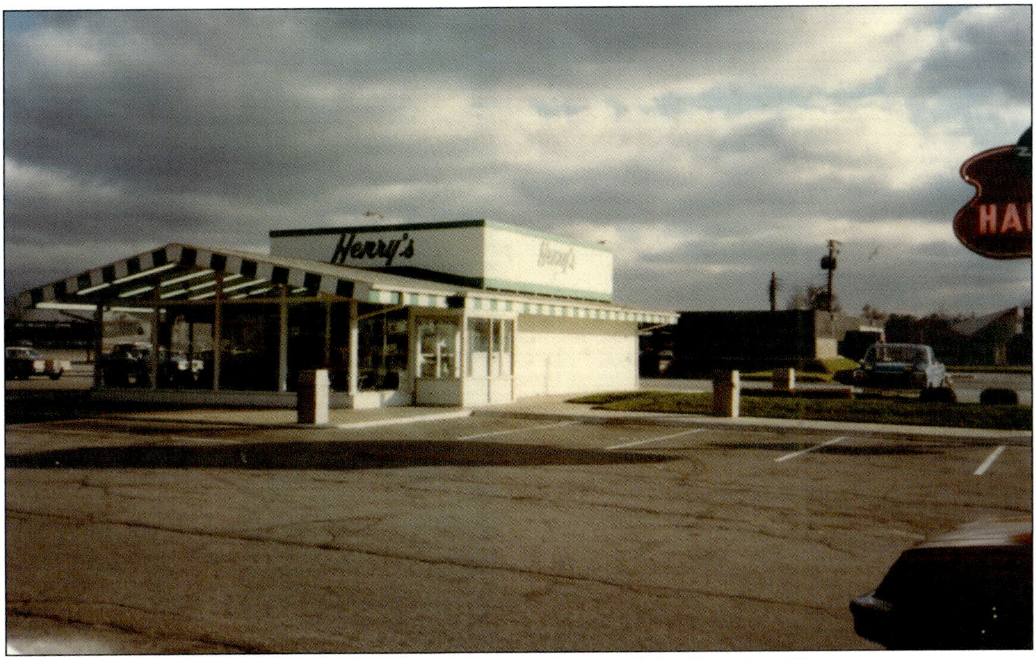

Every midcentury youth scene needs its hamburger joint, and the Fairplain Plaza was no exception. Henry's Hamburgers was the favorite hangout. A Chicago franchise, Henry's opened in 1959, preceding McDonalds in the area. It remains today, across the street from its original location, the only Henry's restaurant still in business. (Courtesy of Bob Catania.)

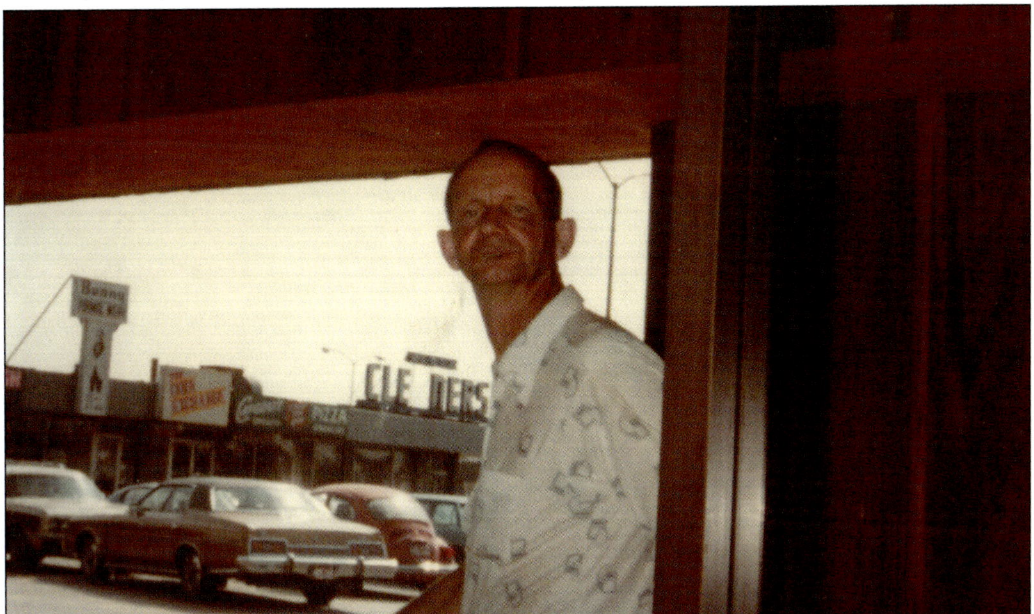

Every town has its legends. John Robert Boelcke, a gentle eccentric, was known and loved by several generations. Friends and family commend him as a Korean War veteran and former Whirlpool employee. A devoted people watcher, he is shown here in the late 1970s in the Brick Alley section of the plaza. (Courtesy of Martin Bishop.)

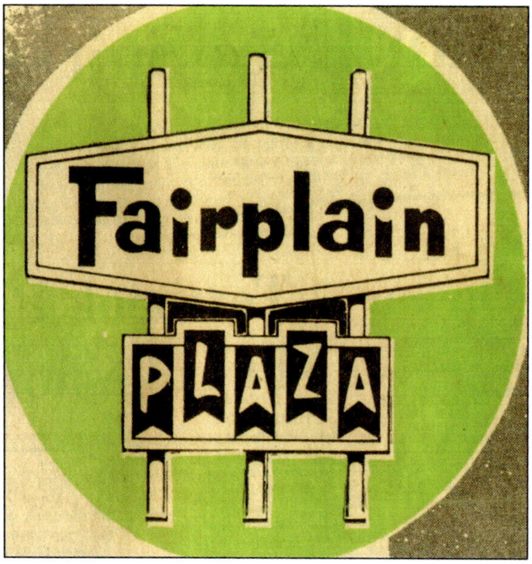

This vintage advertisement for the Fairplain Plaza depicting its sign at left and the sign for the nearby Starlite Drive-In Theater below, are good examples of the lively midcentury signage that was once common in American towns. Opened in 1948 by Walter and Gustav Eisner in the then-rural area of M-139, just south of where the plaza was later to be built, the Starlite Drive-In provided family-oriented movies until the late 1960s. During the mid-1960s, a playground and pony rides were added to expand family recreational opportunities. Like many other such theaters facing lower revenues in the 1970s, the Starlite turned to more adult, grind house fare. It was torn down sometime in the early 1980s. (Left, courtesy of Theresa Angelo-Immoos; below, author's collection.)

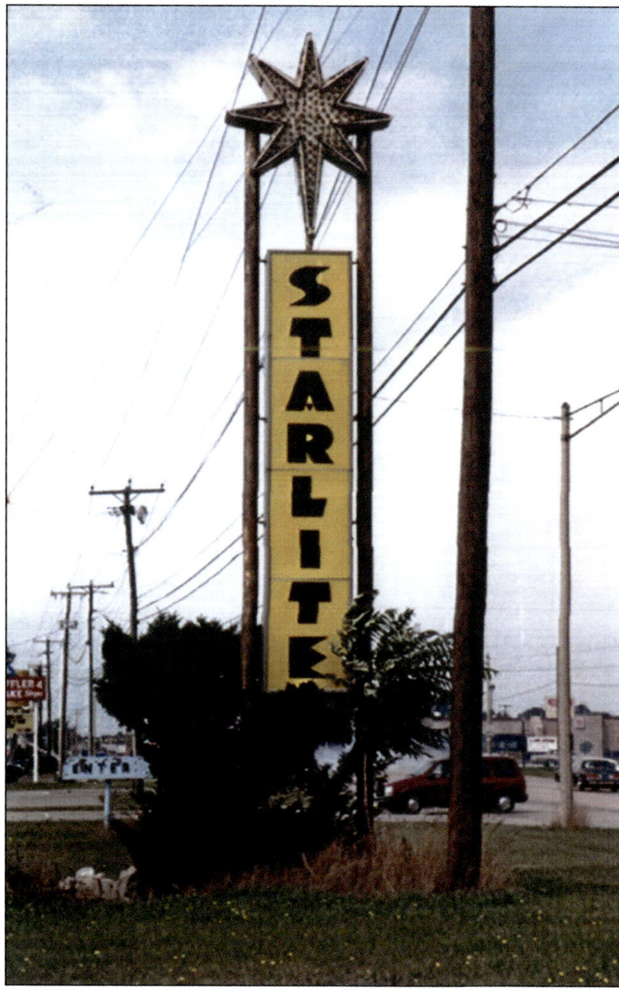

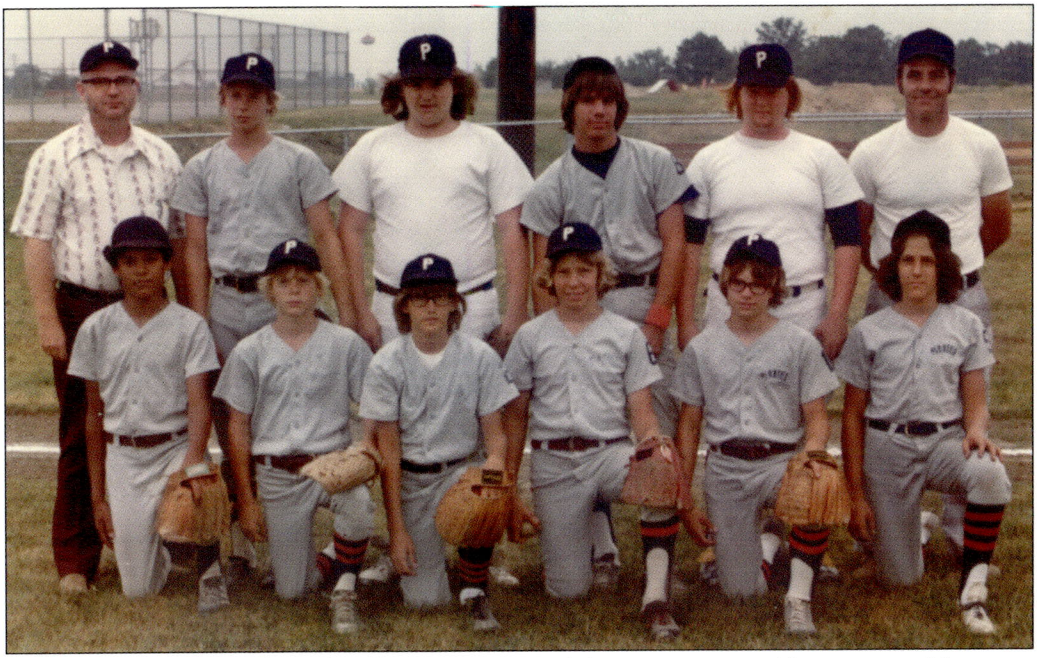

Young people did other things besides cruising around shopping centers. Above is one of the many local baseball teams, about 1975. From left to right are (first row) Fred Henry, Chopper Roloff, two unidentified, Jim Walder, unidentified, and Larry Podjan; (second row) Doc Maxwell (coach), Jeff Phillips, Dave Maxwell, Scott Mucia, Richard Maxwell, and Jack Mucia (coach). This Babe Ruth team played on Union Field. The image below shows a classic 1970s indoor recreational space—the paneled basement "rec room." This one belonged to the Willmings on Lonesome Pine Trail, a St. Joseph subdivision. Rick Willming (left), a glazer, worked for Twin Cities Glass. Larry Podjan (right) collected most of the beer signs on the wall from grocery stores where he worked. (Both, courtesy of Larry Podjan.)

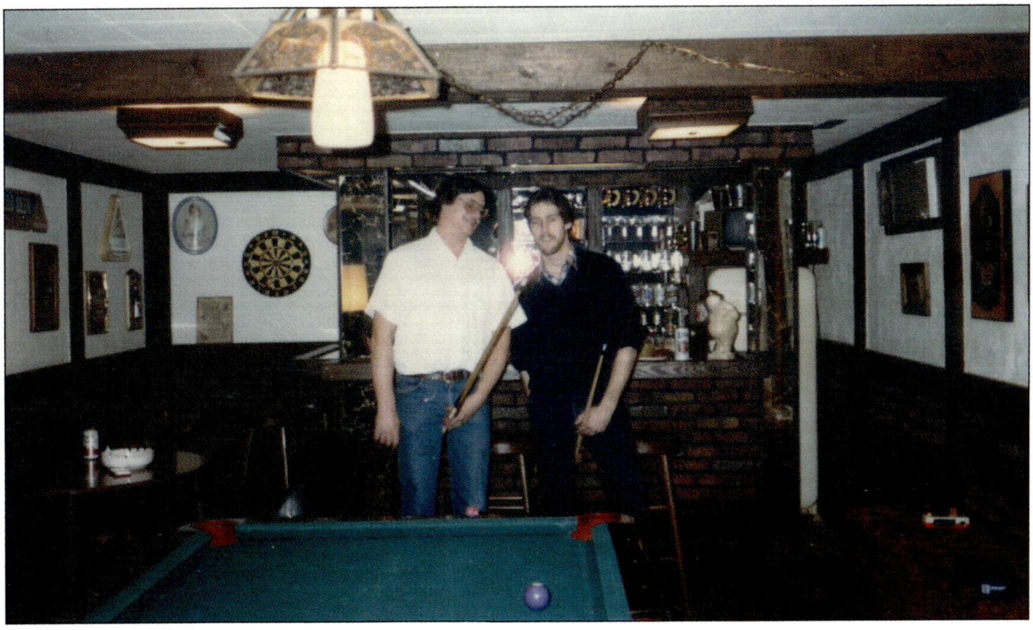

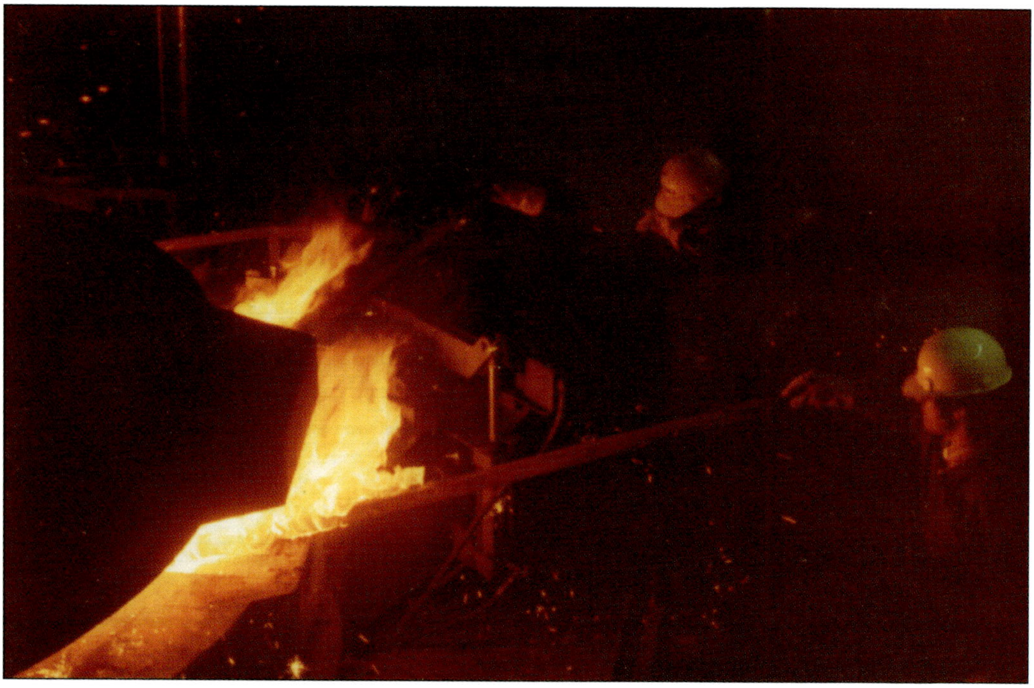

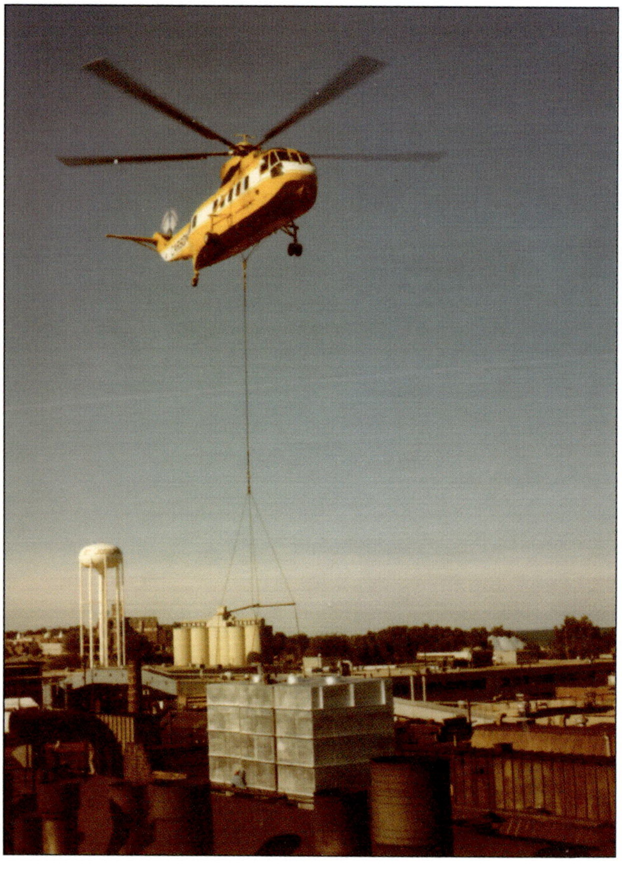

In the early 1970s, the Environmental Protection Agency responded to rising concerns about water and air quality with a series of mandatory anti-pollution measures. Steel manufacturing was particularly hazardous. Auto Specialties, the largest foundry in the area, had been working since the 1960s to reduce toxic emissions, and complied with the costly new regulations. Above is the first pouring from the high-efficiency, state-of-the-art 40-ton Ajax Magnathermic Vertiplex Induction furnace AUSCO installed in the St. Joseph foundry in 1977, at a cost of $750,000. At left is a photograph taken July 11, 1978, of a helicopter delivering a new $80,000 dust collector for installation on the roof of the same plant. Despite massive expenditure and the company's best efforts, AUSCO facilities were designated Superfund sites in 1989. (Both, courtesy of James and Edward Tiscornia.)

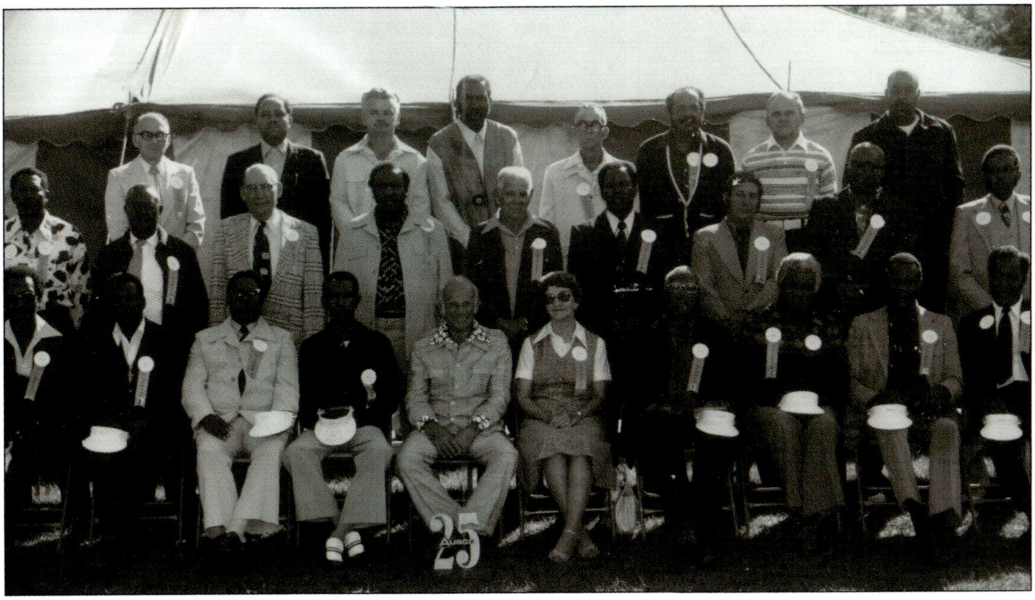

Auto Specialties, like other Northern manufacturing companies after World War II, actively recruited black workers escaping the Jim Crow–era South. They sent down buses to bring back workers and their families, provided temporary housing, and offered good wages, paid benefits, union representation, and long-term stability. These images of the proud members of AUSCO's 25 Year Club of 1977 and 1978 being commemorated for their success after a lifetime of hard work attest to Benton Harbor's retention of a black middle class. Shortly thereafter, prohibitive environmental regulations, automotive industry slowdown, prolonged labor strikes, and the energy crisis devastated manufacture-based economies. AUSCO closed its Riverside plant in 1980 and declared bankruptcy in 1988. In the 1980s, several other plants, including Whirlpool, closed operations in the city, thus decimating Benton Harbor's economy. (Both, courtesy of James and Edward Tiscornia.)

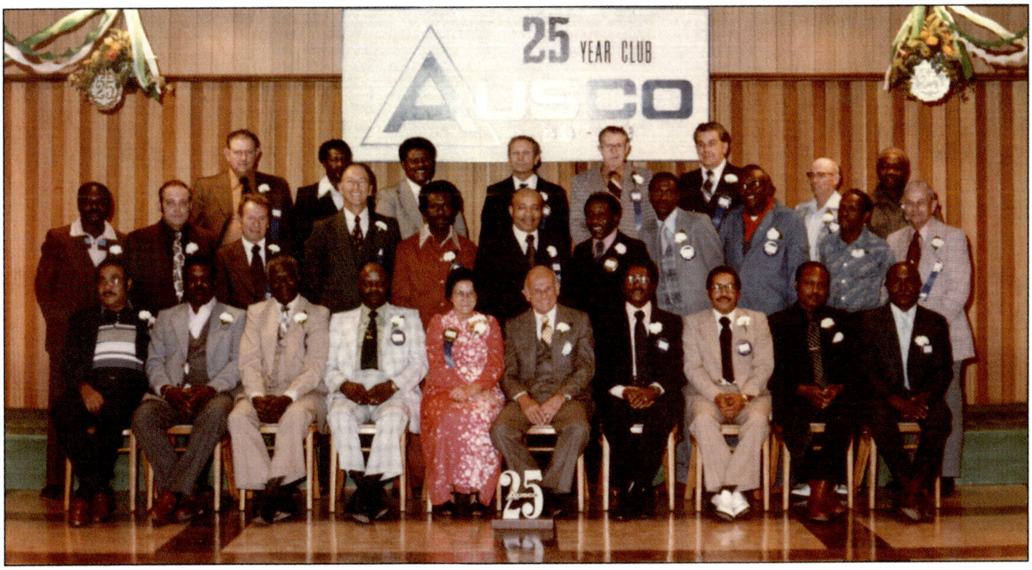

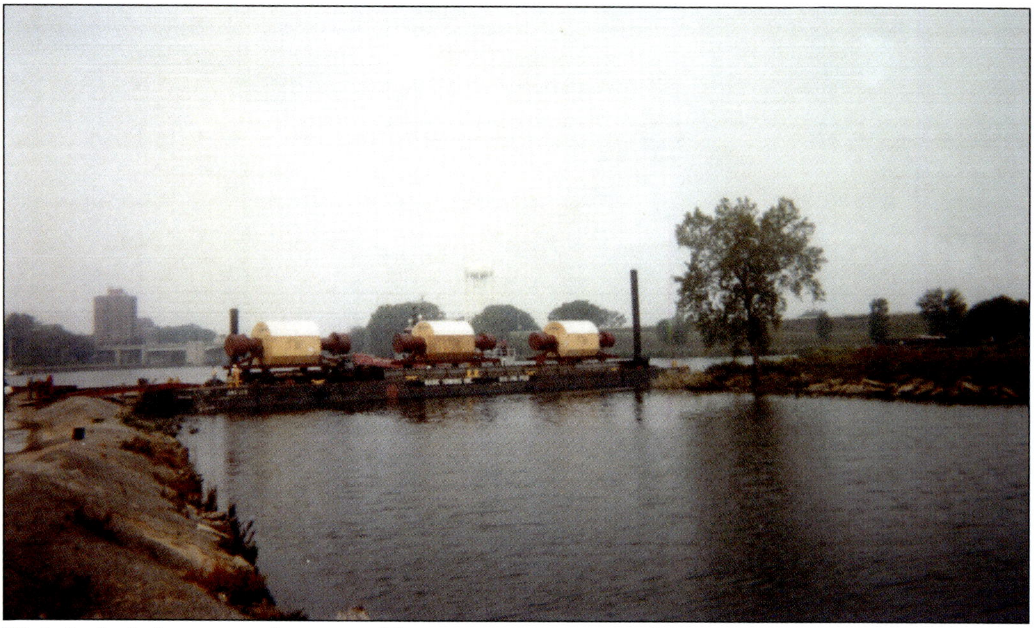

With high fuel prices and an unstable energy economy, nuclear energy seemed an increasingly attractive, if controversial option. These images show two barges in the St. Joseph River Channel in October 1968, delivering parts for construction of the Palisades Nuclear Plant in Covert, 18 miles north of Benton Harbor. The cylindrical parts in the image above are likely for the generator-alternator assembly. The Palisades Plant opened in 1971. After operating without incident for its first year, it was plagued for the next two years with a series of radioactive leaks, leading to 19 months of shutdown and a lawsuit leveled against Bechtel, the manufacturer of its ultimately defective parts. (Both, courtesy of Jack Kinney.)

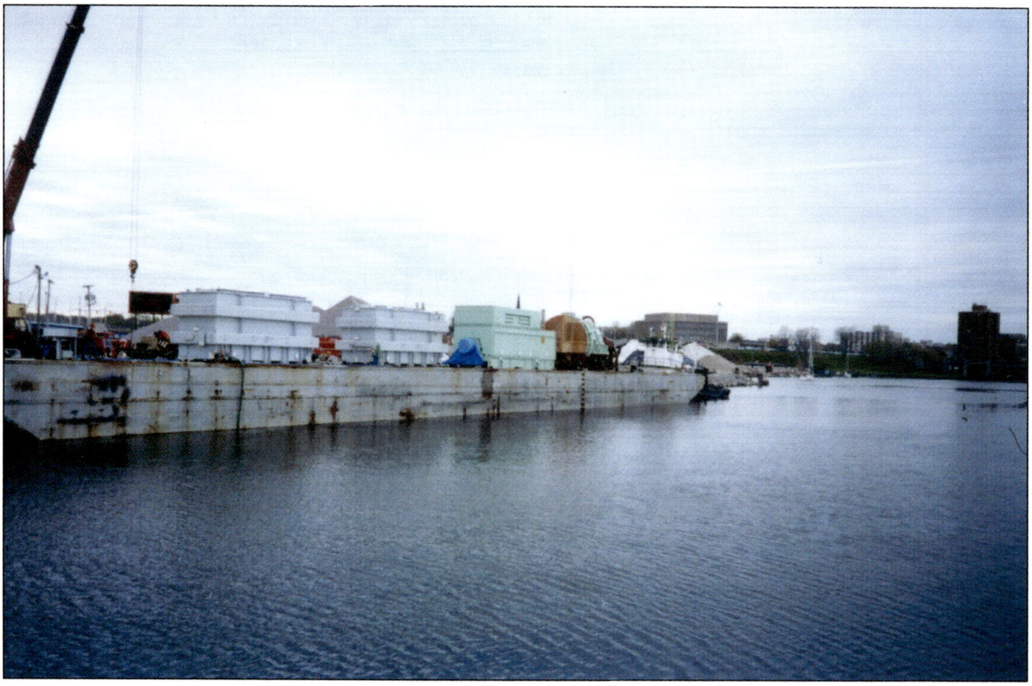

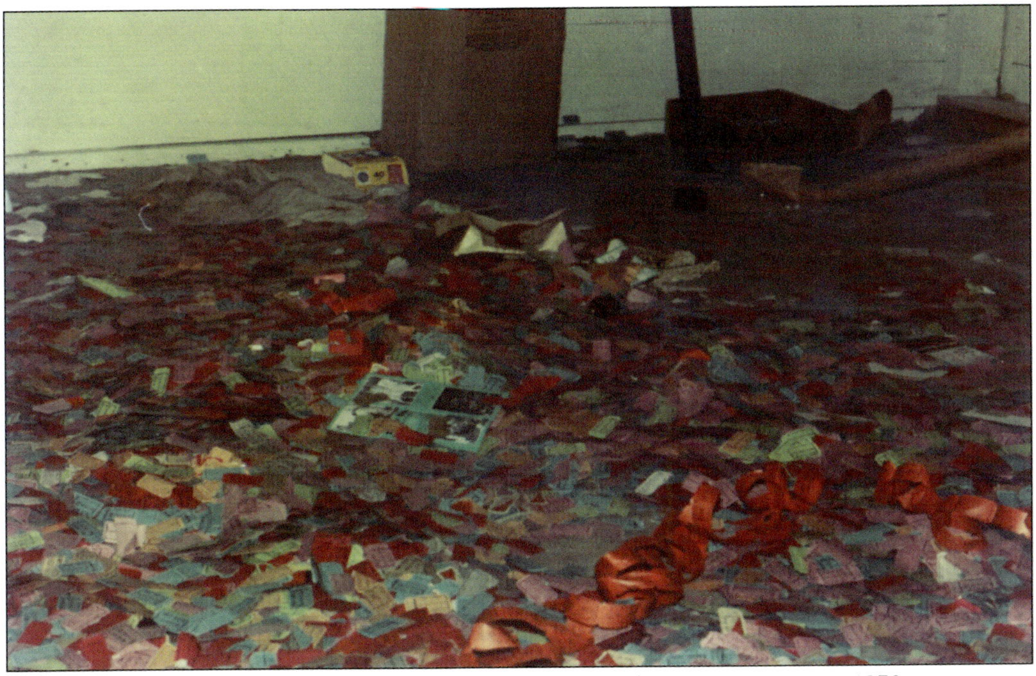

Less reliant on manufacturing, St. Joseph's struggles in the recession-prone 1970s were more localized. Hit hardest by increased crime and an aging infrastructure was the beloved Silver Beach Amusement Park. On Saturday, July 5, 1969, the park shut down when a gang of out-of-town teenagers caused a melee in which 64-year-old ticket seller Mildred Pribbernow and two other elderly employees were injured. In 1972, faced with increasing crime and prohibitive maintenance costs, the park did not reopen. The rollercoaster was demolished over several months in 1974. The wood was sold off or donated locally. Above is the floor of the ticket booth. Below is what was left of the rollercoaster before the last of it was hauled away. (Both, courtesy of Joseph Lodyga.)

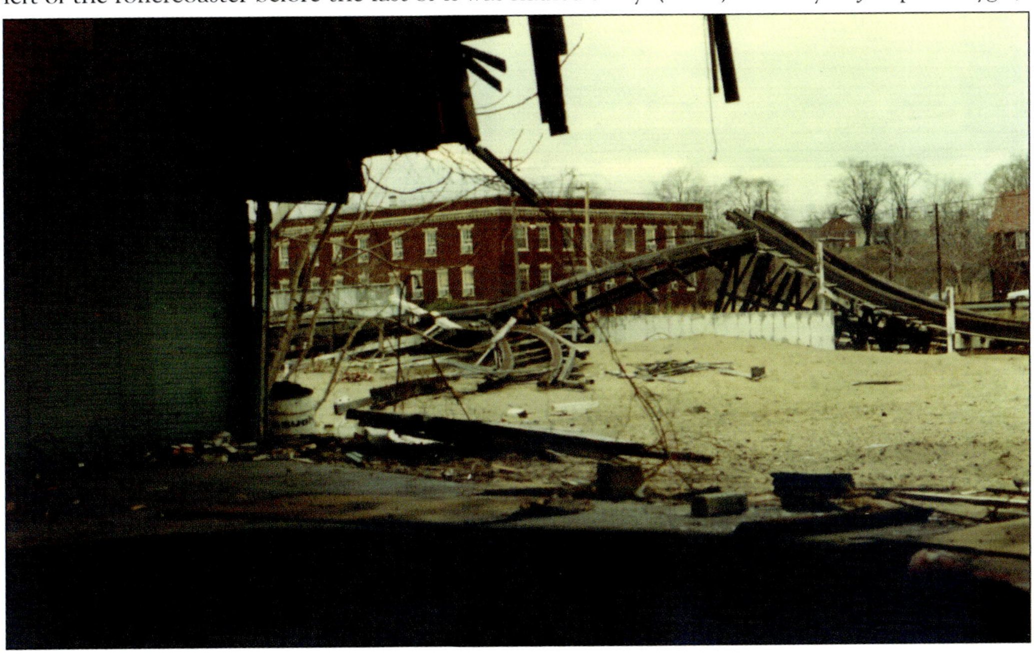

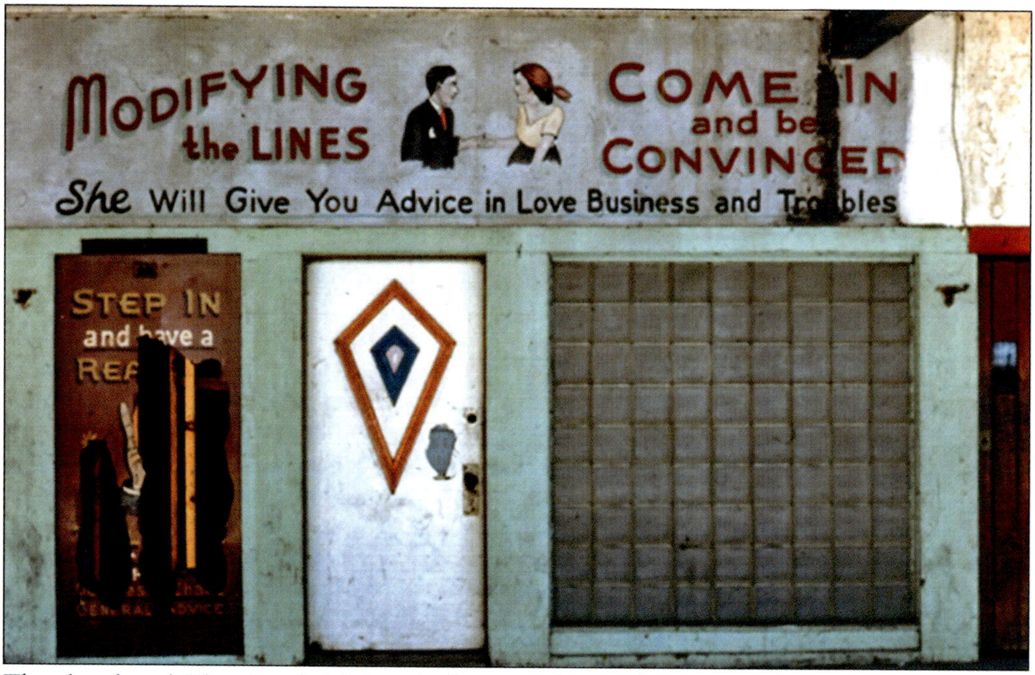

The abandoned Silver Beach Midway had its own haunted carnival beauty, as shown in these images from 1974. Above is the fortune-telling concession of Bessie George, known to her friends as "Juanita." Her husband, Joseph George, and their sons Eddie and Johnny, according to Daryl Schlender, ran several other concessions, including "Spill the Milk," a bottle-toss game shown below, a souvenir shop that sold handmade wire jewelry, a dart balloon game, and the High Striker. For some reason, the laughing clown from the old mirror maze remained operational. The amplified echo of his incessant, maniacal laugh through the decaying midway and his mechanical rocking form behind glass still haunts those who remember it. (Both photographs by Harry Blesy, above courtesy of Daryl Schlender; below, courtesy of Joseph Lodyga.)

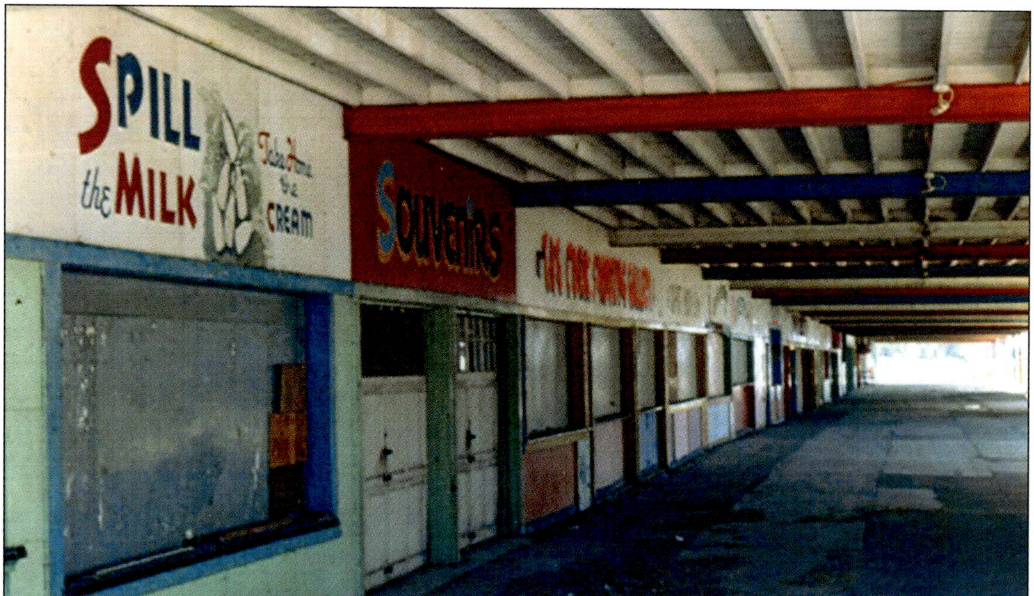

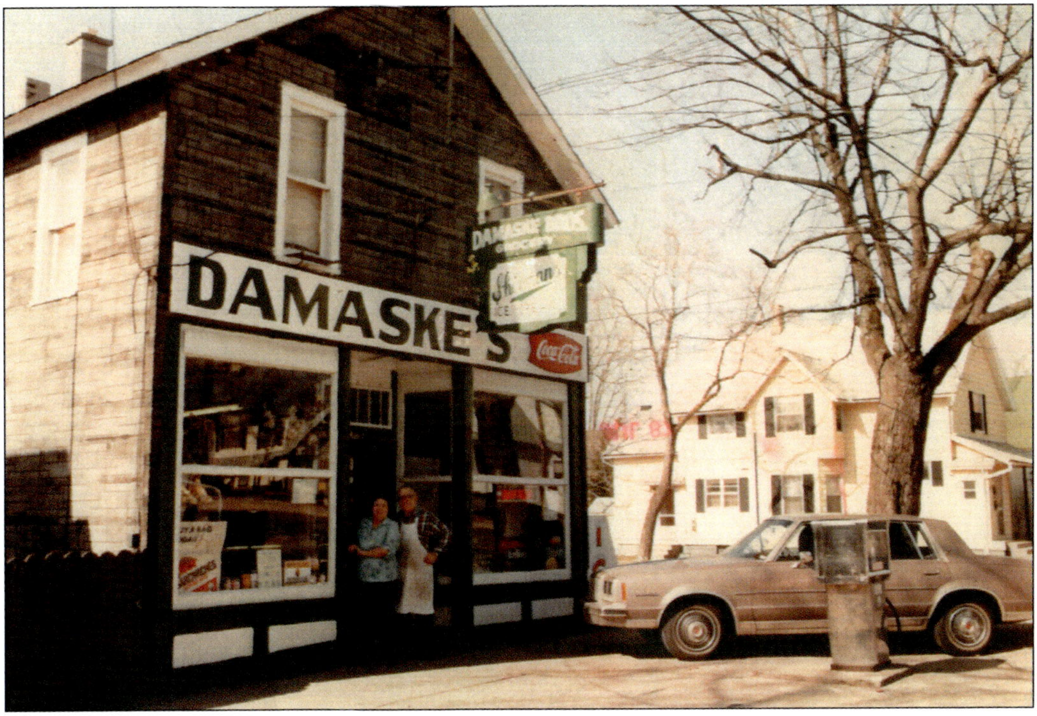

In the 1970s, St. Joseph retained other beloved neighborhood institutions. Above are Mabel and Edwin Damaske in front of their grocery store at 800 Pine Street. Gustav Damaske, Edwin's father, started the store in 1938. Edwin ran the store with his brother Albin "Beans." Below is Philip "Flip" Springsteen, owner and proprietor of Flips Donuts on 607 Broad Street, with Santa, played by Tom Mance. Various Santas maintained Christmas headquarters in the donut shop. Flips, only open at night, was the favorite haunt of police officers, newsmen, and bemused high school students. Flip made fresh donuts every night, cheerfully served with hot coffee and off-color comments. The shop walls were lined with historical photographs, old postcards, and various oddities. (Above, courtesy of the Heritage Museum and Cultural Center; below, courtesy of Joseph Lodyga.)

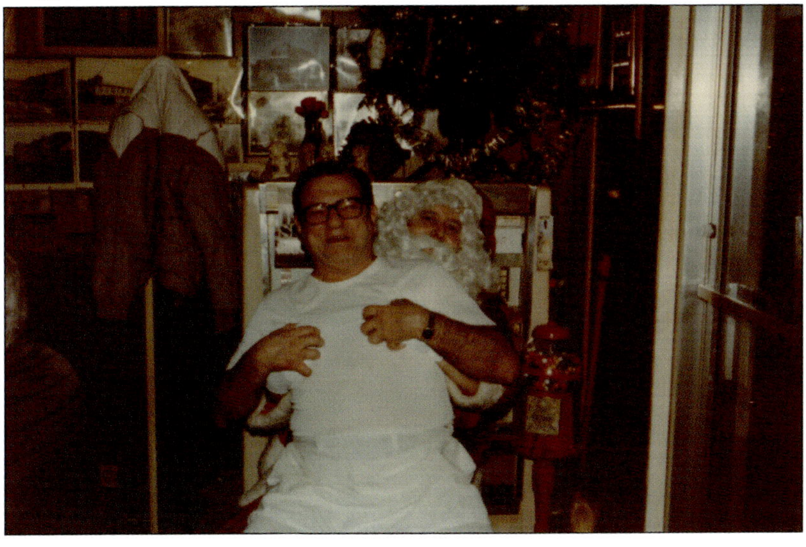

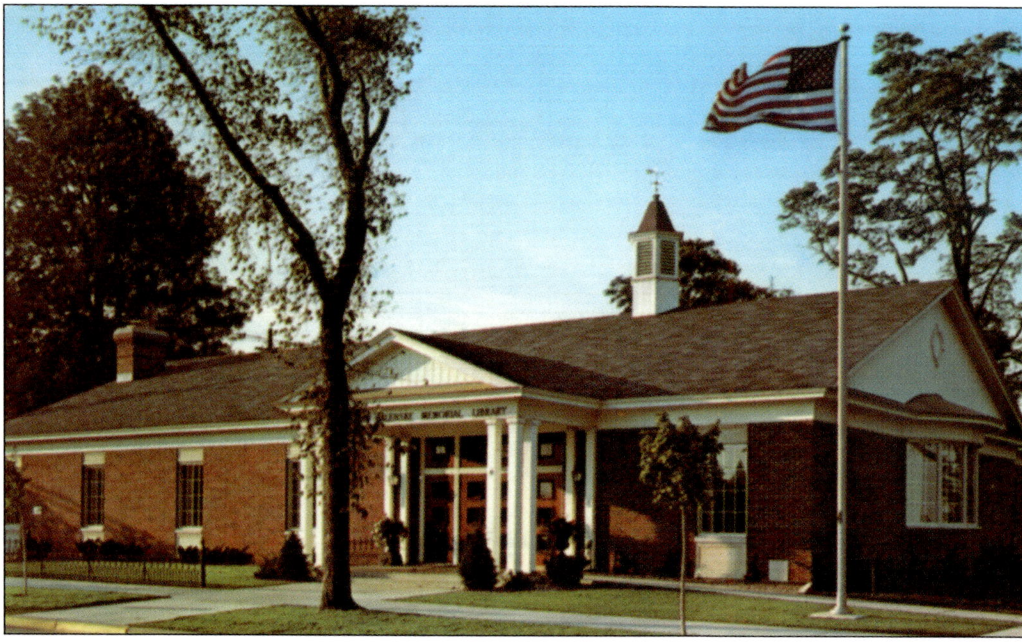

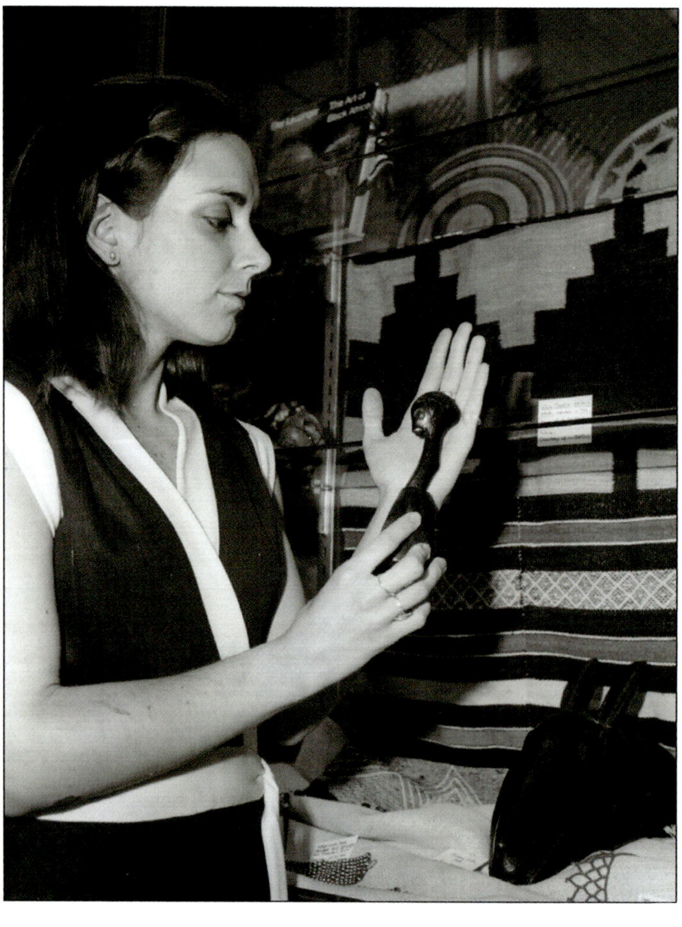

The public library movement in the United States is credited to Andrew Carnegie, industrialist and philanthropist. His goal was to facilitate free public education. Funded by Fred Palenske in memory of his wife and overseen by Harry Rimes, St. Joseph businessman and library president, the new Maude Preston Palenske Memorial Library, above, was dedicated Friday, September 3, 1966. Art and cultural exhibits were also part of the public education mission. On the left is Barbara Paxson, a St. Joseph artist, holding a sample from her collection of African arts and crafts on library display in July 1975. Her interest in African art originated from research trips and volunteer experience in the Peace Corps. (Above, photograph by Penrod Studio; both, courtesy of the Maude Preston Palenske Memorial Library.)

Midcentury education specialists emphasized multiple learning styles, and libraries also sought to encourage young patrons. In this era of youth culture and rock-and-roll, the preferred method was current audio technology, a dedicated listening area, and shelves well stocked with various audiovisual materials. The library kept a good mix of popular and classical music as well as recorded books. In the image on the right, taken during National Library Week in April 1975, Virginia Petrick shows Lake Michigan Catholic high school student Scott Brutsche a sample of the library's collection of cassette tapes and a cassette player available for loan. Below, another young student listens to a record in one of the listening carrels. (Both, courtesy of the Maude Preston Palenske Memorial Library.)

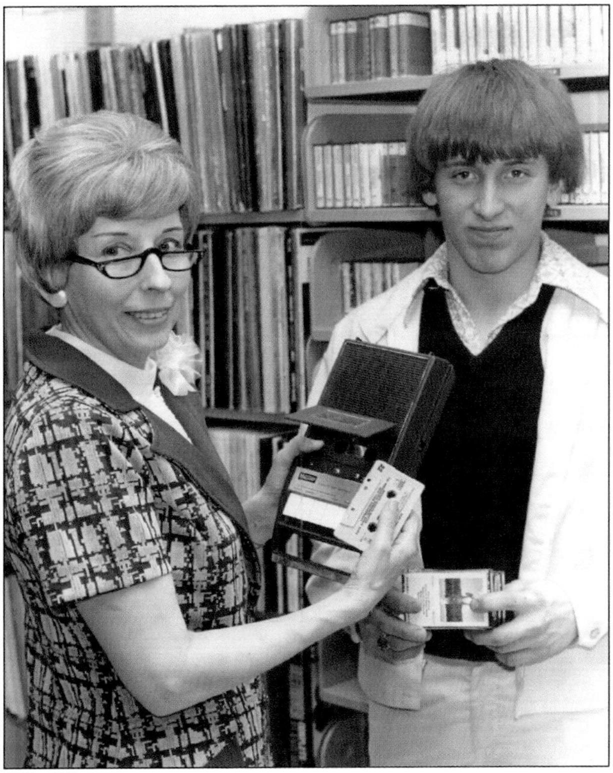

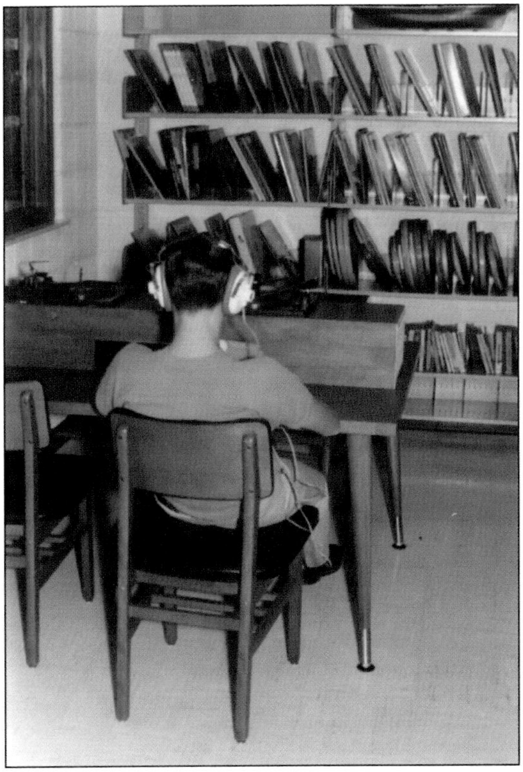

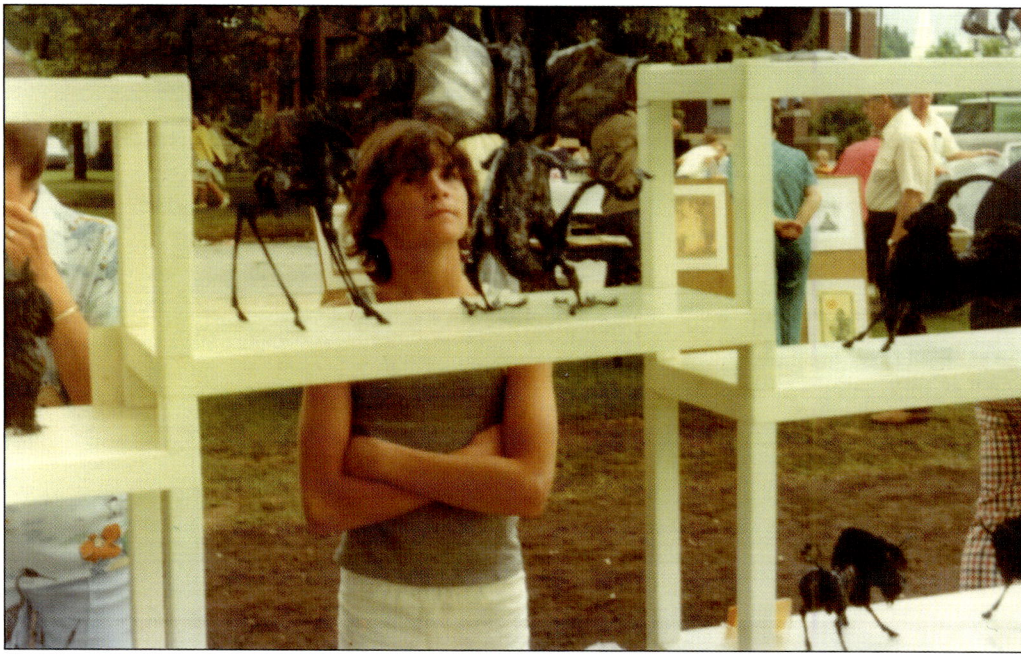

In 1962, three local arts organizations organized the first annual art fair. Under the leadership of Phyllis Rhoads, their goal was to foster a strong arts community through ongoing exhibits and education. The fair, held on the bluff on Lake Boulevard, became an important annual summer event, evolving to a nationally ranked juried exhibit. Above is Patrick McRae examining fanciful metal sculptures at the 1976 fair. In 1972, Olga Krasl, then-president of the St. Joseph Art Association, raised funds to set up the St. Joseph Art Center in an old house at 600 State Street, where artists taught classes for children and adults. Below is the new Krasl Art Center, which opened in 1980. (Above, author's collection; below, photograph by Don Ames Photography, courtesy of the Maude Preston Palenske Memorial Library.)

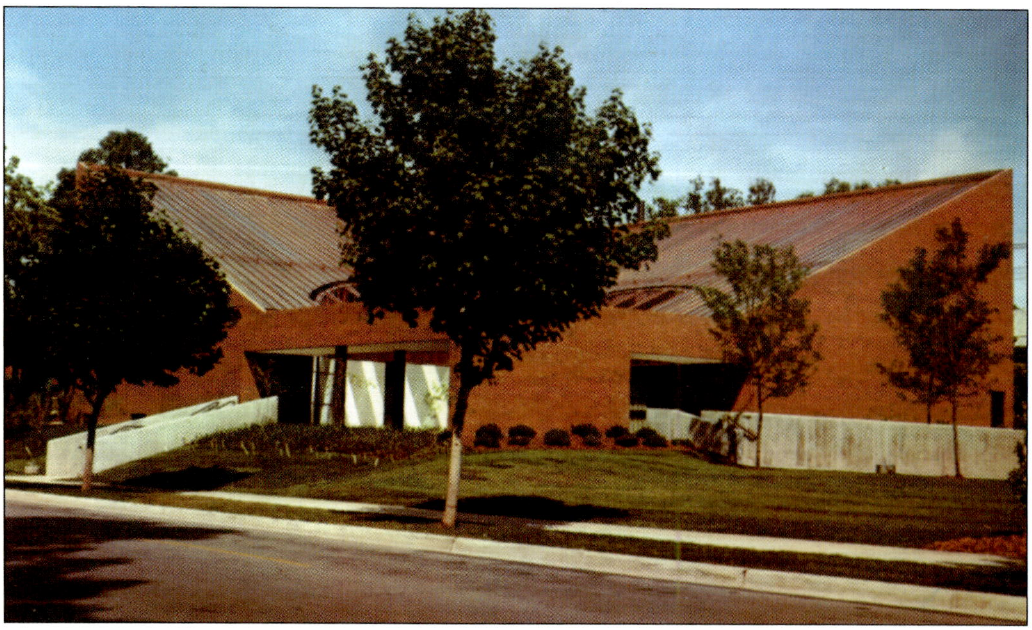

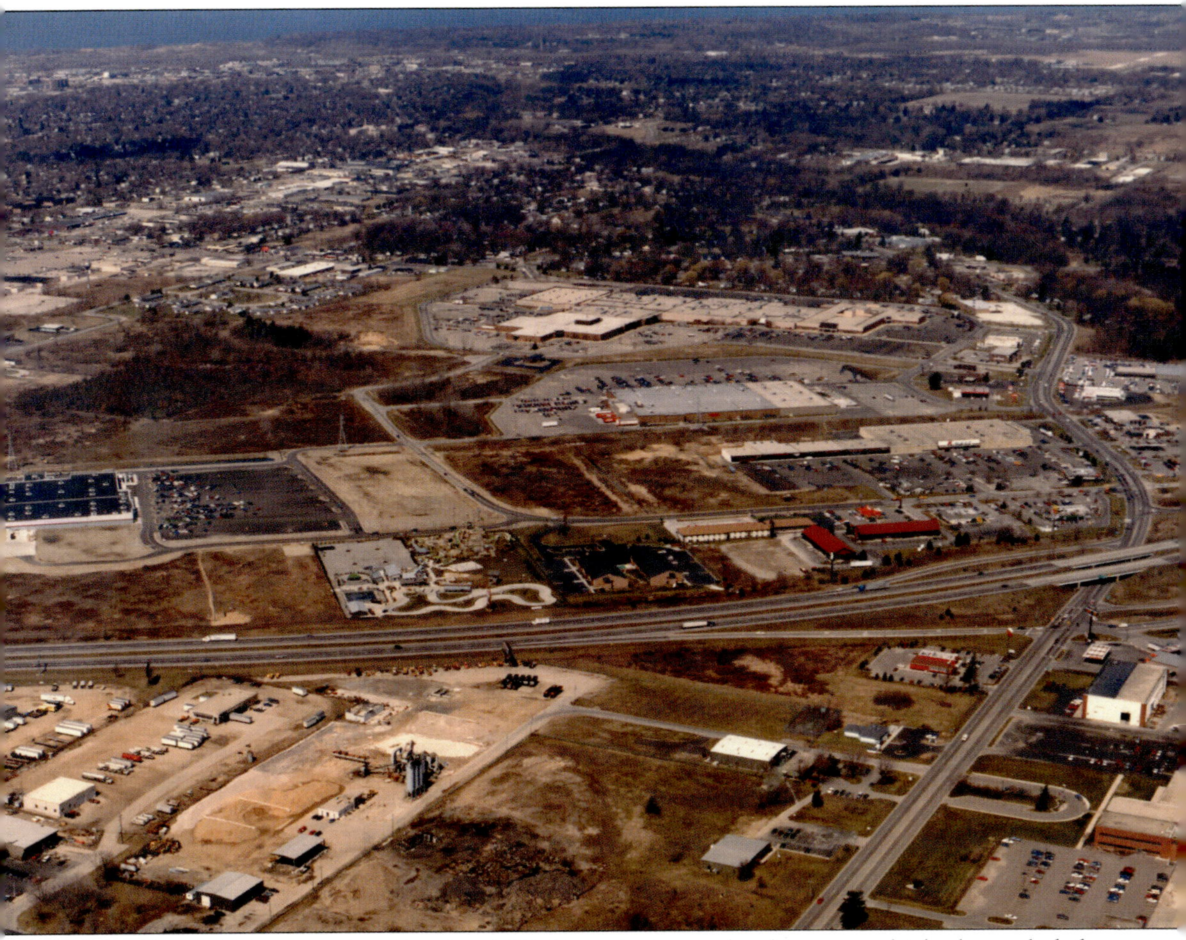

The Orchards Mall opened in October 1979. Part of a larger development, which also included a strip mall and a new Kmart, the project was first proposed in 1974. Among sites originally discussed for its location was the demolished Benton Harbor Flats neighborhood, as part of the revitalization plan that never materialized. Located adjacent to Interstate 94 and populated with a larger percentage of national chains than local retail, this mall drew business away from the Fairplain Plaza as well as remaining downtown shops. In keeping with the typical late-20th-century retail life cycle, nearby big-box developments such as Wal-Mart and other similar franchises now at the old Fairplain Plaza site in turn contributed to the eventual deterioration of the mall. (Photograph by Don Ames Photography, courtesy of Jack Kinney.)

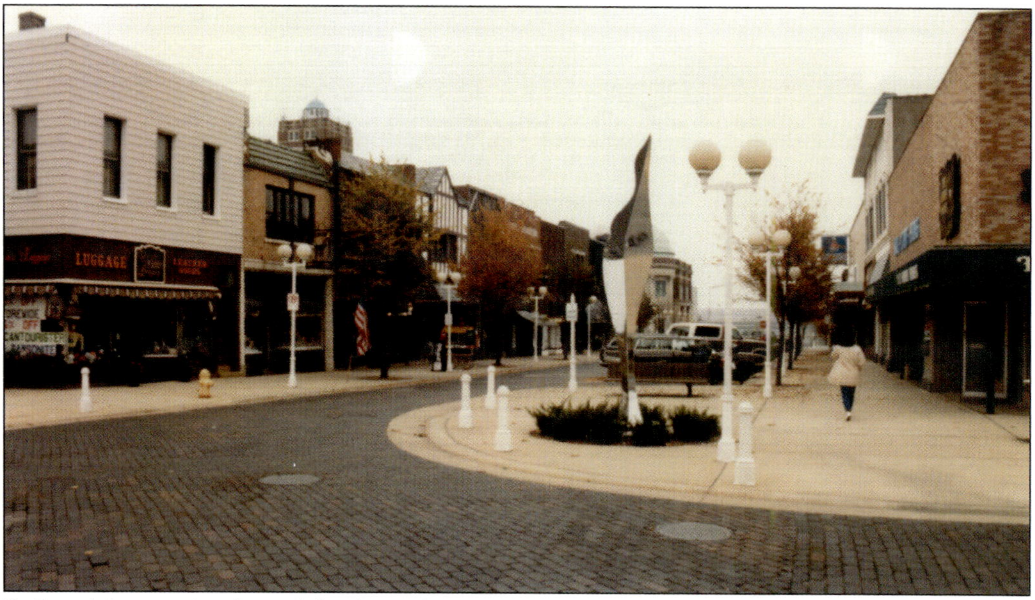

St. Joseph began a local, carefully planned renovation program designed to draw tourists and shoppers back downtown. In 1976, the downtown development authority, comprised of civic and business leaders, began improvements. The plans, focused on recovering St. Joseph's small-town charm, included improved parking, tree planting, new streetlights, vintage-looking street furniture, and renovations designed to invite customers to local businesses. Public art was another key component of downtown beautification. Above, on the corner of State and Pleasant Streets, is the sculpture *Nimbus Flight*, by California sculptor James Russell, who won a national competition for the public installation in 1982. Below is Jan Zebell, assistant to the police chief, standing next to the new planters installed during Broad Street's 1986 renovation. (Both, courtesy of Kathryn Zerler.)

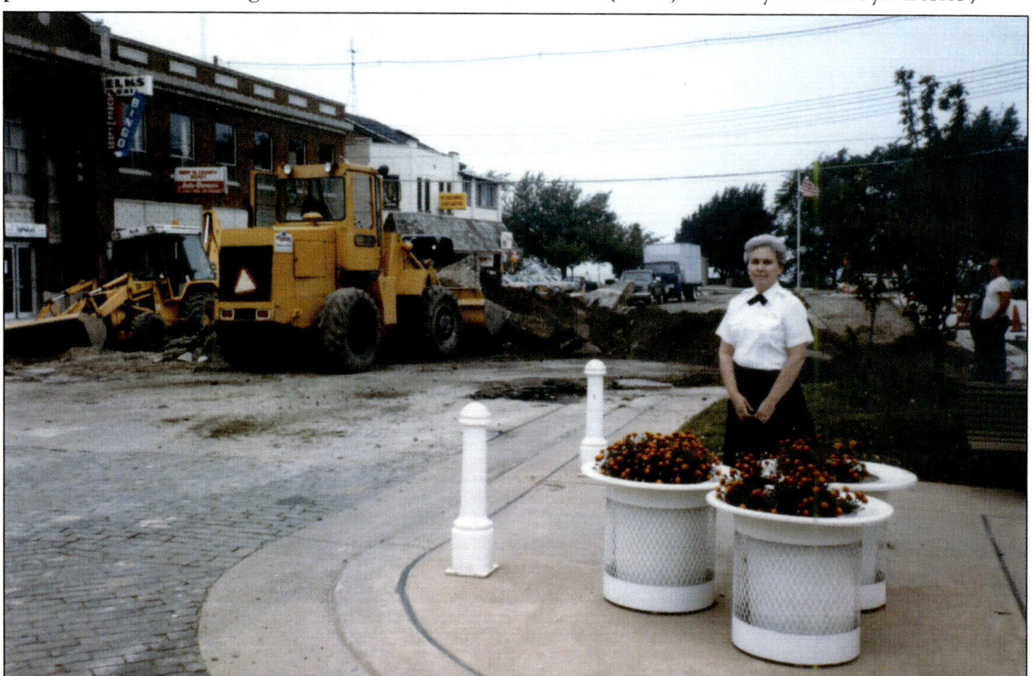

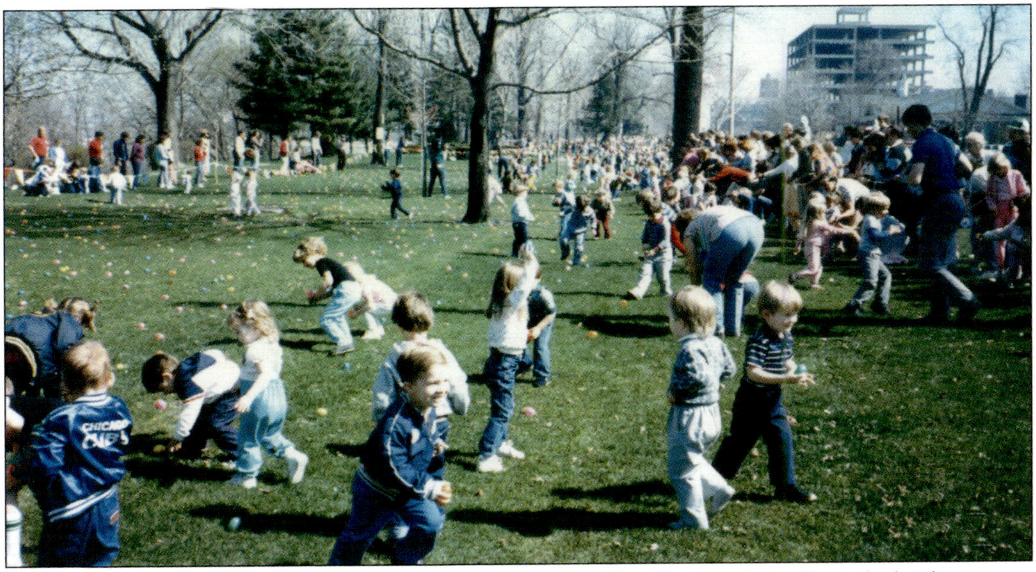

Formed in 1979, the civic organization St. Joseph Today worked in coordination with the downtown development association, as former executive director Kathryn Zerler explains it, "to advance the interest of retailers, property owners, business and professional people, and consumers" in ongoing downtown improvement and events promotion activities. Many of the events were family-focused, involving the entire community. Above are small children along the Bluff Park enthusiastically chasing down Easter eggs on April 18, 1977. Below, joining in on the 1988 Easter festivities are police officer Rick Smiedendorf as an Easter bunny and Carol Fassbender, of Fassbender-Pierce & Walden financial advisers, accompanying him as a clown. (Both, courtesy of Kathryn Zerler.)

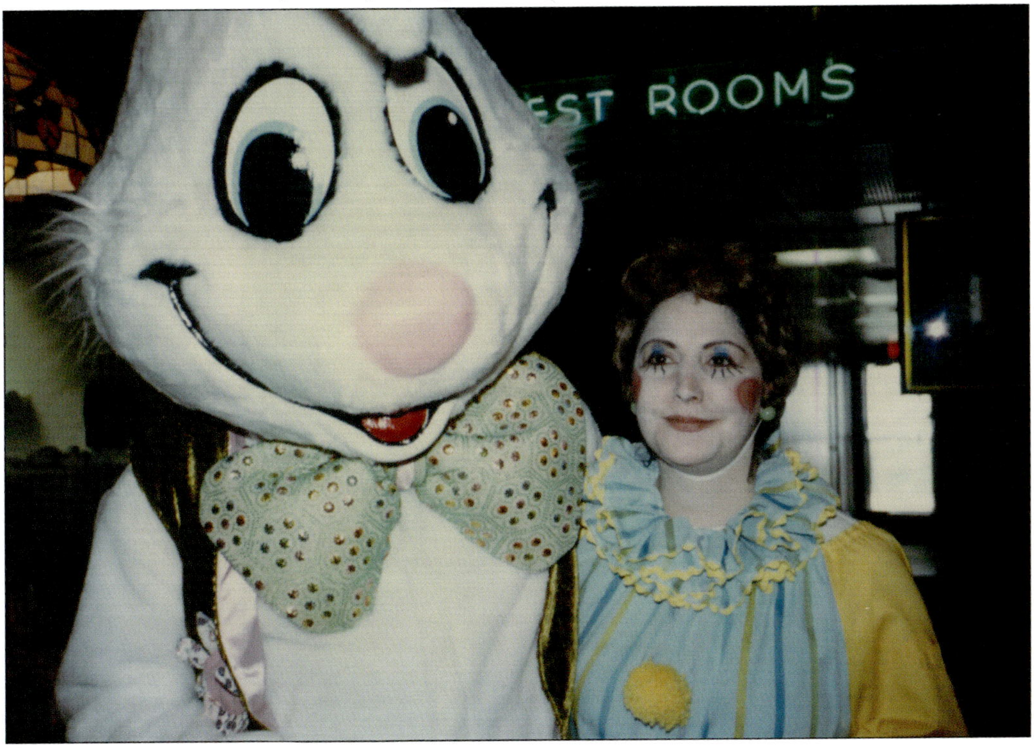

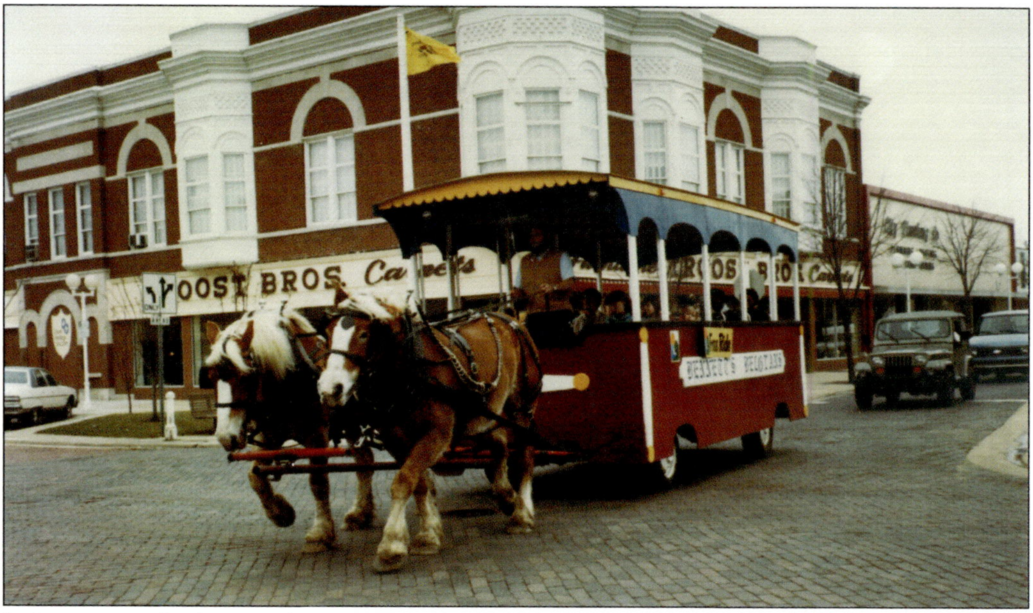

In keeping with the new focus on restoring St. Joseph's 19th-century charm, quaint summer tourist activities such as this horse-drawn trolley ride received enthusiastic support. The trolley was owned by Dennis and Mickey Bennett, who called their business Bennett's Belgians. Dennis, who built the trolley, is seen here driving it. Free rides for year-round events were sponsored by the Frederick S. Upton Foundation. (Courtesy of Kathryn Zerler.)

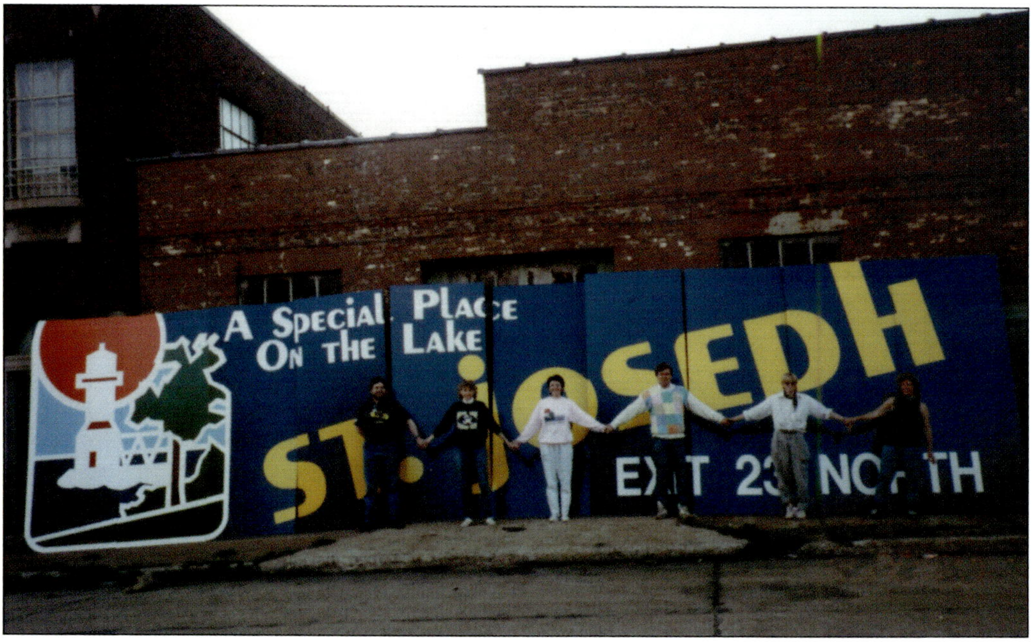

Members of St. Joseph Today proudly stand in front of the billboard they constructed in 1990 for display on I-94. Pictured are, from left to right, Patrick Ohmann, Lee Passaro, Kathryn Zerler, Jack Engelhardt, unidentified, and Cynthia Cooke. The logo, representing St. Joseph's lake, sunsets, public parks, and lighthouse was designed by Don Johnson, cofounder of Johnson-Rauhoff, a local promotions and marketing company. (Courtesy of Kathryn Zerler.)

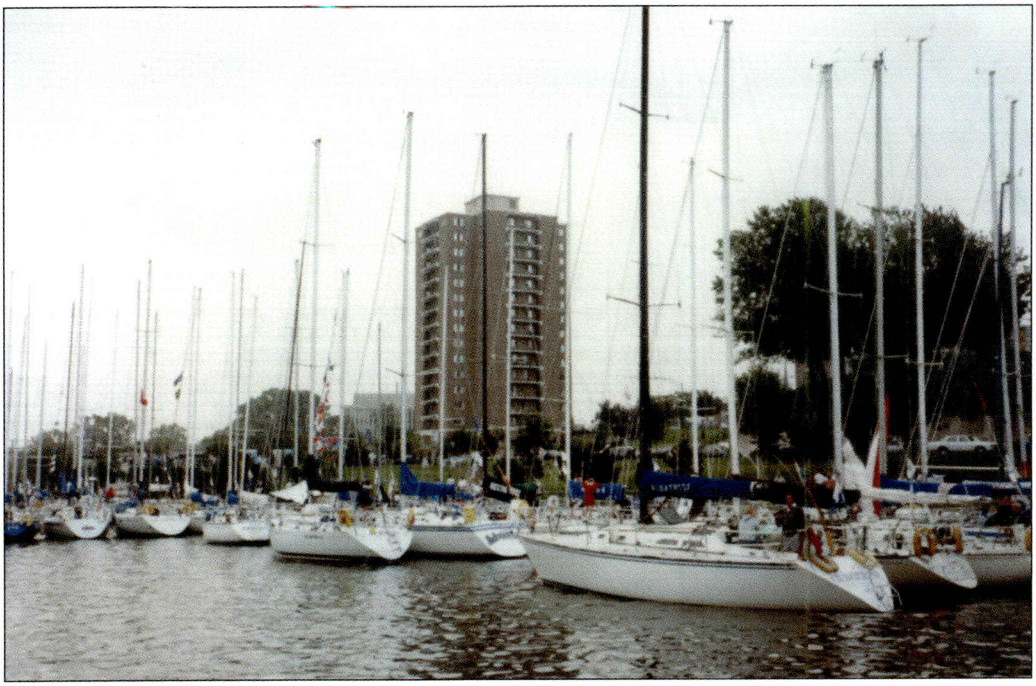

Among St. Joseph's other accomplishments in self-reinvention was the institution of major festivals that celebrated the area's waterfront heritage. The image above is of sailboats in the St. Joseph River Channel on Labor Day weekend in 1985, ready for the second leg of the Tri-State Regatta. An annual event sponsored by Chicago Yacht Club, the race starts on Friday night in Chicago. Sailors spend Saturday night in St. Joseph, leave for Michigan City, Indiana, then back to Chicago. Below, photographed in July 1987 during St. Joseph's Venetian Festival, the USS *Oliver Hazard Perry*, a 455-foot Navy frigate, is docked along the north pier for a passenger cruise. The Venetian Festival was held every third weekend in July. (Both, courtesy of Kathryn Zerler.)

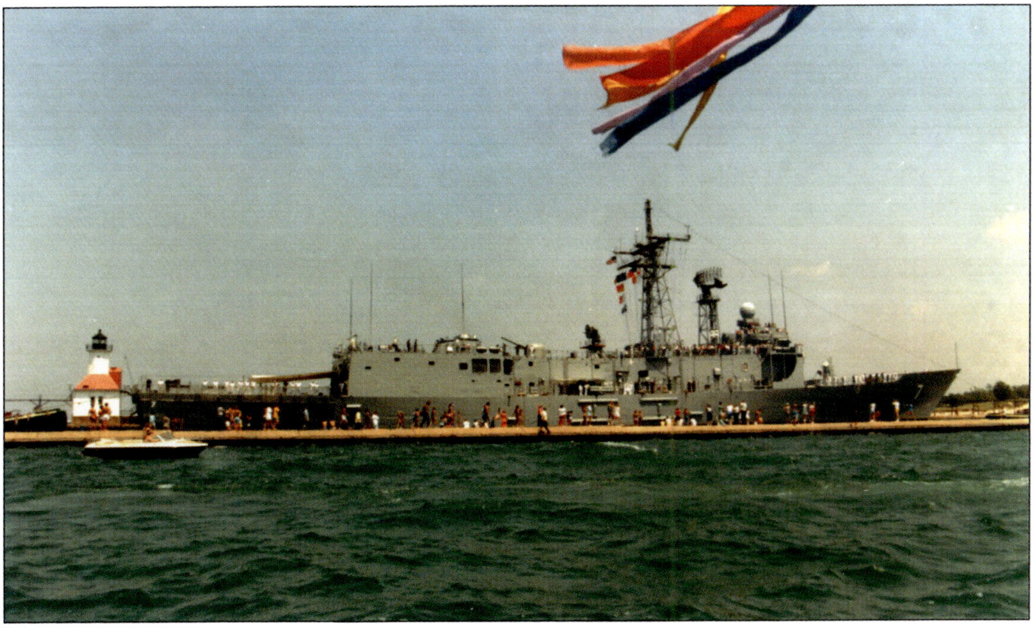

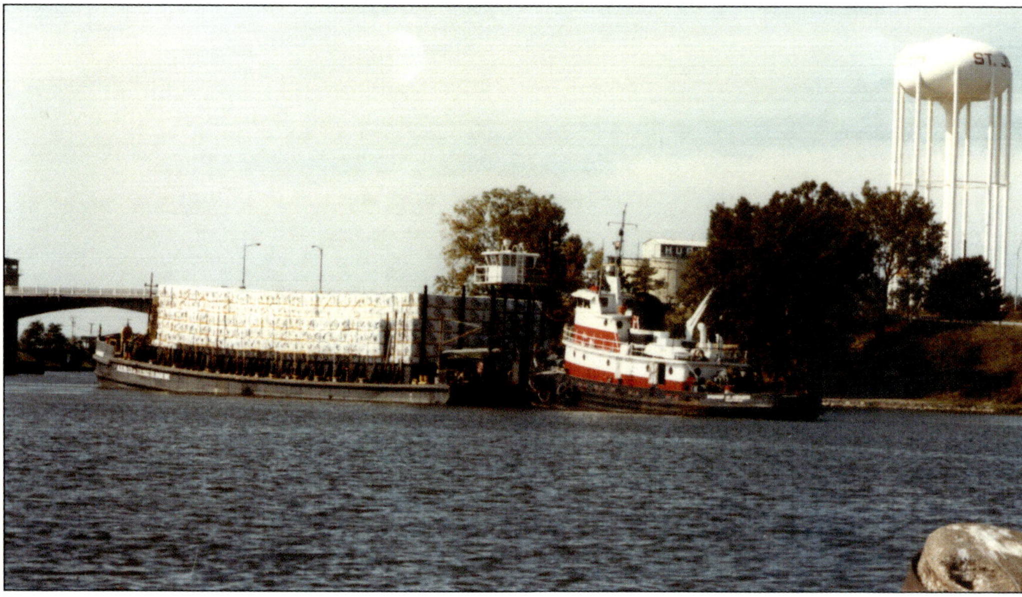

Between major events and successful revitalization efforts, life in St. Joseph continued more or less as always. As these two peaceful scenes from the 1980s show, Lake Michigan and the St. Joseph River remained the vital centers for work and play. Above, Great Lakes towing tug *Wilfred M. Cohen* pushes a load of lumber to the Central Dock. Below, Whirlpool executive Glenn Zerler pilots his Uniflight the *Lady Z* down the St. Joseph River Channel toward Lake Michigan in the late 1980s. Zerler, a lifelong St. Joseph resident, bought and rebuilt his first boat, a 16-foot wooden Lyman, when he was 12 years old. (Above, courtesy of Jack Kinney; below, courtesy of Kathryn Zerler.)

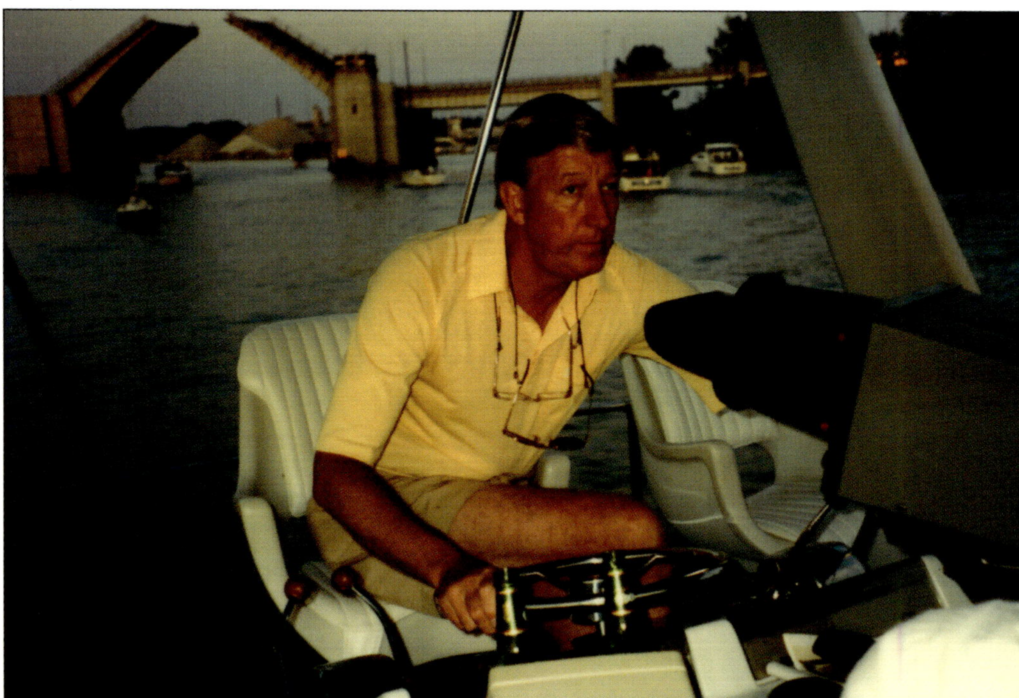

Four

New Territory, New Beginnings

Benton Harbor's turn came in the early 1990s. Like St. Joseph, its renaissance was local. But the scale was smaller, the focus was more localized, and the mood was different—less American hometown and more urban frontier.

By the 1990s, the pretty, busy downtown Benton Harbor seen in the earlier images was long gone. Now vacant lots and empty warehouses ringed abandoned and collapsing buildings—many of them condemned as hazardous or toxic sites.

Now among the poorest and most crime-ridden cities in Michigan, city and state officials and even the federal government sought recovery plans. Through a fortuitous combination of philanthropy, state and federal grants, vision, sheer love for the city, and shared passion for the arts, a group of local artists and entrepreneurs began to bring it back.

Crucial to this effort were Herbert and Audre Mendel, a philanthropic local couple—an industrialist and a ballet dancer—who loved the arts. When one of their earlier projects, helping rebuild the Globe Theatre in London, spurred a renewal in the blighted neighborhood around it, they were inspired to do the same for Benton Harbor. In 2000, the Mendels offered $500,000 via an organization called the Cornerstone Alliance to provide grants to artists who wished to renovate property in downtown Benton Harbor. The Whirlpool Foundation matched the Mendels' donation.

The program, originally called Community Renewal though the Arts, provided support to the grassroots efforts of local artists, arts educators, and entrepreneurs who eventually formed the New Territory Arts Association with the aim of creating a new Benton Harbor Arts District. Recently, other like-minded citizens, businesses, and organizations have joined in, working to build the promised "city of the future" together.

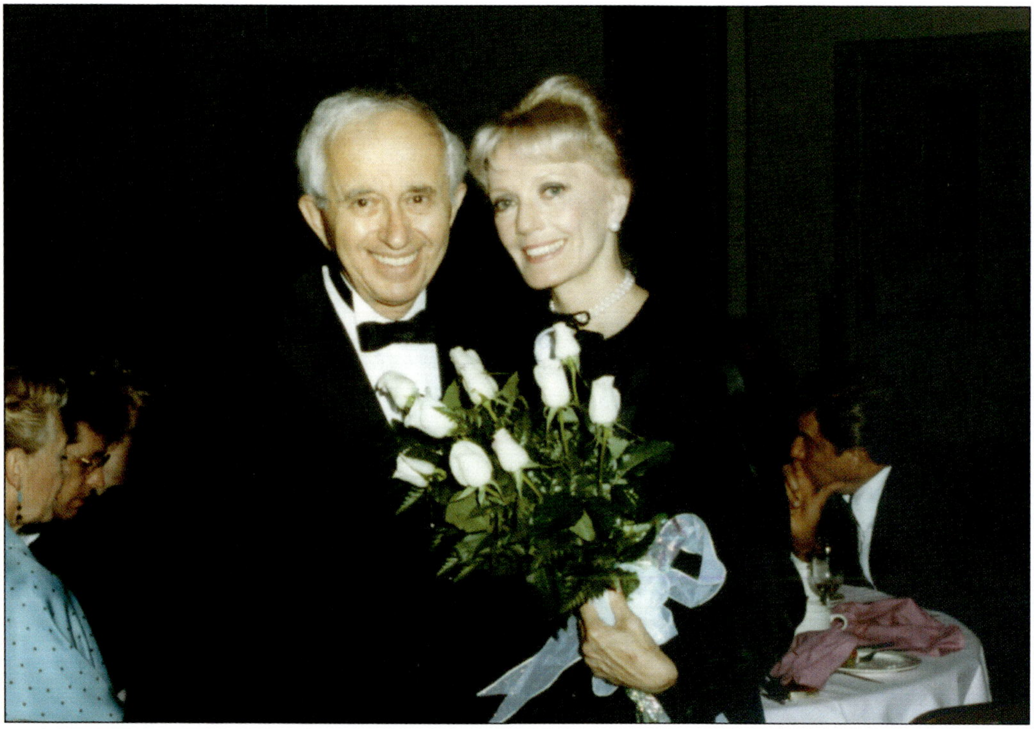

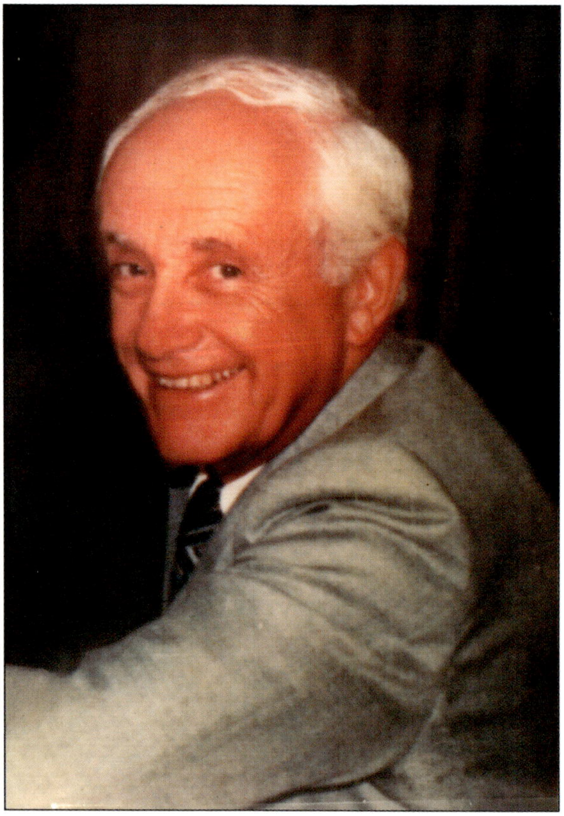

Above are Herbert and Audre Deckmann Mendel. Born in Chicago, Herbert Mendel moved to Benton Harbor after World War II and founded Michigan Standard Alloys. Audre was a Balanchine dancer and later danced for the American Ballet Theater. The couple financed the completion of the Mendel Center for the Arts and Technology at Lake Michigan College as part of a larger revitalization plan for Benton Harbor. The grant was given on the condition that the new center be named after Herbert's late brother Edwin, pictured at left. The center had its grand opening in 1992. According to an article in the *Herald Palladium* dated June 20, 1999, Audre was responsible for bringing the American Ballet Theater to perform in the Twin Cities—a rare appearance outside of major venues. (Both, courtesy of Lake Michigan College.)

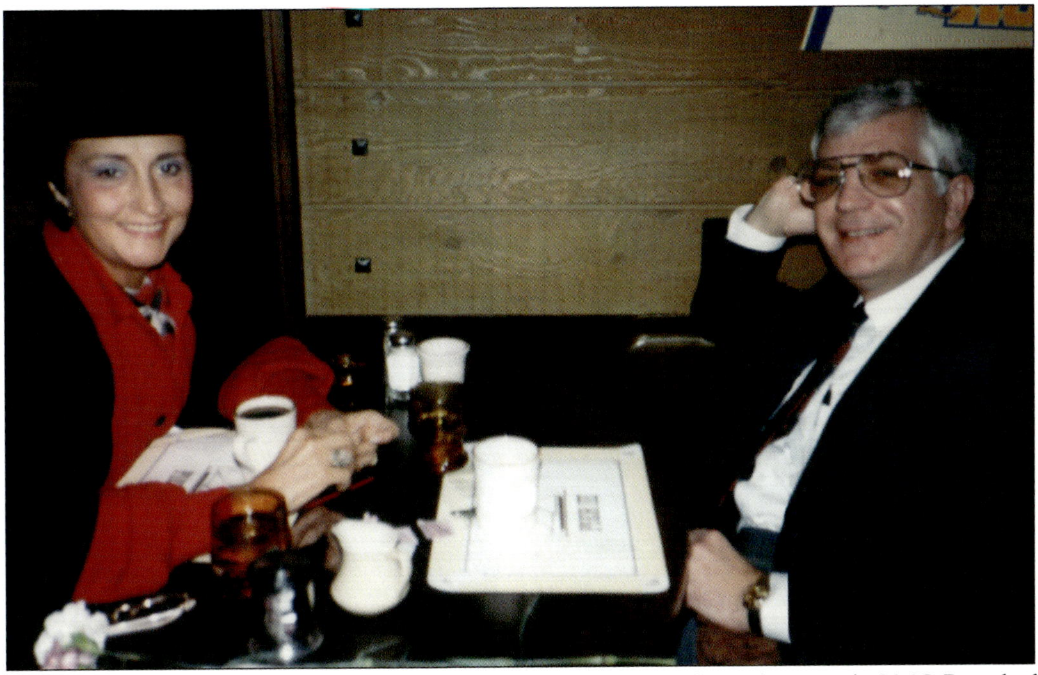

Above are Anne Mulder, Lake Michigan College president, and Frank Pastrick, LMC Board of Trustees and Chevrolet dealership owners, at Holly's Landing in St. Joseph. In August 1989, Dr. Mulder announced plans to finish construction on a campus arts and community center. In 1990, Herbert and Audre Mendel donated $1 million toward the project. Whirlpool matched the grant, and the People's State Bank also contributed. Hired in 1985 as the first woman president of the college, Dr. Mulder retired in 1993. Below are members of the Lake Michigan College Foundation Board of Directors at the Mendel Center groundbreaking on May 17, 1991. Pictured from left to right are (first row) Steve Silcox, unidentified, Sylvia Coleman, Nan Taylor, unidentified, Anne Mulder, Judy Zacha, and unidentified; (second row) Bill Mahrone, unidentified, Dick Schanze, and Warren Gast. (Above, courtesy of Kathyrn Zerler; below, courtesy of Lake Michigan College.)

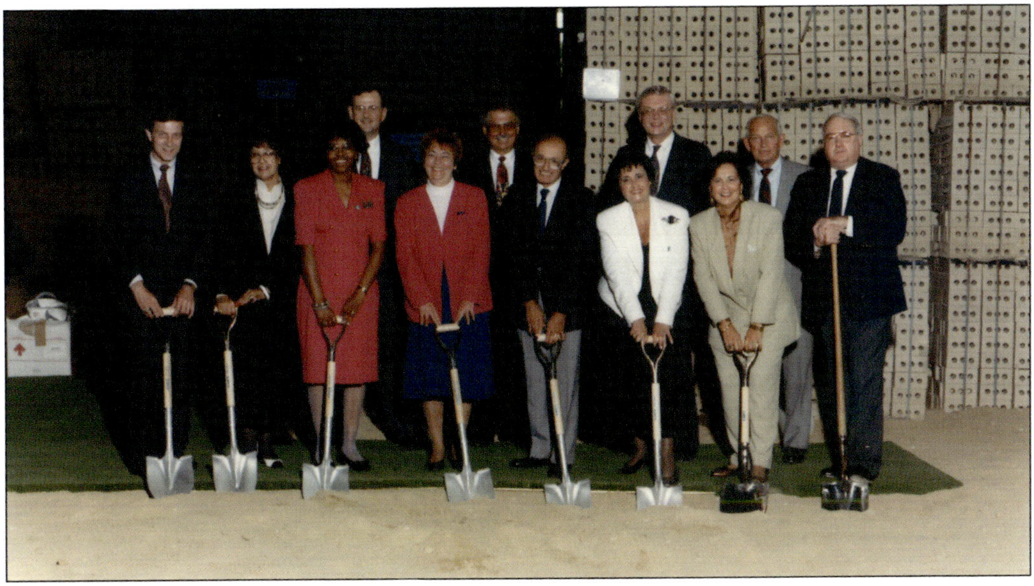

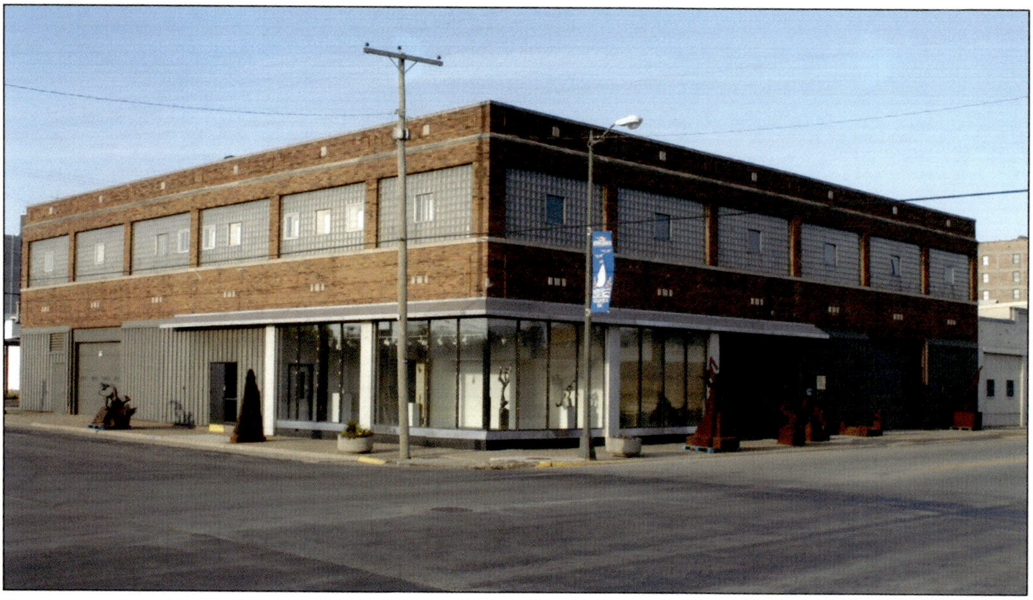

On December 15, 1995, world-renowned Chicago-based metal sculptor Richard Hunt opened a studio in a former warehouse on 258 Territorial Roard in Benton Harbor. Hunt, who had fond childhood memories of the area, became interested in the Community Renewal Through the Arts program through local gallery owner John Wilson and Evan LeDuc, architect and then-executive vice president of the Cornerstone Alliance. Inocencio and Flynn Design Inc. renovated the studio façade. The winter evening scene below depicts *And You Seas*, which Hunt installed in St. Joseph at the point where the St. Joseph River meets Lake Michigan, in 2002. The 50-foot welded-steel sculpture echoes the rhythms of the lake. Its name is taken from a poem of the same name by French surrealist poet St. John Perse. (Above, courtesy of Dixie Inocencio; below, photograph by Joshua Nowicki.)

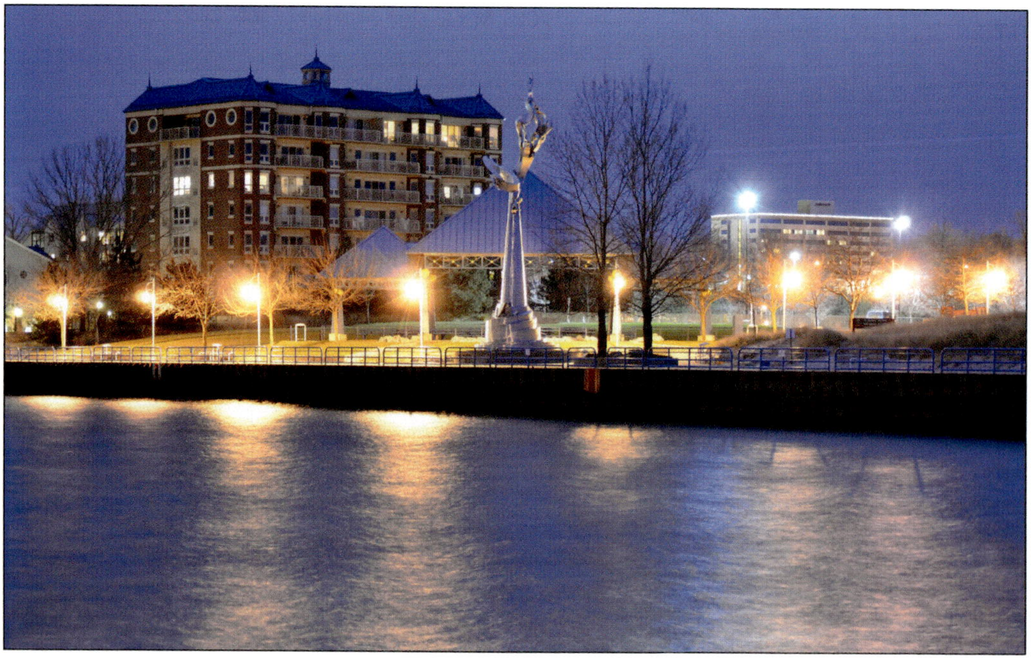

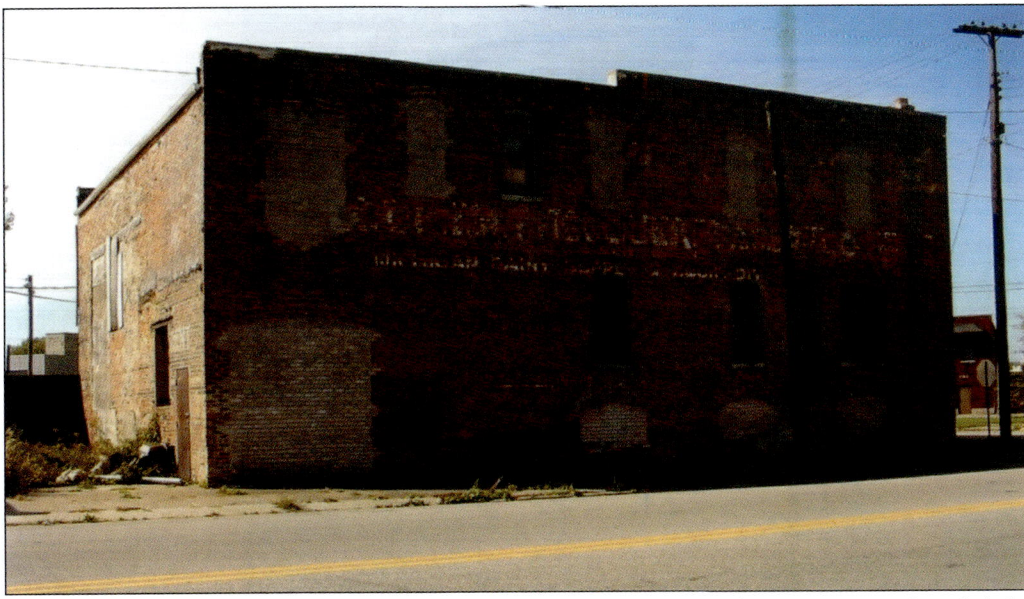

In 1998, Benton Harbor's small community of artists, architects, and entrepreneurs founded the New Territory Arts Association, and many of them live and work in the area they have revitalized. The Livery Microbrewery on 190 Fifth Street doubles as a local community center. Locals gather for fresh microbrews and café fare to discuss art, politics, or current events. The Livery hosts fantasy football, movie nights, community meetings, nationally known musical acts, and weekend jam sessions. In summers, the outdoor beer garden doubles as a CSA garden exchange. Above and below are before-and-after shots of the building. Originally a livery stable, the building stood abandoned until Leslie Pickell, Michael Gardner, Tim Flynn, and Dixie Inocencio purchased it in 2003. Renovated by Inocencio and Flynn Design Inc., it opened for business in 2005. (Above, courtesy of Dixie Inocencio; below, courtesy of Ken Ankli.)

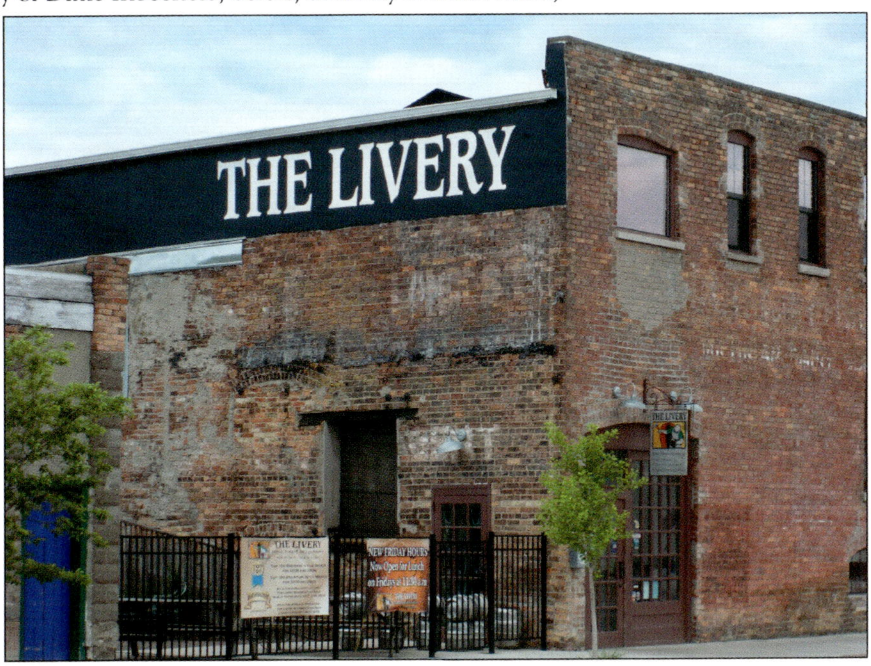

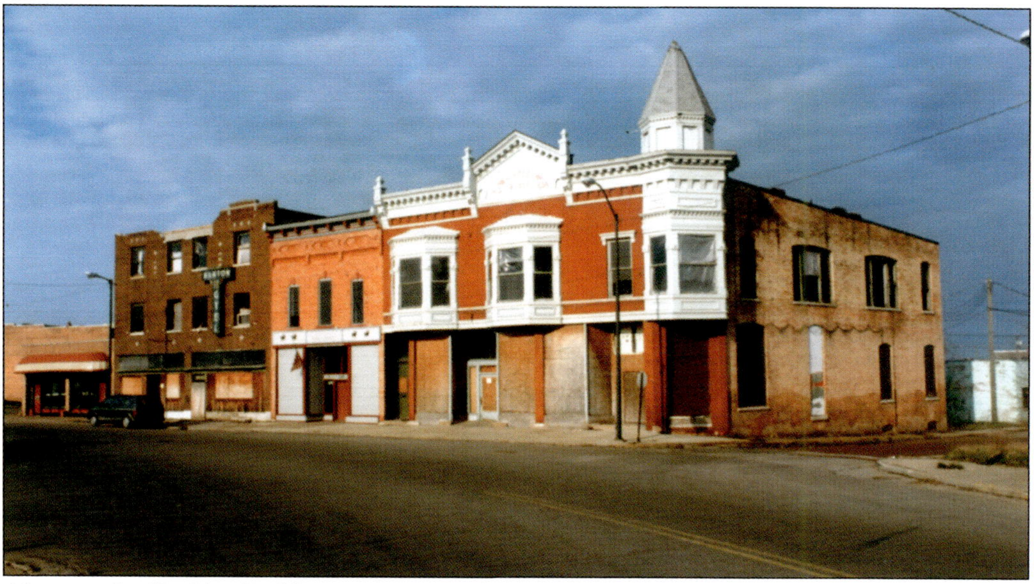

Above is the Hinkley Building in 1997. Far from its venerable 19th-century origins, or even its 1970s repurposing described in the previous chapter, the building was collapsing when Kathy and Jerry Catania purchased it in 1997. Envisioning the perfect space for their glass studio, the Catanias spent the next eight years renovating. Their biggest obstacle was the caved-in roof, which no local company would repair until Inocencio and Flynn Design Inc. devised a way to support it. The old Benton Hotel below, on the same block, also languished until Brad and Regina Emberton renovated it into the Phoenix Café. Keeping with the neighborhood spirit, Scott Elliott supplied the whimsical figures by nationally known urban sculptor Red Grooms, shown below decorating the outside of the decayed former hotel. (Above, photograph by Gloria Badiner; both, courtesy of Kathy Catania.)

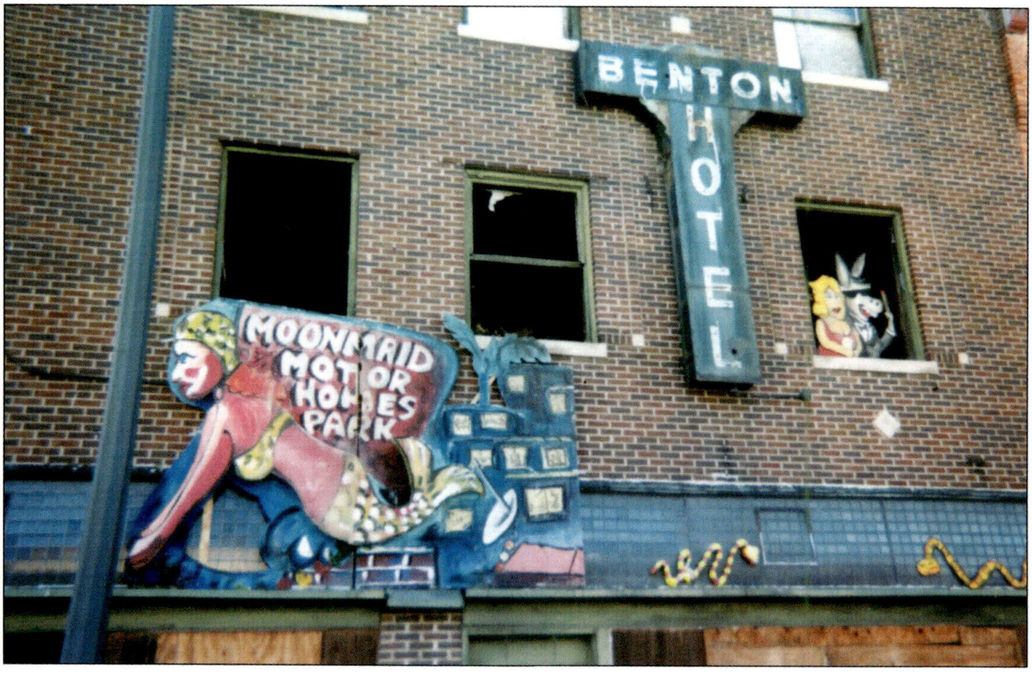

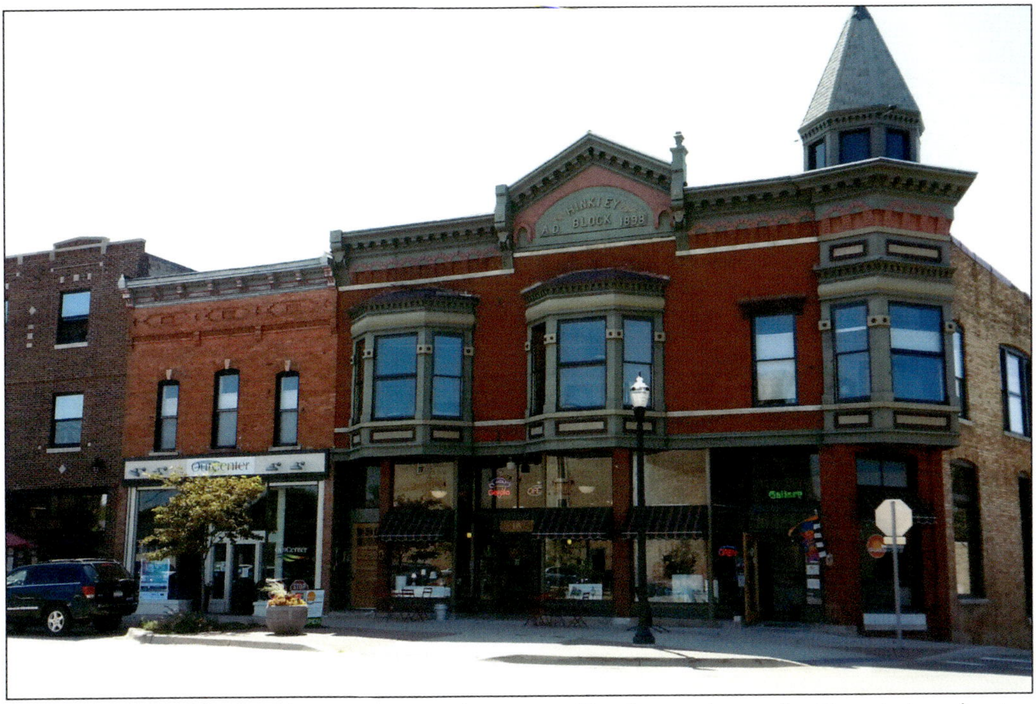

Above is the Hinkley Building as it currently appears. Besides serving as the Catanias' production studio, Water Street Glassworks sponsors Fired Up!, an after-school program that trains Benton Harbor teens in the art of glassblowing techniques. Glass-working and metal-casting classes are also available for adults. Next door are Gelato Works, which serves Palazzolo's gelato and doubles as gallery space, and the Out Center for LGBT youth. Below are local musicians having a session in the Phoenix Café, while other patrons enjoy fresh-brewed coffee, deli sandwiches, and free WiFi. Local business owners, tourists, and students frequently congregate here for lunch or afternoon coffee. (Both photographs by Stephen Brandon.)

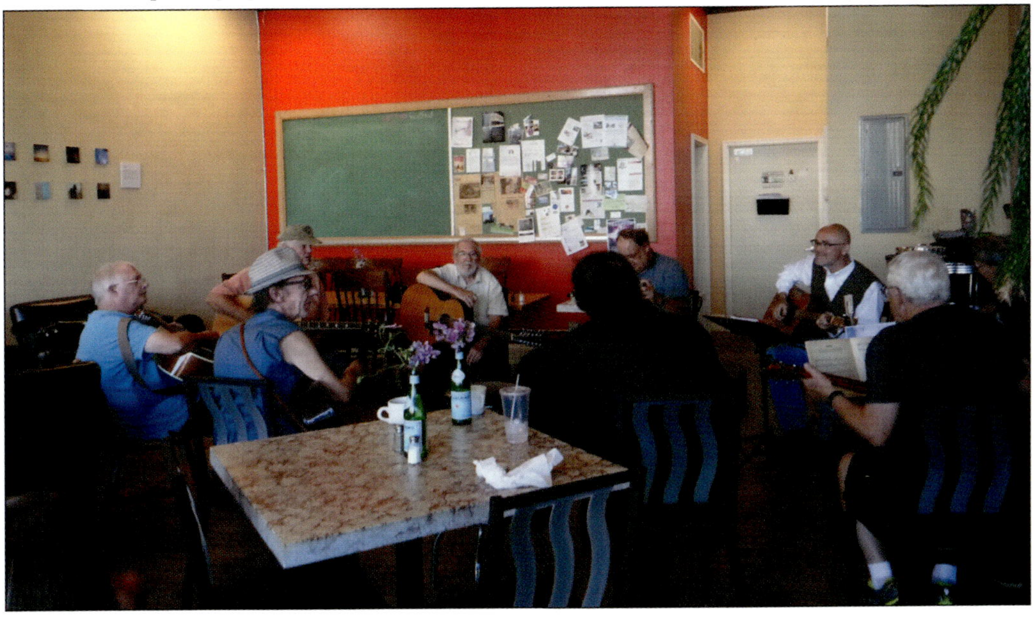

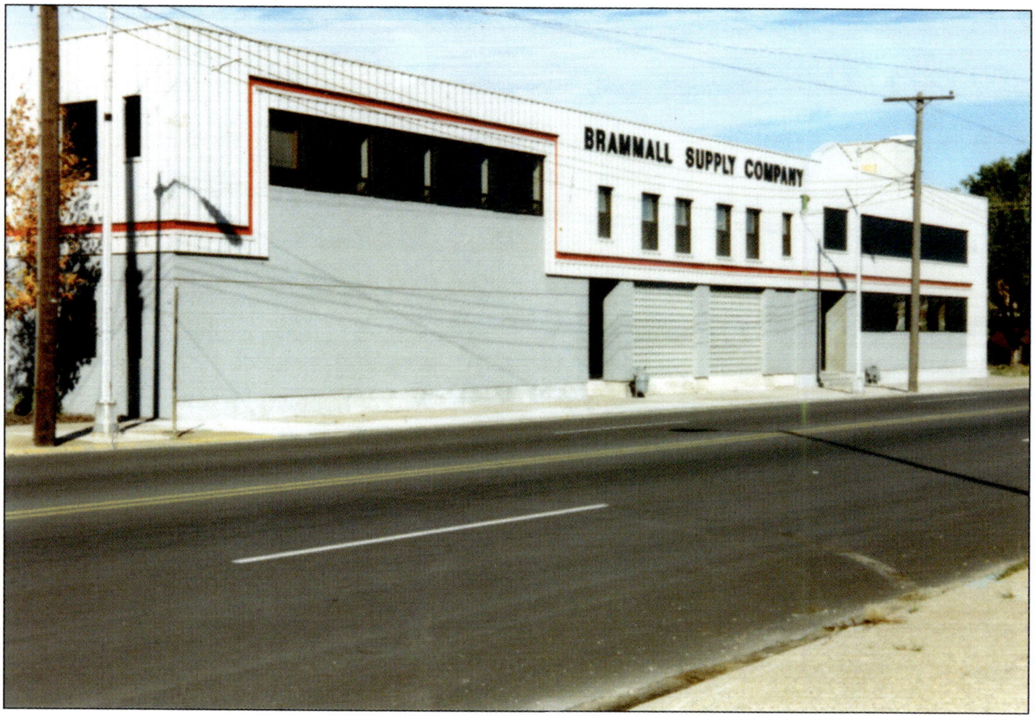

Founded by Edward Brammall in 1873 as a farm implement dealer, Brammall Industrial Supply at 196 Water Street, now a wholesale distributor of industrial supplies, is the oldest business remaining in Benton Harbor. Ken Ankli, its president, is also the current president of the New Territory Arts Association. Above is a photograph of the building as it was refaced in the 1990s. Below is the mural on the front of the revamped Brammall building, which also houses high-end Quarternote Lofts apartments, and the Citadel Dance & Music Center complex. One of three commissioned through a major arts grant from the W.W. Kellog Foundation, the mural was painted by Tony Hendrick of Lansing, Michigan, in collaboration with locals Chris Dicicco and Sally Ross in 2005. It depicts the city of Benton Harbor, the fruit market, and local industry. (Both, courtesy of Ken Ankli.)

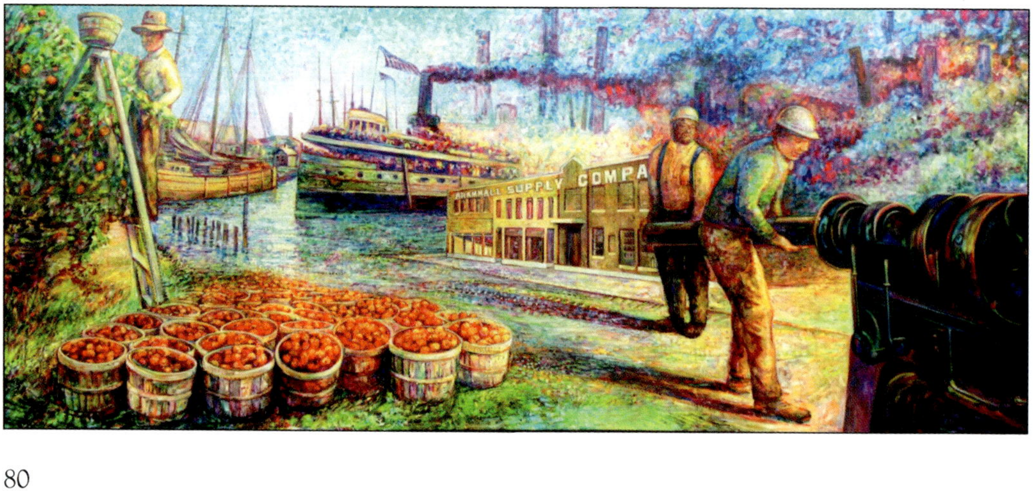

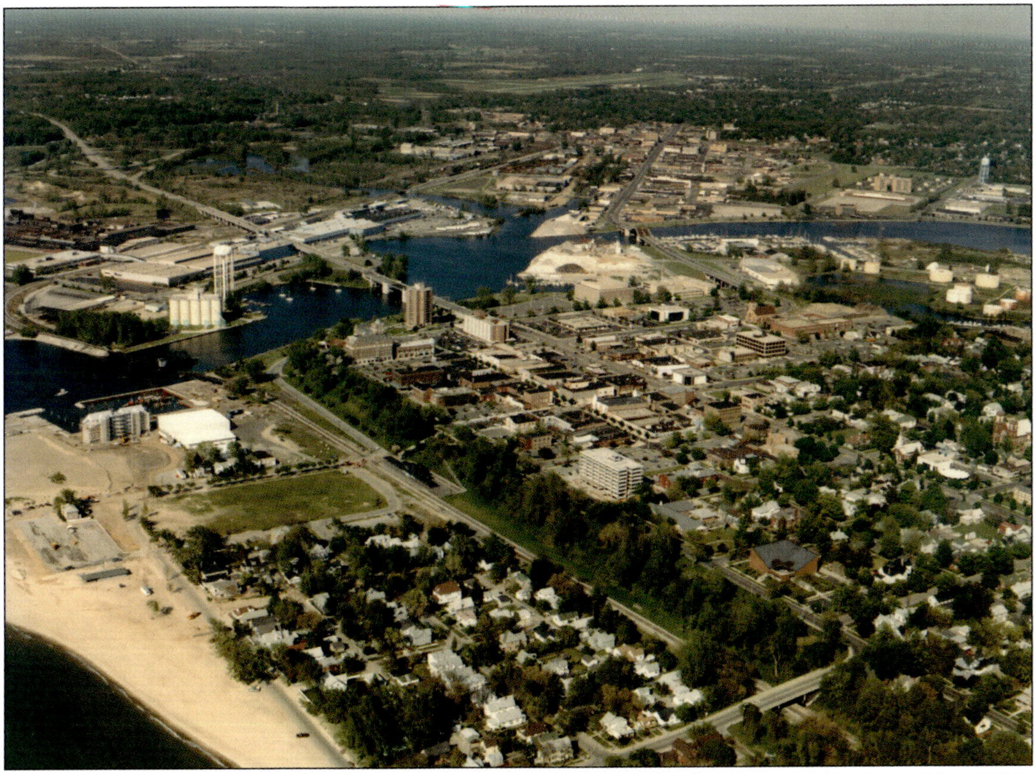

The New Territory Arts Association was so named because desolate Benton Harbor of the 1990s offered a new frontier for visionary experiments. St. Joseph, by contrast, was now positioned for large-scale investment development. Since St. Joseph's development efforts through the 1980s focused on emphasizing its hometown feel, recreating the too-long and sadly deserted vacancy of Silver Beach into a newer, bigger, and better multiuse development seemed the logical next step. The upscale Waterfront Condominiums, completed in 1988, aimed toward a perceived future of high-end investment. The project proved controversial, as the towers obscured the panoramic lakefront view key to the city's charm. The aerial shot above shows the near-complete Waterfront complex and the void of Silver Beach. The postcard view below shows the just-complete condos in 1988. (Both, courtesy of the Maude Preston Palenske Memorial Library.)

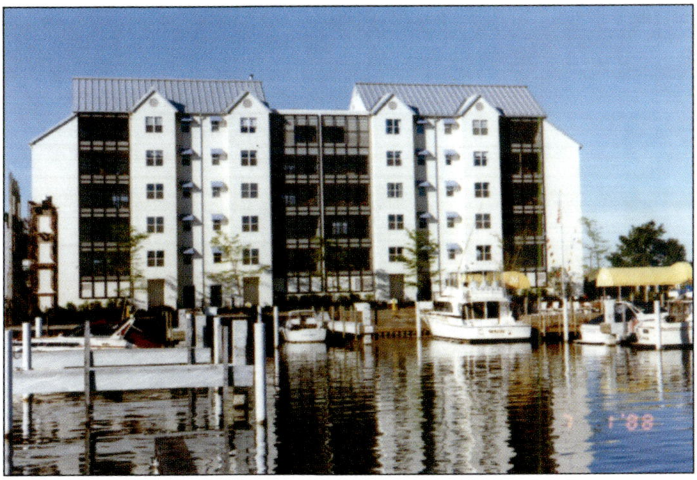

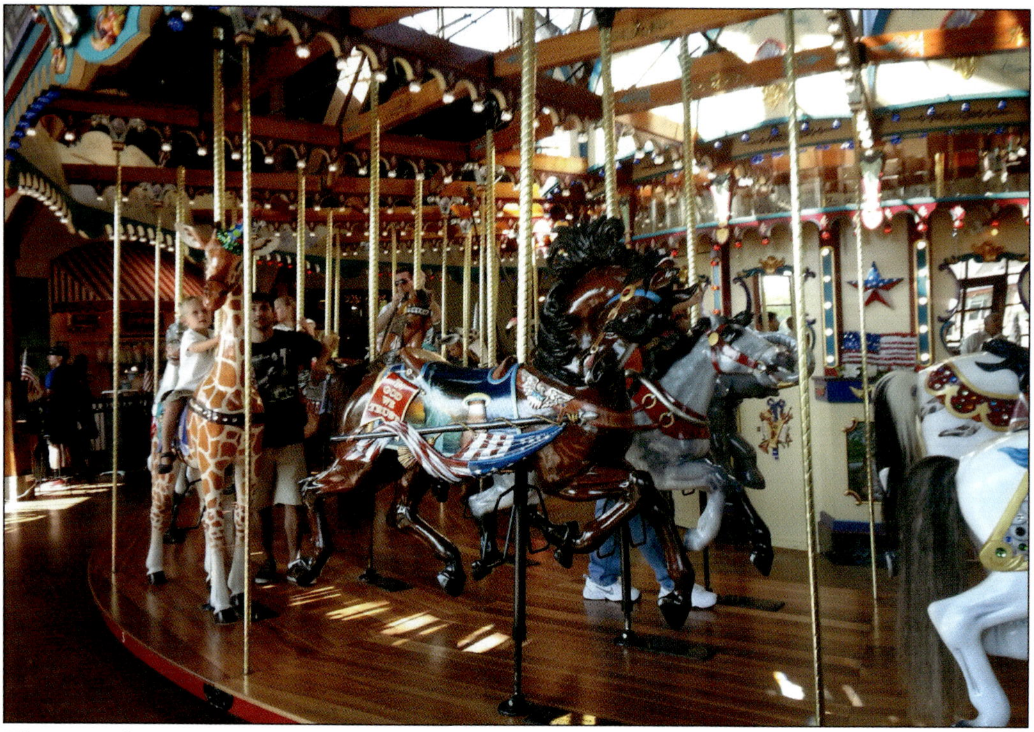

The new Silver Beach carousel was far better received. The original carousel, which ran at Silver Beach from 1910 until 1971, when the park closed, was sold to collector Marianne Stevens of Roswell, New Mexico. In 1995, the carousel society began fundraising to buy it back. Unable to secure sufficient funding on time, the society turned to Carousel Works of Mansfield, Ohio, to produce hand-carved originals. Sponsored by community donors, each unique horse represents a different local attraction, and each of the 18 rounding boards illustrates a moment in community history. Above are fathers and babies enjoying the carousel, which opened in 2010. Below is the new Silver Beach Center, with the carousel, the arched roof of the new Curious Kids Museum, and the Compass Fountain. (Above, author's collection; below, photograph by Joshua Nowicki.)

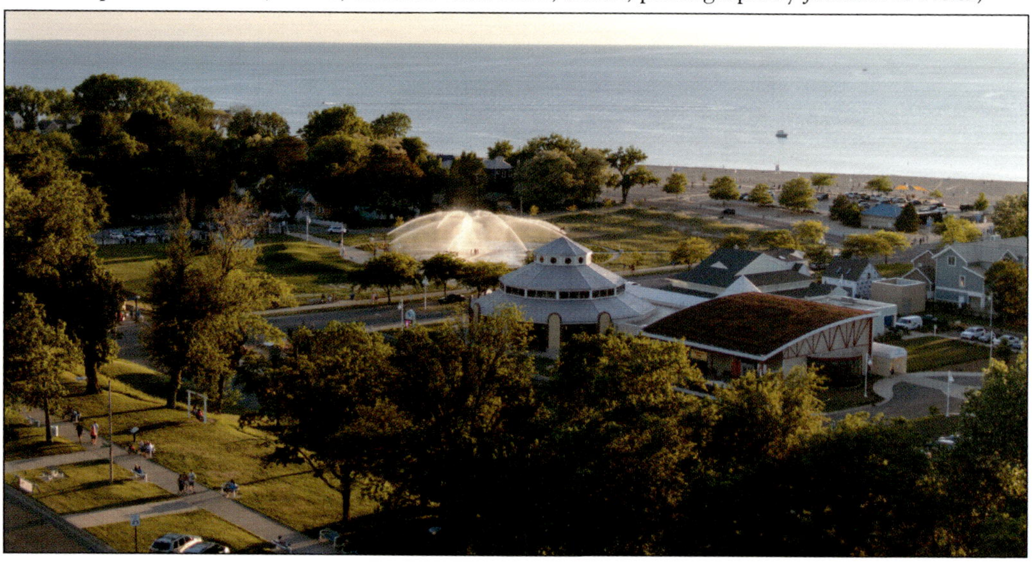

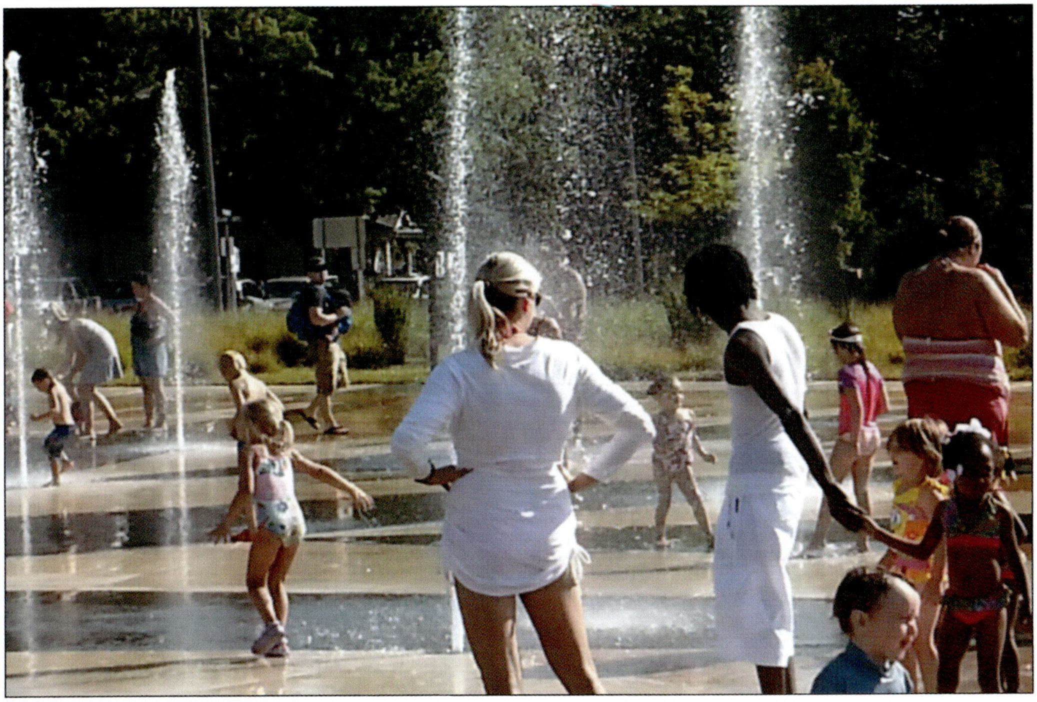

To the delight of visiting and local children, the jets of the Whirlpool Compass Fountain were turned on for the first time on Saturday, September 5, 2009. In summer, families such as those above splash, free of charge, among the 28 water jets, while children eagerly await the 75-foot blast of the eight water cannons every 15 minutes. Those wishing to stay dry can still enjoy the beauty of the fountain, complete with the shining lake and summer sunsets, over margaritas in the bar of Silver Beach Pizza, which opened in 2003 in the historic Amtrak station. (Above, author's collection; below, photograph by Joshua Nowicki.)

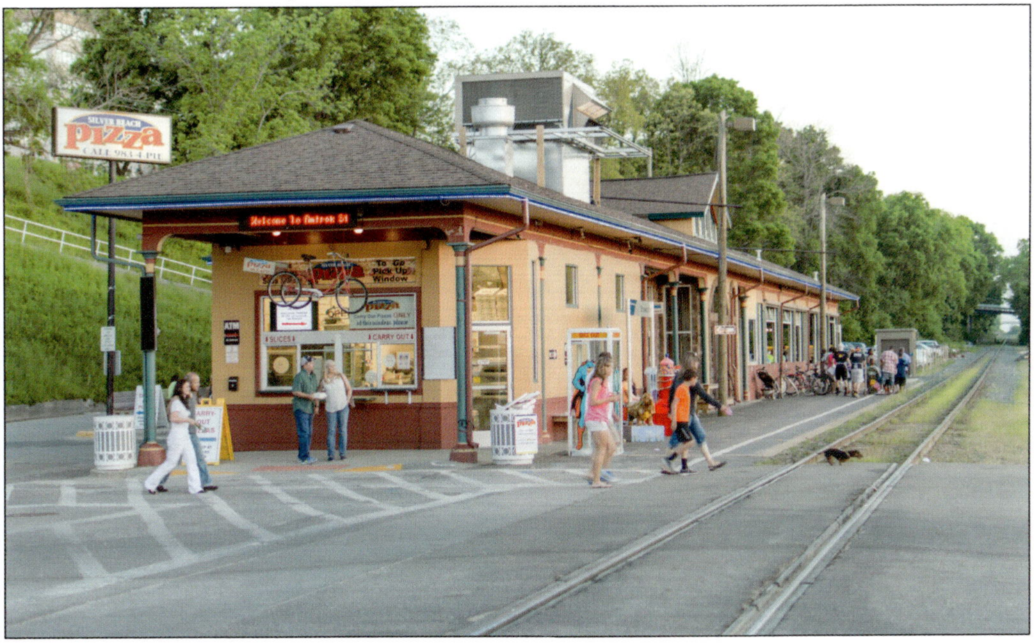

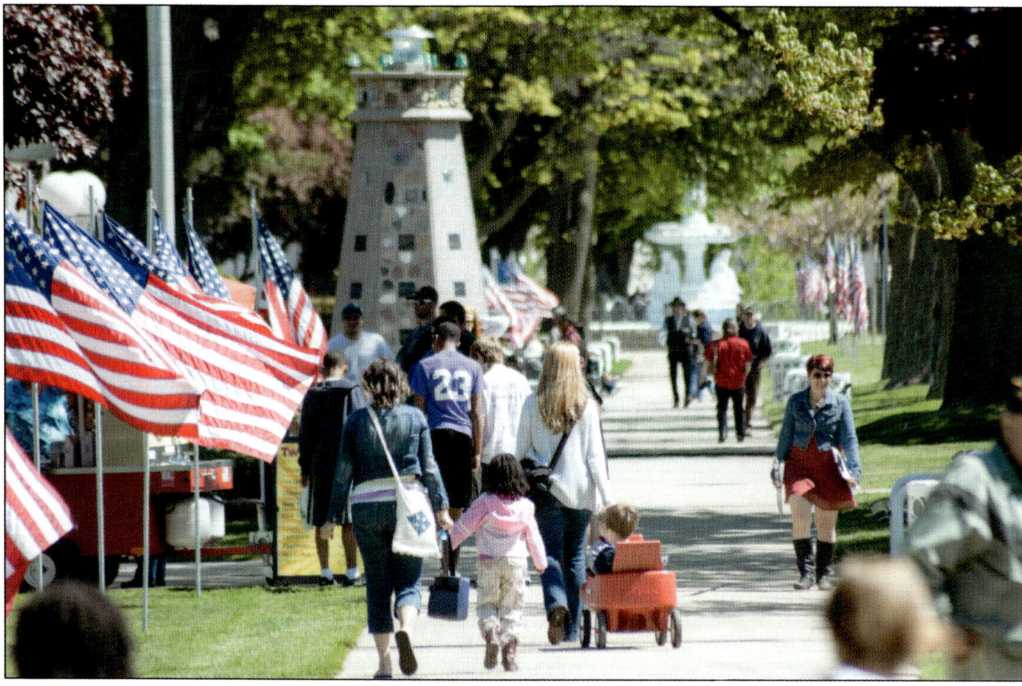

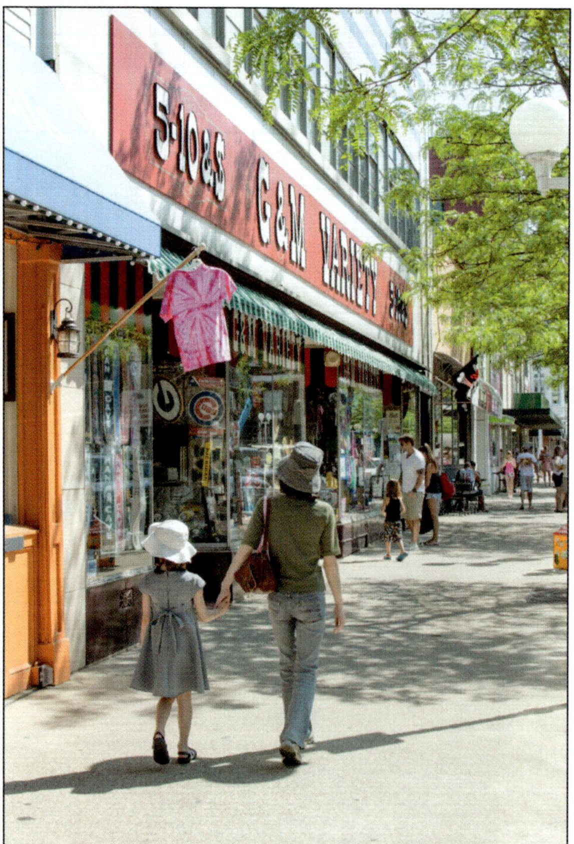

These two recent images of St. Joseph show the town's characteristic of preserving the old while incorporating the new. Above is the Bluff Park as it appears in 2014, with the Maids of the Mist fountain in the background. In the foreground is a lighthouse sculpture by Grand Rapids stonemason Rod Davis. Embedded with stones from Lake Michigan and engraved with Michigan's animals and lighthouses, it was brought to the city as part of a fundraiser to preserve St. Joseph's historic lighthouse. At left, a young mother and her daughter stroll past the G&M Variety Store at 307 State Street. Formerly the G.C. Murphy Company, this old-fashioned five-and-dime has changed little since moving to its present location in 1939. (Both photographs by Joshua Nowicki.)

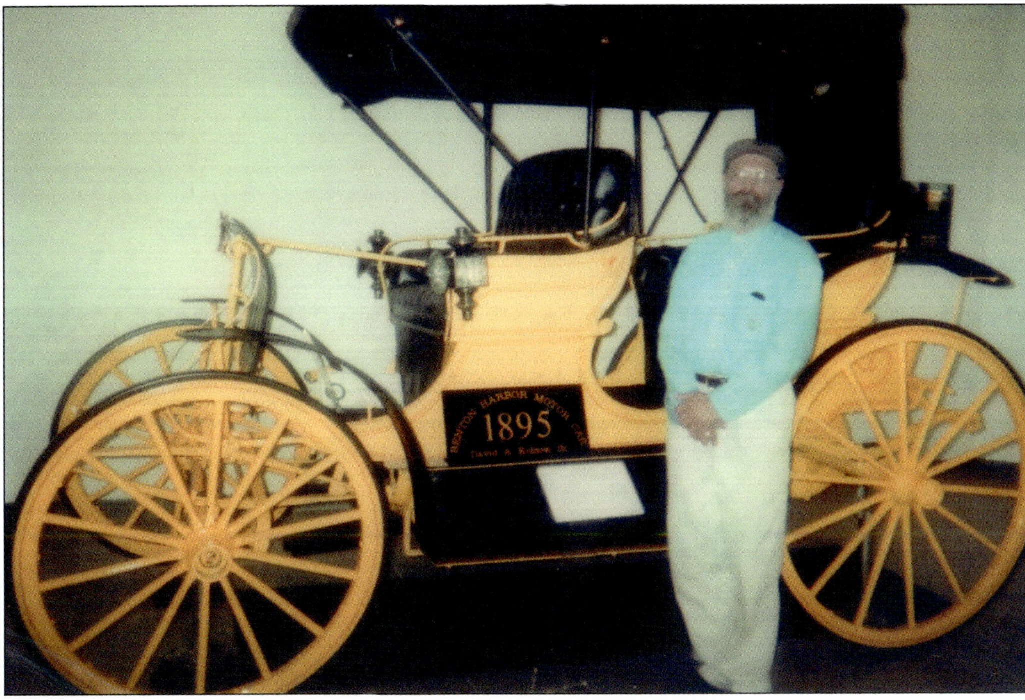

In 1997, Ron Taylor of Mary's City of David (reorganized from the Israelite House of David by Mary Purnell in 1930) opened the long-secluded colony site for public tours. Taylor also brought vintage baseball to Benton Harbor and supplies water from the onsite spring to the Livery for Silver Queen Helles ale. In this 2005 photograph, Taylor stands near a car built in 1894 by brothers Lewis and Albert Baushke, who were members of the House of David. (Courtesy of the Maude Preston Palenske Memorial Library.)

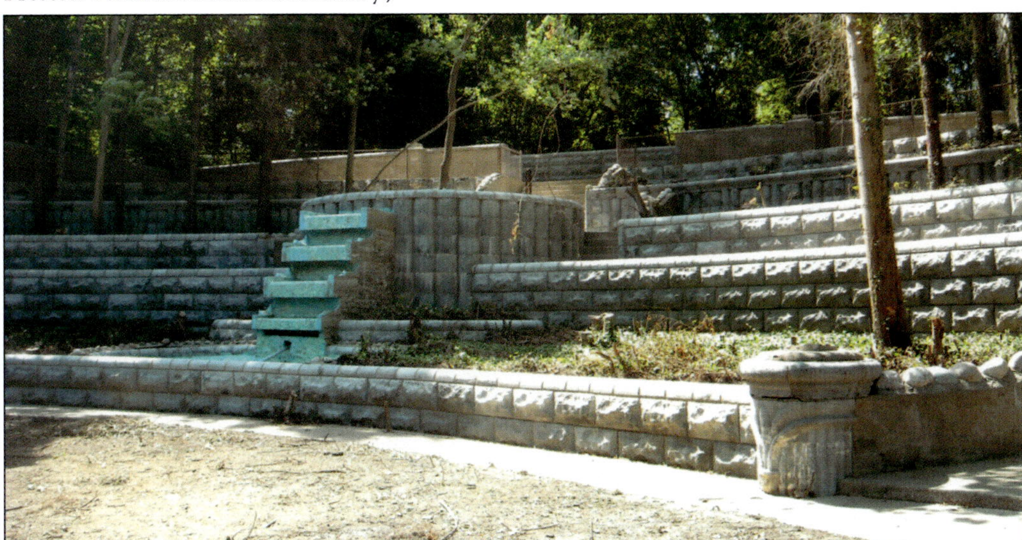

In the meantime, out-of-state train enthusiasts Carey Williams and George Dixson purchased the long-abandoned House of David amusement park in 2009. Working with local preservationists and volunteers, they began the hard recovery work. Pictured here is the newly-restored park fountain. (Photograph by Stephen Brandon.)

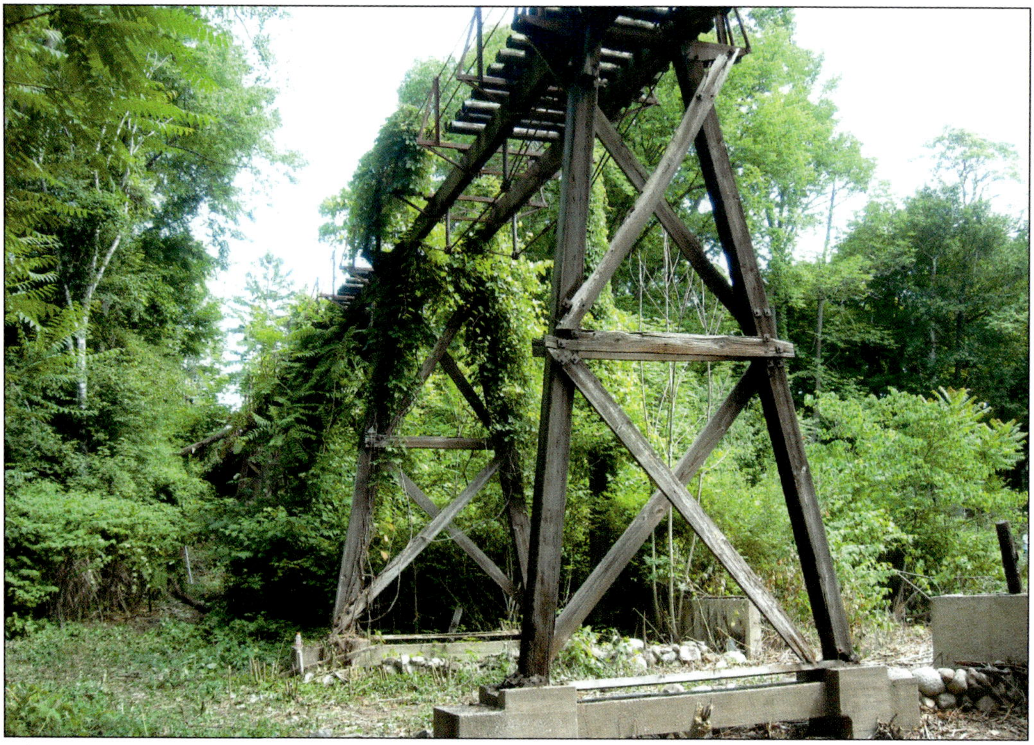

Above is the old House of David train trestle as it appeared in 2009, prior to restoration. Vivid childhood memories of crossing that trestle in one of the colony's miniature trains later inspired local industrialist Merlin Hanson to purchase and restore two of the original steam engines. Shown below is the 903 on a trailer in Hanson's Riverside warehouse in 2007, in the final stages of restoration. Early plans to run this train, or its twin, the 902, around the Silver Beach Center, never materialized. Engineers, toolmakers, and craftsmen themselves, Hanson's volunteers marveled during restoration at the top quality of both engines, built by colony members in the 1940s. (Both author's collection.)

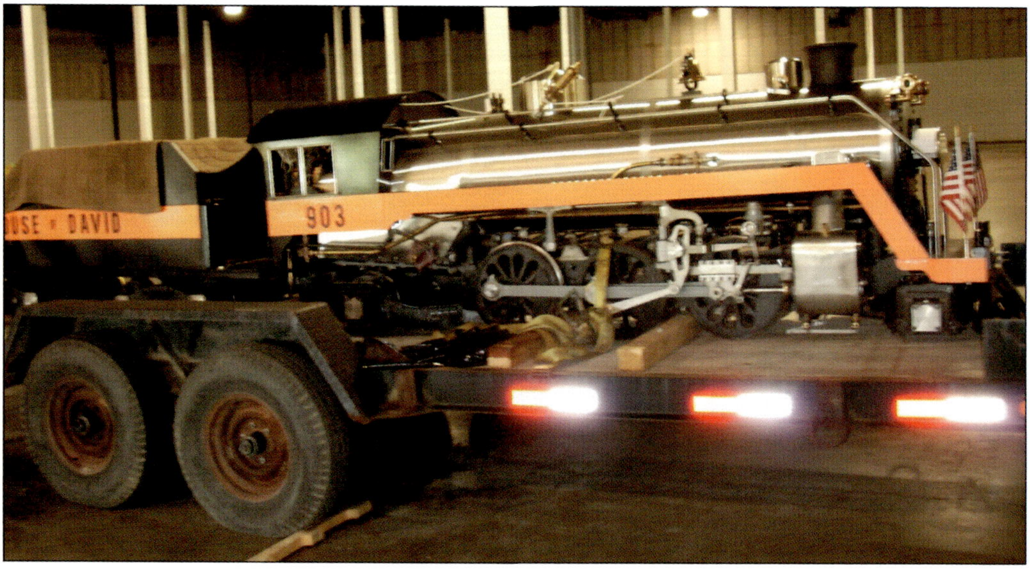

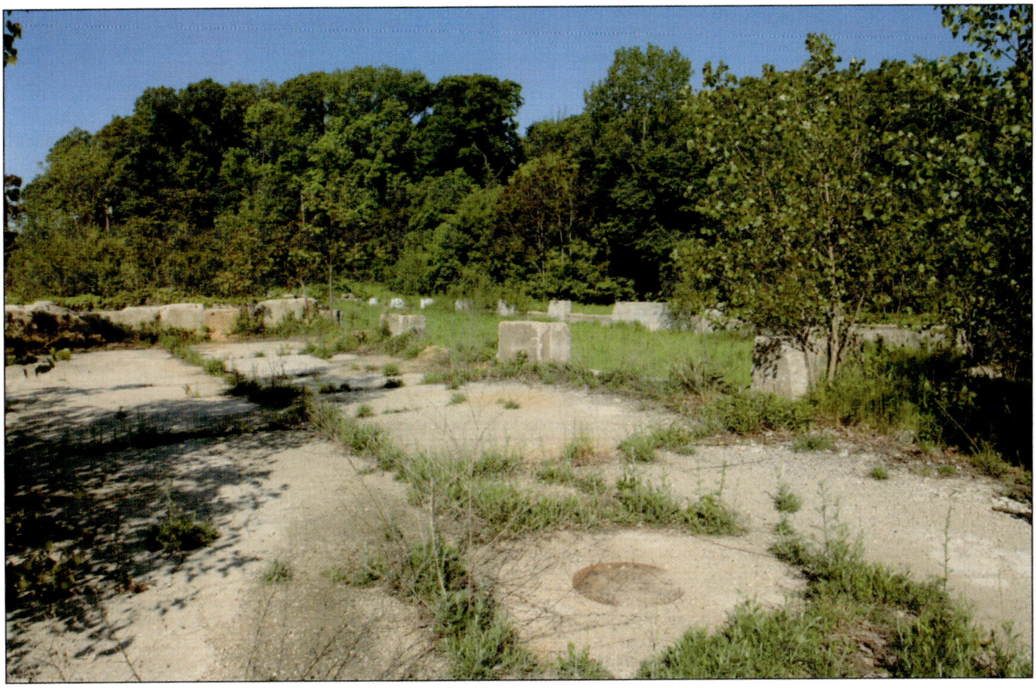

Revitalizing Northern industrial cities for the 21st century means addressing the unfortunate 20th-century manufacturing legacy of contaminated land. The largest number of polluted sites in Michigan belonged to Benton Harbor. In 2002, Pres. George W. Bush signed an act providing federal assistance to entrepreneurs willing to rehabilitate such sites. In 2005, plans began for the Harbor Shores project, a massive revitalization plan involving the 530-acre development of Benton Harbor's heavily polluted former industrial zone. This project included a Jack Nicklaus signature golf course, housing developments, a hotel, marina, and restaurants. Above is the concrete foundation left after the toxic former Superior Steel site was razed. On the right is the 14th hole of the public golf course built in its place, with the Paw Paw River shining in the background. Each hole is named after an indigenous plant; this one is Vervain. (Both, courtesy of Whirlpool Corporation.)

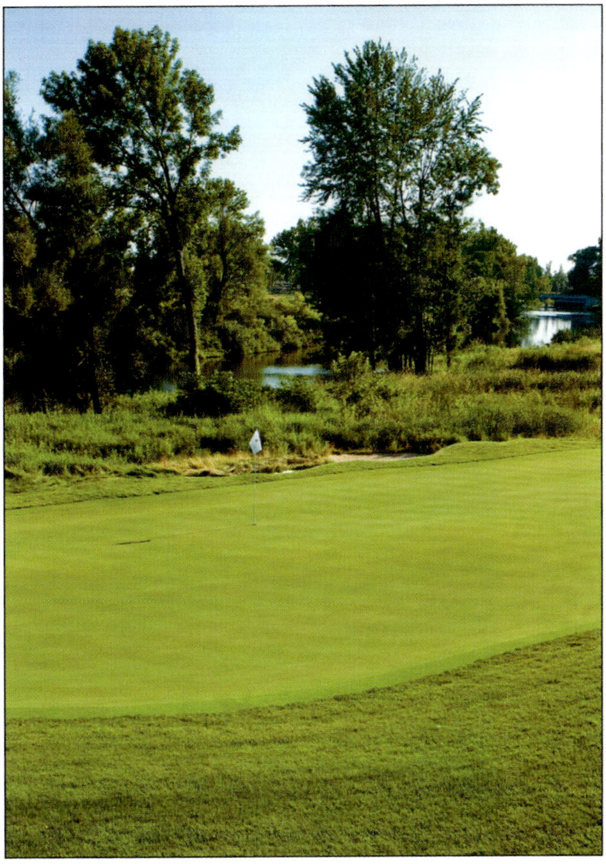

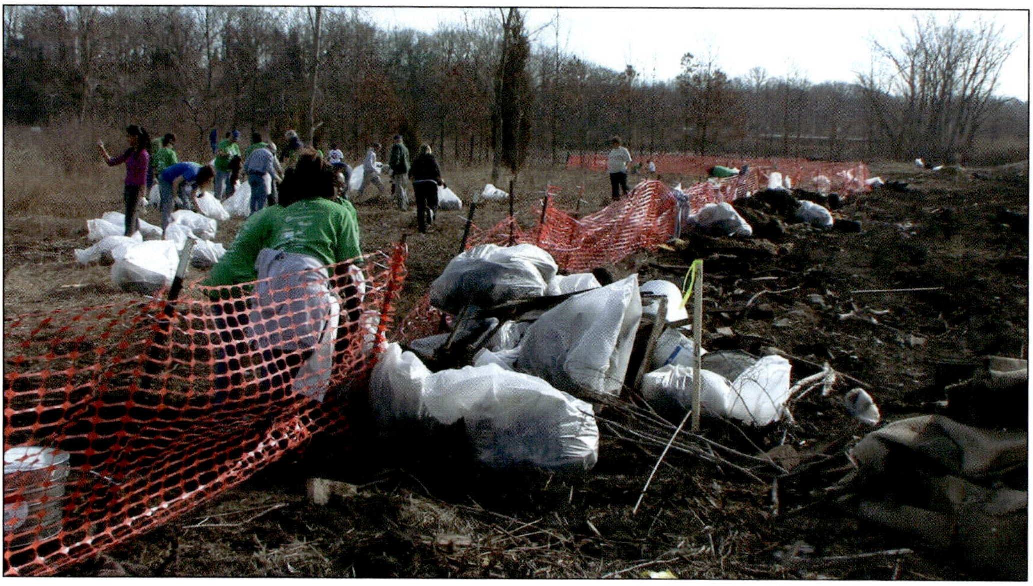

One of Harbor Shores's goals was to increase the amount of public use within Jean Klock Park. To this end, they invested over $3.7 million in non-golf related improvements, including updates to the existing bath house, concession area, and pavilion; a new entry road and beach boulevard to access the park; additional lights; walking trails; and environmental and trash clean-up. In the image above, taken on Earth Day, April 18, 2009, Harbor Shores sponsored a beach cleanup in which several community organizations participated. Altogether, the Harbor Shores project removed over 117,000 tons of trash, solid waste, and concrete, including 20,000 tons of contaminated soils. Below, families enjoy the newly-renovated Jean Klock Park. (Both, courtesy of Whirlpool Corporation.)

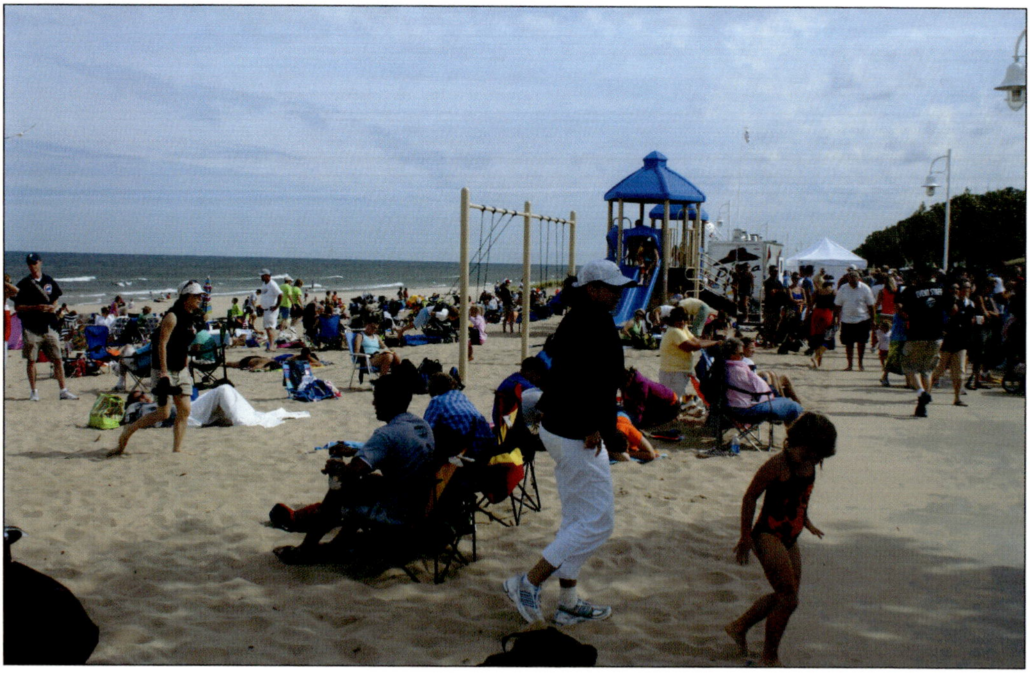

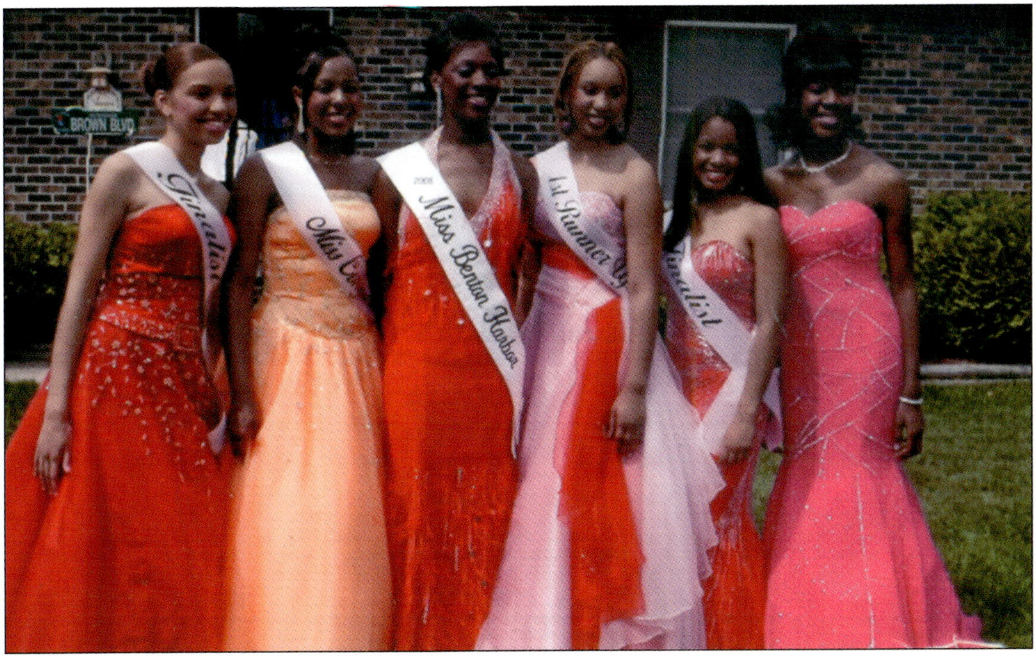

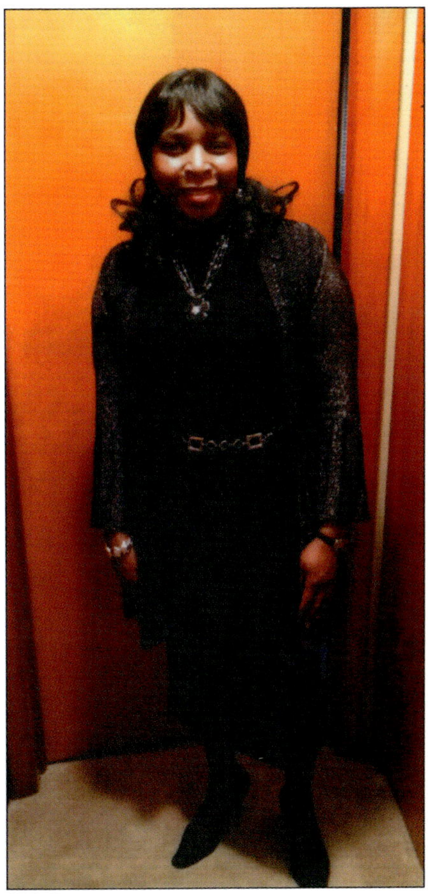

Benton Harbor residents love their hometown. Above is Ashley Hampton, Miss Benton Harbor 2005, with her court. From left to right are Brianna Hill, Siobhan Williams, Hampton, Leah Choyce, Alexandria Leonard, and Taleah Adams. Hampton, who studied political science and has a master's degree in criminal justice from Western Michigan University, returned home to devote herself to her community. She works as a senior consultant at Whirlpool and as a field trainer for Hewlett-Packard, and has volunteered with the Boys and Girls Club since 2004. On the right is her mother, Joyce Hampton, who works in admissions at Lakeland Health Center and runs her own housekeeping service. Joyce remembers being one of the first black students to attend the newly integrated Fairplain schools in the 1960s, and the teachers who helped her excel. (Both, courtesy of Ashley Hampton.)

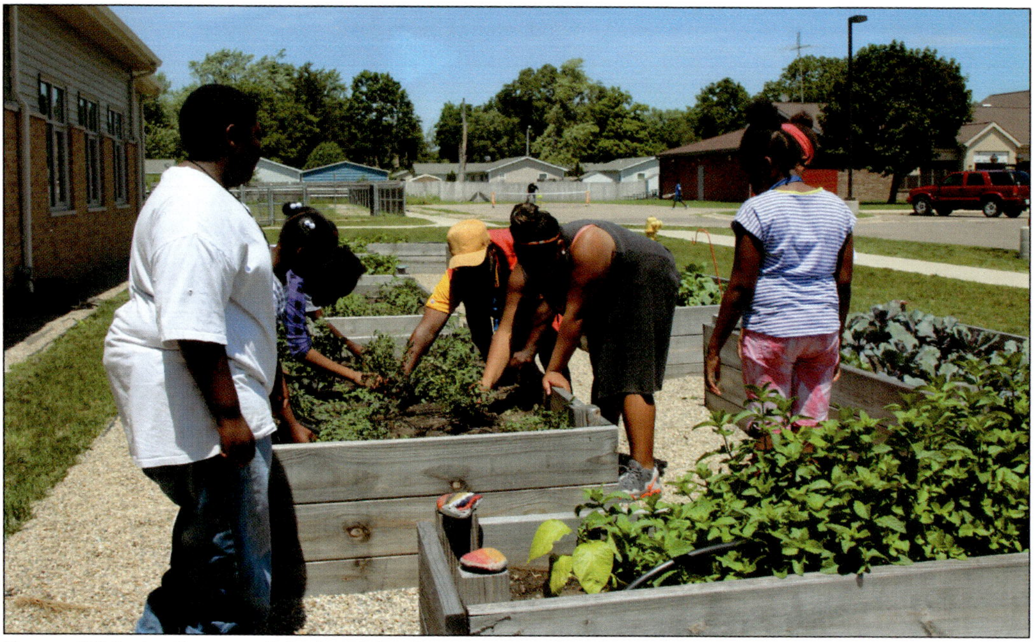

Since 1999, the Boys and Girls Club of Benton Harbor has provided after-school education and recreational facilities for children and teenagers. In 2012, two new facilities opened, one for elementary and middle school children, the other for teenagers. Besides expert classroom tutoring in airy, pleasant spaces, the children benefit from practical hands-on experience. Above, young members tend the club gardens with the guidance of foster grandparent Nate Whitelow. Below, boys perform in a drum line at the outdoor Saturday Harbor Market. From left to right are Darius Sallie, Christopher Ferguson, Timothy Nichols, Kamarion Halliburton, William Suggs, and Quindarius Davis. The group performs at area festivals and events and has accompanied the local high school in a Southwest Michigan Symphony Orchestra concert at nearby Lake Michigan College under the supervision of Freddie Robinson, senior program coordinator. (Above, courtesy of the Boys and Girls Club of Benton Harbor; below, author's collection.)

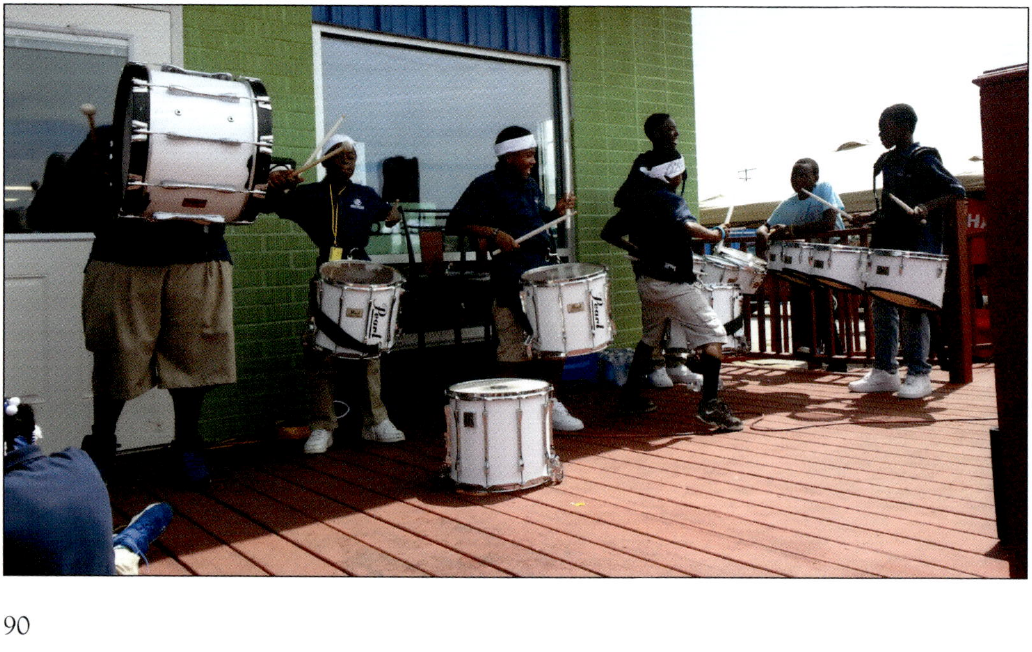

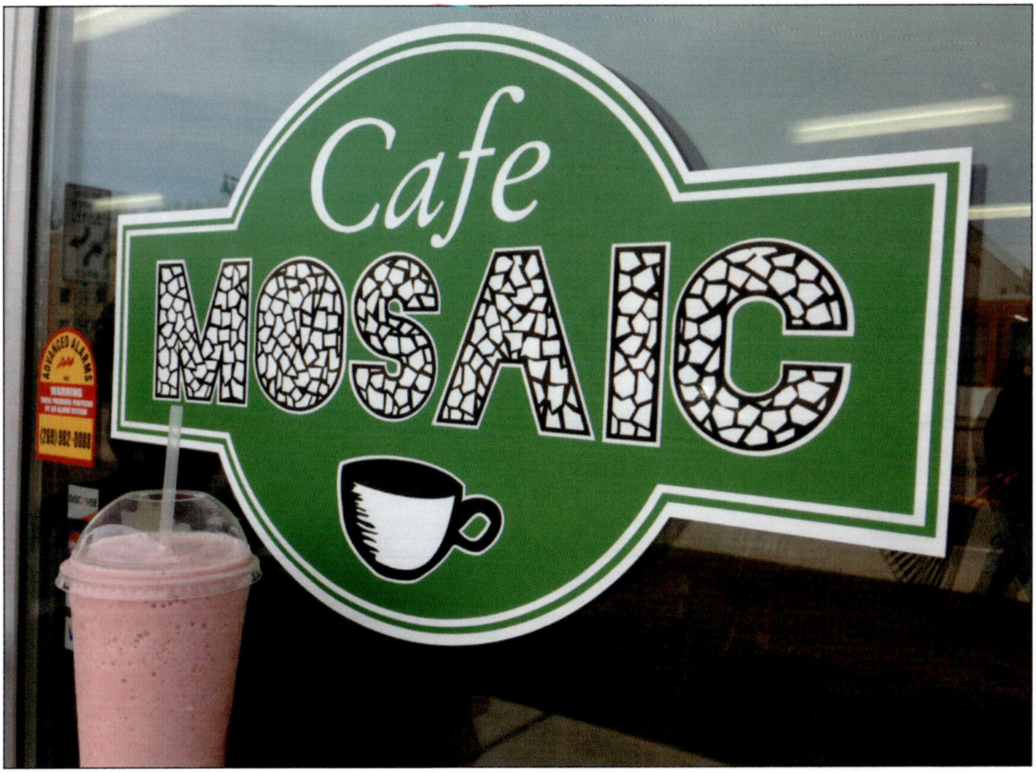

Faith organizations are key to community organization and service. Beginning in 2009, Rev. Brian Bennett of the Overflow Church, in cooperation with 15 other local church partners and over 30 community organizations, formed the nonprofit Overflow Christian Community Development Association (OCCDA). The social enterprises of the OCCDA are Harbor Shine Lawncare and Snow Removal, Cafe Mosaic, and the Mosaic Resale Store at 510 Main Street. Besides selling clothing, books, and household goods at reasonable rates and fresh, locally roasted coffee, pastries, and lunches, the center provides training, employment, and support for those who struggle against various barriers to employment. Above is the café door, with one of its delicious drinks on display. At right are two dedicated shop workers, Tra'Shawna (assistant café manager) and Rachel Eaton (bookstore employee). (Both, courtesy of the OCCDA.)

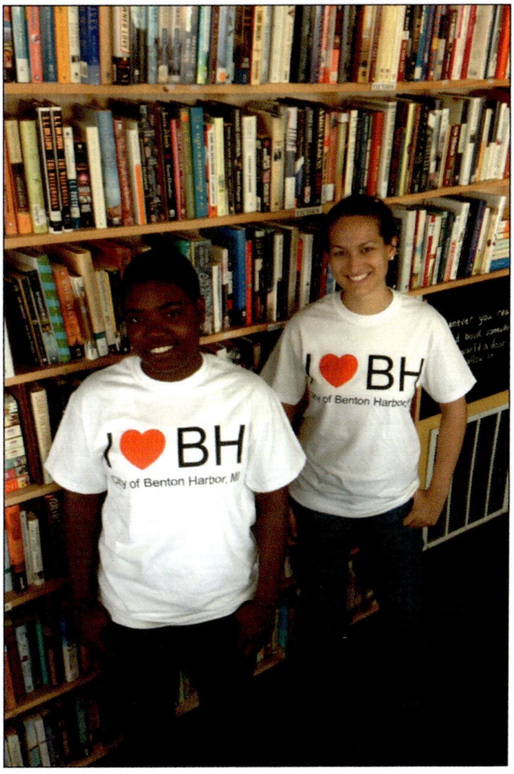

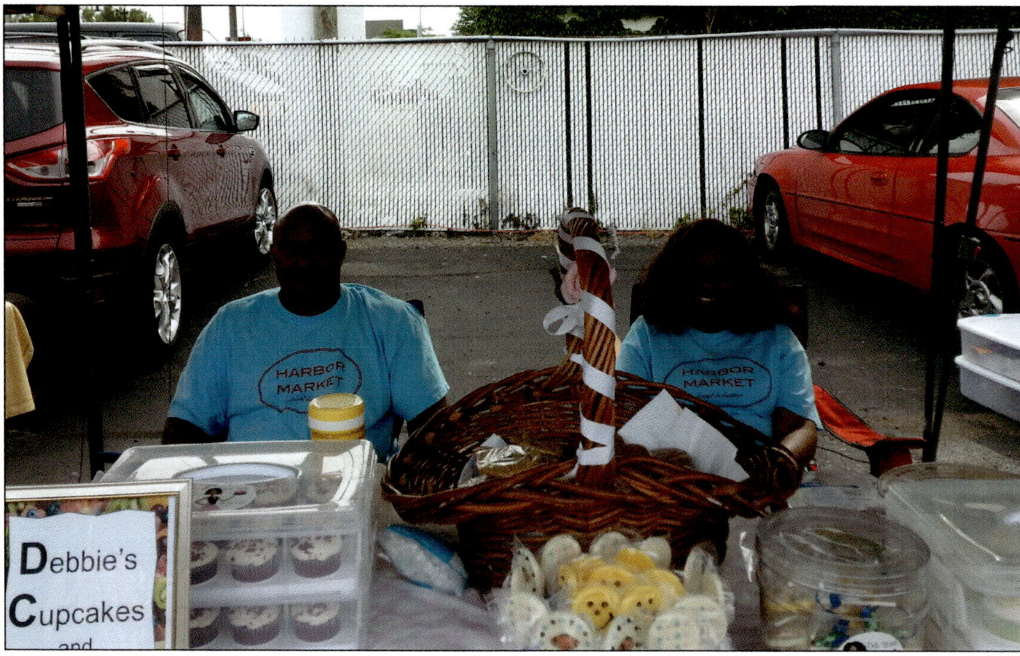

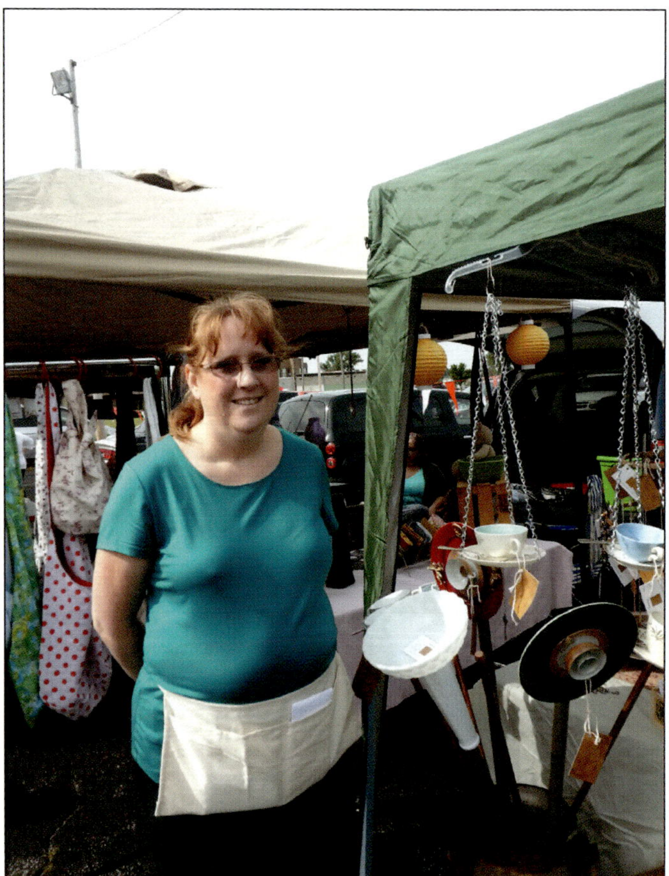

From the first weekend in June to Labor Day weekend, the OCCDA sponsors the Harbor Market in the parking lot of Mosaic, where local farmers, bakers, artisans, and craftspeople sell their produce, baked goods, and handmade wares. Above are Deborah Webb and her husband, Philip, selling her cupcakes. She started Debbie's Cupcakes when her son was a baby. To supplement the family income, she began baking delicious cakes, cupcakes, and treats for friends, who encouraged her to go into business. At left is Laurie Lewis. She started her business, College Feed, selling bird feeders and yard ornaments made from vintage pottery, jewelry, and antiques in order to raise money to send her daughter Megan to school. (Both, author's collection.)

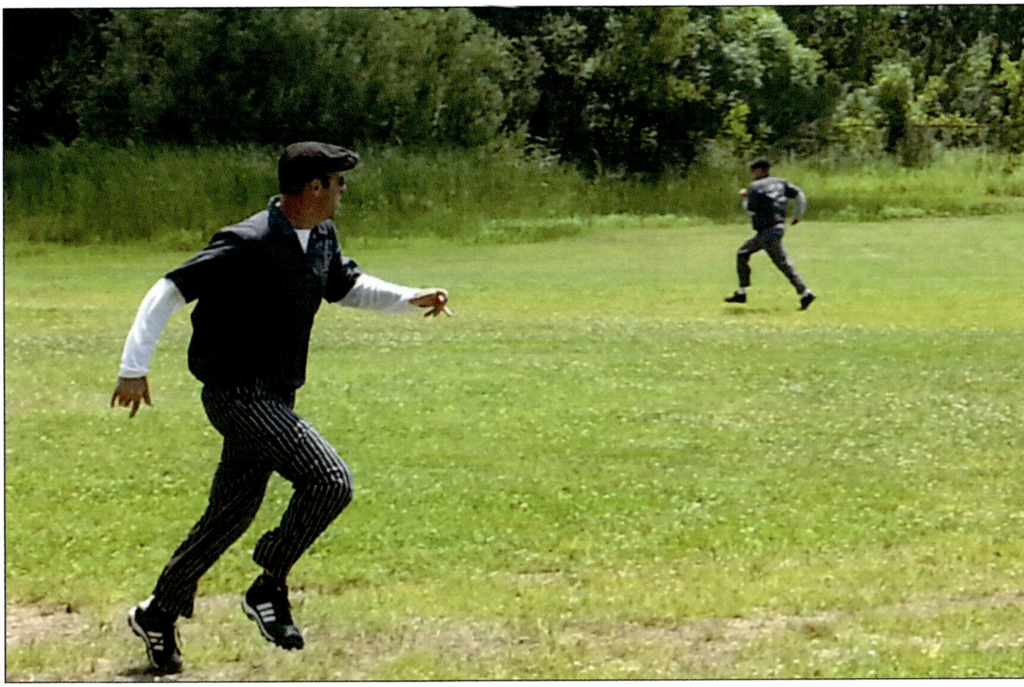

Any given summer Sunday afternoon in downtown Benton Harbor, one might come across local sporting events such as these in Hall Park. Above are the Benton Harbor Livery Brewers, one of several local vintage baseball teams. They play by 1858 rules, wear authentic uniforms, catch bare-handed, charge fines for swearing on the field, and begin and end each game with a hearty "Huzzah!" Their closest local rivals are the House of David Echoes. Benton Harbor also boasts an all-woman vintage team, the Lil Fillies. Below, on the nearby basketball court, young men play an energetic pickup game. (Both author's collection.)

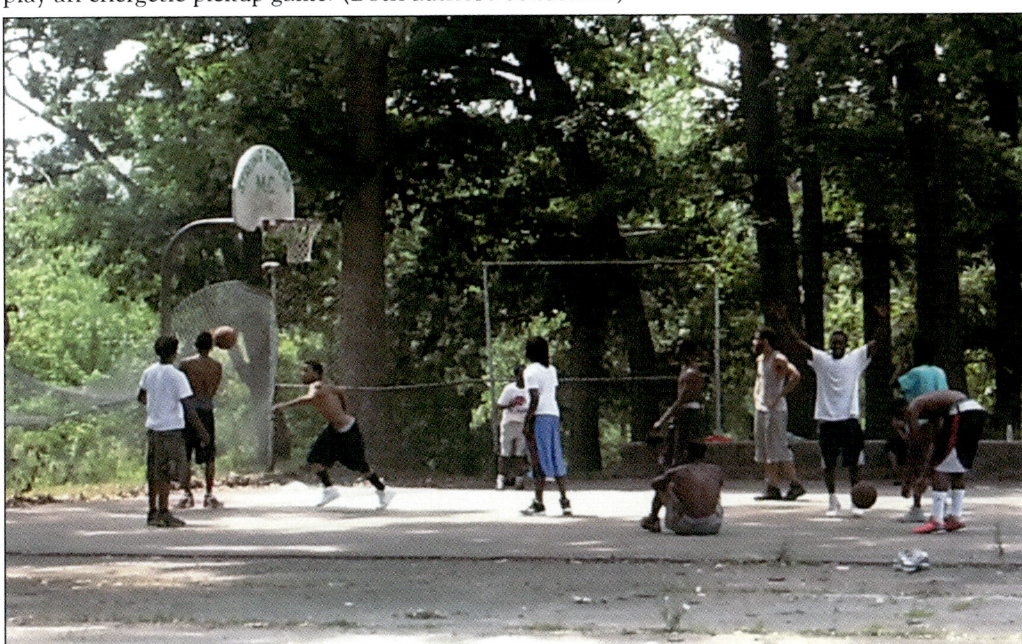

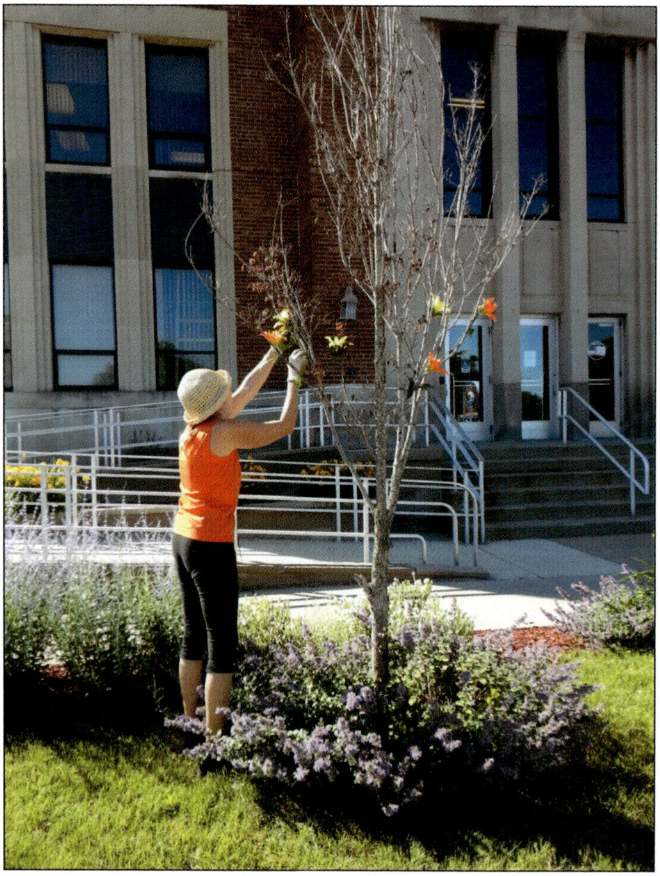

Benton Harbor remains a city of hope, creativity, and community spirit. In the image at left, in the summer of 2014, St. Joseph writer, historian, and civic leader Kathryn Zerler decorates the dead tree in front of Benton Harbor City Hall with paper flowers. While this photograph was taken, a city employee went inside to fetch her a ladder. Zerler, along with cousins A.J. and Ed Heiden, planted a new live tree in the fall. Below, leaving off where the story began 50 years ago, is a final panorama of the Twin Cities in 2014: fully grown, brand new, and thanks to the vision, cooperation, and hard work of their citizens, ready for their shared futures. (Left, author's collection; below, photograph by Joshua Nowicki.)

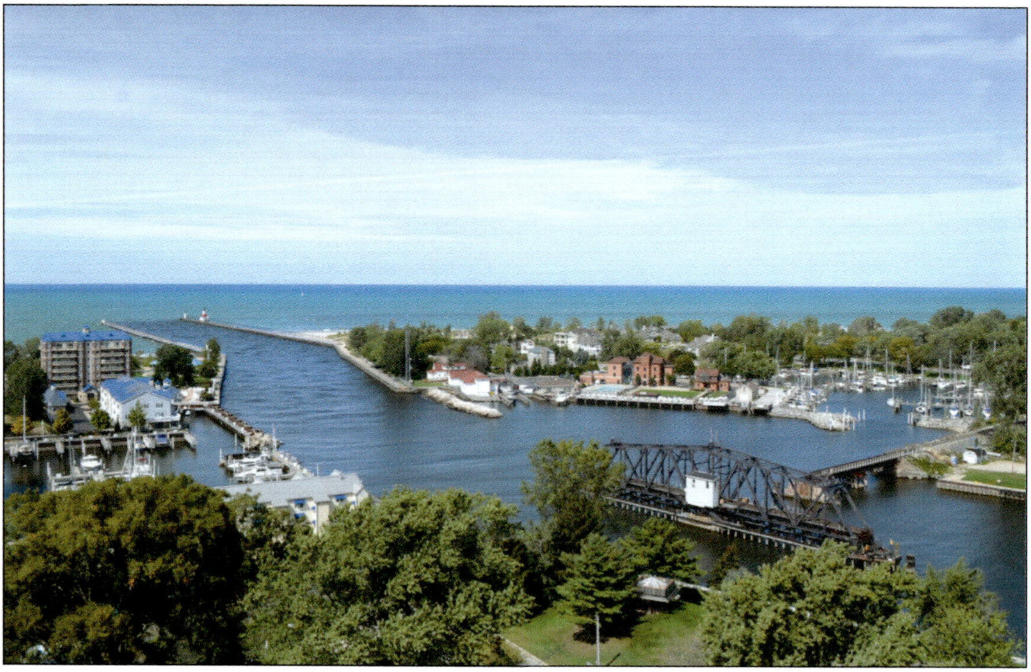

Bibliography

Schlender, Daryl T. *Silver Sands and Golden Memories: The History of Silver Beach Amusement Park*. St. Joseph, MI: Schlender Publishing Co., 2008.

Thomopoulous, Elaine Cotsirilos. *St. Joseph and Benton Harbor*. Charleston, SC: Arcadia Publishing, 2003.

Zerler, Kathryn S. *On the Banks of the Ole St. Joe: A Selected History of the Twin Cities of St. Joseph and Benton Harbor Michigan*. St. Joseph, MI: St. Joseph Today, 1990.

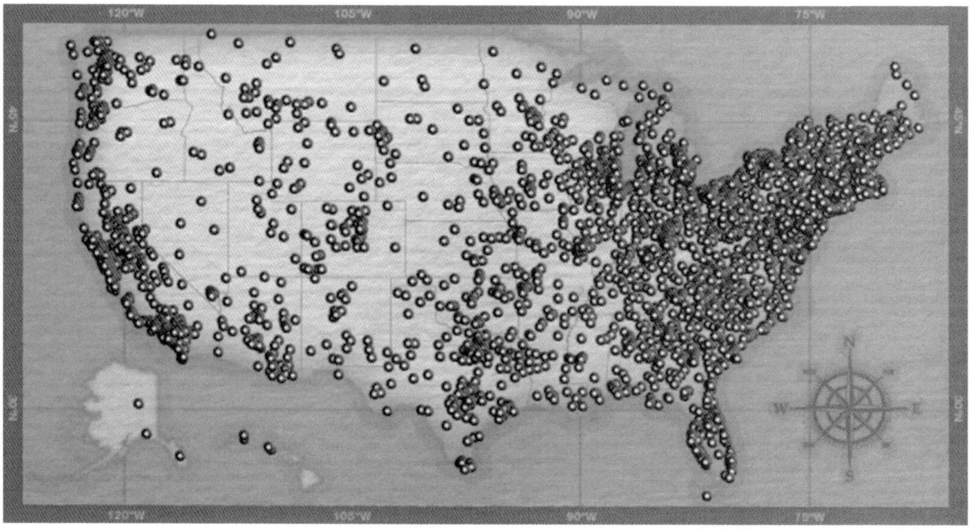